Aderyn y Nos

Nofel gyntaf mewn trioleg
i ddysgwyr gan
PAT CLAYTON

GWASG Carreg Gwalch

Argraffiad cyntaf: Gorffennaf 1997

ⓟ   *Pat Clayton*

Ni chaniateir defnyddio unrhyw ran/rannau
o'r llyfr hwn mewn unrhyw fodd
(ac eithrio i ddiben adolygu)
heb ganiatâd perchennog yr hawlfraint yn gyntaf.

Rhif Llyfr Safonol Rhyngwladol:
0-86381-445-X

Cynllun y clawr: Alan Jones
Darlun y clawr: Andrew Maclean

Argraffwyd a chyhoeddwyd gan Wasg Carreg Gwalch,
12 Iard yr Orsaf, Llanrwst, Dyffryn Conwy LL26 0EH
☎ (01492) 642031

Diolchiadau

Diolch i Gymdeithas Hanes Sir y Fflint am bob cymorth, yn enwedig yr ysgrifenyddes Nora Parker a'i gŵr John Parker a gynlluniodd fap y gwersyll. Roedd monograff y Gymdeithas, *The Kinmel Park Camp Riots 1919* gan Julian Putkowski hefyd yn ddefnyddiol iawn i mi yn fy ymchwil. Diolch unwaith eto i Cynthia Davies am ei chyngor parod, i Elwyn Hughes am ei gymorth parhaol ac i Esyllt a Myrddin yng Ngwasg Carreg Gwalch am eu gwaith hwythau.

Er cof am Mansel Davies

Geirfa filwrol

Wedi ei nodi yn y testun â *(m)* ar ôl y gair.

ar wyliadwriaeth – *on guard duty*
brwydro – *to battle*
bwth gwarchodwr – *sentry box*
byddin – *army*
cadfridog – *general*
cadoediad – *armistice*
cantinau gwlyb – *wet (beer) canteens*
catrawd – *regiment*
cwt/cytiau y fyddin – *army hut(s)*
cyhuddiad – *accusation*
cyrch – *attack*
disg enw – *name tag*
dwyn cyhuddiad – *to bring a charge*
enciliwr – *deserter*
ffens derfyn – *boundary fence*
ffos/ffosydd – *trench(es)*
gorchymyn – *order*
gwarchodwr – *guard*
gwersyll – *camp*
heddlu milwrol – *military police*
heddychwr – *pacifist*
'lladdwyd mewn brwydr' – *killed in action*
milwr – *soldier*
rhyfel – *war*
sifil – *civilian*
swyddog – *officer*
taith hyfforddi – *route march*
terfysg – *riot*
tŷ gwarchod – *guard house*
ymosod – *to attack*

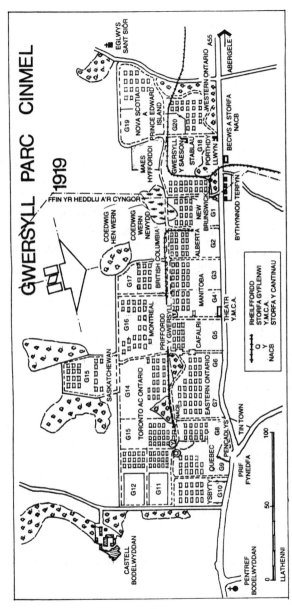

GWERSYLL PARC CINMEL
1919

EGLWYS SANT SIÔR

NOVA SCOTIA
PRINCE EDWARD ISLAND
MAES HYFFORDDI
GWERSYLL Y SAESON
STABLAU
PORTHDY LLWYN
BECWS A STORFA NACB
A55 WESTERN ONTARIO
ABERGELE

G19
G20
G18
G1

FFIN YR HEDDLU A'R CYNGOR

COEDWIG HEN WERN
COEDWIG WERN NEWYDD
BRITISH COLUMBIA
ALBERTA
BRUNSWICK NEW

BYTHYNNOD TERFYN

G17
G2

MANITOBA
G3

MONTREAL
G16

THEATR Y.M.C.A.
G4
CAFALRI
G5

PRIFFORDD Y GWERSYLL

SASKATCHEWAN
G15
TORONTO AC ONTARIO
G14
G15

EASTERN ONTARIO
NACB
G6
G7

TIN TOWN

PENCADLYS
G8
QUEBEC
G9

YSBYTY
G10

PRIF FYNEDFA

G12
G11

CASTELL BODELWYDDAN

PENTREF BODELWYDDAN

LLATHENNI

0   50   100

RHEILFFORDD
STORFA GYFLENWI
Y.M.C.A.
STORFA Y CANTINAU

Y
NACB

7

Pennod 1

Roedd traed Danny'n oer fel rhew. Roedd gwisgo ei esgidiau yn y gwely wedi bod yn gamgymeriad. Doedd o ddim wedi cysgu chwaith. Roedd o'n rhy nerfus ac yn rhy oer. Faint o'r gloch oedd hi? Byddai Jackson yn gwybod. Doedd Jackson byth yn cysgu'n dda. Insomniac oedd o. Yn y tywyllwch, trodd Danny'n araf tuag at Jackson yn y gwely nesaf. Doedd o ddim eisiau gwneud sŵn, dyna pam roedd o wedi gwisgo ei esgidiau yn y gwely. Syniad Jackson oedd hynny.

Sibrydodd Jackson, 'Waeth i ti fynd, Danny, mae hi'n bedwar o'r gloch.'

'Rwyt ti'n iawn. Oes rhywun yn effro?' sibrydodd Danny. Roedd Jackson yn adnabod pob sŵn yng nghwt y fyddin (m) gyda'r nos.

'Neb. Maen nhw'n cysgu fel babanod.'

Yn ddistaw, safodd Danny ar ei draed a chodi'r gôt fawr oedd ar y gwely.

'Cofia, rho gusan i'r briodferch oddi wrtha' i,' sibrydodd Jackson.

'Iawn. A chofia fy esgus bore fory – y gaseg wael,' atebodd Danny.

'Dim problem. Pob lwc, Danny.'

'Wela' i di yn y bore.' Pwnsiodd fraich ei ffrind fel diolch.

Sleifiodd Danny'n ofalus rhwng y rhesi o filwyr *(m)* tawel. Ddeffrodd neb. Aeth allan drwy ddrws y cwt ac anadlodd yn drwm. Roedd o wedi cynllunio sut y byddai'n mynd allan o'r gwersyll *(m)* ers dyddiau. Gadawodd gytiau Montreal y tu ôl iddo. British Columbia oedd nesaf, ac wedyn y ffens derfyn *(m)*. Cadwodd ei ben i lawr dan lefel y ffenestri wrth fynd heibio i'r cytiau. Y tu allan i gwt B.C., ciciodd garreg. Rhewodd ac aros. Ddigwyddodd dim byd. Rhedodd dros y glaswellt tuag at y ffens derfyn. Roedd o wedi gwneud twll ynddi hi y diwrnod cynt. Y tu ôl i'r ffens roedd rhywun yn ceisio goleuo lamp y tu mewn i un o gytiau B.C. Gwasgodd Danny drwy'r ffens a'i rhoi hi'n ôl yn ei lle eto. Byddai arno angen defnyddio'r un llwybr ar ei ffordd yn ôl. Rhedodd tuag at goedwig Hen Wern. Roedd ei galon yn curo fel gordd, ond roedd o allan.

Cododd Danny goler ei gôt. Doedd gaeaf Cymru ddim fel gaeaf Canada. Roedd yr awyr yn sych yng Nghanada ond roedd hi'n llaith bob amser yng Nghymru. Roedd y lleithder yn mynd drwy'ch esgyrn. Byddai'n rhaid iddo ddod i arfer â hyn. Cychwynnodd i fyny'r bryn dros y caeau. Roedd ganddo tua dwyawr i gyrraedd y ficerdy. Doedd 'na ddim brys. Pan gyrhaeddodd Danny ben y bryn, edrychodd yn ei ôl. Roedd Gwersyll Parc Cinmel yn gorwedd o dano fo. Rhesi o gytiau, ychydig o olau, a channoedd o filwyr yn aros am y llong i fynd â nhw adref. Roedden nhw wedi bod yn aros yn hir.

Roedd y Canadiaid wedi cyrraedd Gwersyll Parc Cinmel ar ôl y cadoediad *(m)* ym mis Tachwedd. Roedd rhai ohonyn nhw wedi mynd adref, ond yn ddiweddar doedd neb wedi cael mynd. Roedd eu llongau wedi cael eu rhoi i'r Americanwyr – yr olaf i fynd i ryfel *(m)* oedd y cyntaf i adael meddai'r milwyr. Doedd hi ddim yn deg. Roedd y milwyr wedi gwylltio ac yn fuan byddai helynt yn codi. Roedd pawb wedi cael llond bol ar addewidion ac esgusodion. Wrth gwrs, doedd neb yn gwybod pryd fyddai'r helynt yn dod, na sut, ond pan fyddai'n dod, roedd gan Danny a Jackson eu cynlluniau eu hunain.

Erbyn hanner awr wedi chwech, byddai Danny wedi priodi. Cyflymodd ei gamau pan feddyliodd am Megan. Tua thair milltir arall i fynd. Roedd o wedi bod yn lwcus i ddod o hyd iddi, ac roedd o'n lwcus bod ganddi fam mor garedig hefyd. Ond doedd o ddim yn siŵr am y ficer. Roedd mam Megan yn cadw tŷ i'r ficer ac roedd hi wedi dweud bod y ficer yn fodlon eu priodi nhw am ei fod o'n meddwl y byd o Megan ac am ei fod o'n casáu'r rhyfel. Heddychwr *(m)* oedd o, ond roedd o'n gwneud camgymeriad os oedd o'n meddwl y byddai priodas Danny a Megan yn taro ergyd yn erbyn y fyddin. Beth bynnag, os oedd Megan a'i mam yn ymddiried ynddo, roedd hynny'n ddigon da i Danny.

Cyrhaeddodd Danny ffordd gul. Doedd neb o gwmpas. Byddai'n saff iddo gerdded ar y ffordd. Roedd Megan yn meddwl efallai ei bod hi'n feichiog. Roedd Danny'n gobeithio ei bod hi. Roedd o'n edrych ymlaen at ddechrau ei fywyd newydd efo babi. Wrth gwrs, byddai'n rhaid iddo guddio am rai misoedd tan i fyddin y Canadiaid fynd adref. Wedi'r cyfan, enciliwr *(m)* fyddai o. Mi fedren nhw ei saethu o tasen nhw'n dod o hyd iddo. Oedd Megan wedi chwilio am rywle i'w guddio, tybed?

Drwy'r tywyllwch roedd o'n medru gweld tŵr yr eglwys. Trodd oddi ar y ffordd ar hyd lôn fach oedd yn mynd y tu ôl i'r ficerdy. Oedd o'n rhy fuan? Crensiodd ei gamau ar lwybr yr eglwys. Agorodd ddrws y festri a mynd i mewn. Cododd ei galon pan welodd Megan yng ngolau'r gannwyll yn edrych yn smart iawn yn ei gwisg nyrs. Rhuthrodd i'w freichiau.

'Danny, diolch byth dy fod ti wedi cyrraedd.' Tynnodd Danny ei gap a'i chofleidio cyn edrych dros ei hysgwydd.

'Lle mae dy fam, Megan?'

'Mae hi'n paratoi brecwast ar ein cyfer ni yn y ficerdy. Mi fydd hi yma'n fuan.'

Daeth dyn tal allan o'r cysgodion. Trodd Megan ato'n swil.

'Danny, ga' i gyflwyno'r Parch Rees-Davies?' Ysgydwodd y ddau ddyn ddwylo.

'Mae'n dda gen i eich cyfarfod chi, syr,' meddai Danny'n gwrtais.

'Roedden ni wedi bod yn gweddïo y byddech chi'n cyrraedd yn saff fy machgen i. Croeso aton ni.'

Geiriau newydd

addewid – *promise*
anadlu – *to breathe*
beichiog – *pregnant*
cam – *step*
caseg – *mare*
cofleidio – *to hug*
cysgod – *shadow*
ergyd – *blow*
esgyrn – *bones*
gordd – *sledgehammer*
gwasgu – *to squeeze*
gweddïo – *to pray*
gwisg – *dress*
helynt – *trouble*
llaith – *damp*
lleithder – *dampness*
priodferch – *bride*
rhes – *row*
sibrwd – *to whisper*
swil – *shy*
tywyllwch – *darkness*
ymddiried – *to trust*
ysgwyd – *to shake*

Pennod 2

Wrth i'r drws agor y tu ôl iddyn nhw, trodd y tri. Daeth y gwynt oer a mam Megan i mewn gyda'i gilydd. Roedd Myfanwy Jones yn wraig dal a smart ac roedd ganddi gôt, het a siôl lwyd dros ei ffrog ddu.

'Bore da, Mrs Jones,' meddai Danny. Gwenodd Megan ar ei mam yn nerfus.

'Bore da, Danny, neis eich gweld chi.'

'Helô, Myfanwy,' meddai'r ficer. 'Wel, os ydy pawb yma, mi gawn ni fynd i mewn i'r eglwys.' Cymerodd y ficer gannwyll ac arwain y ffordd. Cerddodd parti'r briodas drwy'r eglwys dywyll ac oer. Goleuodd y ficer ganhwyllau ar yr allor a gweddïo ar ei ben ei hun am funud. Yna, trodd at y lleill eto. 'Ydan ni'n barod?'

Estynnodd mam Megan i'w bag a thynnu darn o les ohono.

'Gwisga hwn, Megan,' meddai, gan geisio rhoi y les ar ben cap nyrs ei merch. Ysgydwodd Megan ei phen. Sylweddolodd Danny nad priodas fel hon oedd breuddwyd y fam.

'Tyrd, Megan, gwisga fo i blesio dy fam.' Rhoddodd Megan y les dros ei chap.

Doedd y seremoni ddim yn un hir. Fedrai Danny ddim deall popeth – doedd ei Gymraeg ddim yn dda iawn. Ond cyn bo hir roedd y ficer yn dweud, 'Mi gewch chi gusanu'r briodferch.' Gwnaeth Danny hynny'n fodlon. Llofnododd pawb y gofrestr a mynd i'r ficerdy. Roedd Mrs Jones wedi gosod y brecwast priodas ar fwrdd yn seler y ficerdy.

Plas oedd y ficerdy yn wreiddiol, ac roedd y seler wedi bod yn stablau a thŷ cadw coets. Tynnodd Danny ei gôt. Roedd hi'n gynnes yn y seler. Sylwodd ar y boeler yn y gornel. Mae'n rhaid bod y ficer yn ddyn cyfoethog os oes ganddo fo wres canolog, meddyliodd Danny.

'Eisteddwch Danny, eisteddwch ficer!' meddai Mrs Jones. 'Megan, helpa fi efo'r brecwast.'

Diflannodd y ddwy ddynes i fyny'r grisiau oedd mewn cornel arall. Roedd Danny'n gobeithio na fyddai'r ficer yn gofyn beth oedd ei gynlluniau ar gyfer y dyfodol. Doedd o ddim eisiau dweud celwydd wrtho. Ond roedd y ficer wedi mentro'n barod ar ran Danny a Megan, a doedd o ddim eisiau bod yn rhan o fentro pellach. Roedd y ficer yn gwybod bod Danny wedi cael ei fagu'n Babydd. Holodd y ficer os oedd o'n Babydd da. Roedd yn rhaid i Danny ddweud celwydd wedi'r cyfan.

Daeth Megan a'i mam yn ôl efo potaid o de a phlatiau o wyau, bacwn a thatws wedi eu ffrio. Roedd bara, jam a chaws ar y bwrdd. Bwytaodd Danny'n harti, ond roedd o'n poeni. Roedd o'n siŵr ei bod hi tua saith o'r gloch erbyn hyn.

'Mae'n ddrwg gen i,' meddai Danny gan sefyll ar ei draed. 'Mae'n rhaid imi fynd.'

'Oes gynnoch chi amser i gynnig llwncdestun i'r briodferch?' gofynnodd y ficer gan estyn dan y bwrdd. Cododd botelaid o bort. Edrychodd Megan, Mrs Jones a Danny arno'n syn. Yn gyflym, golchodd mam Megan y cwpanau te efo jwgaid o ddŵr poeth a chododd pawb eu cwpanau o bort i Megan.

'Pob lwc i chi'ch dau, a bendith Duw arnoch chi,' meddai'r ficer. Gorffennodd Danny ei ddiod ac ysgwyd llaw efo'r ficer. Cofleidiodd mam Megan Danny cyn iddo adael y seler. Aeth Megan allan efo fo. Roedd y wawr yn torri'n llwyd, oer a niwlog. Cusanodd Danny Megan.

'Pryd wela' i ti eto, Danny?' gofynnodd Megan.

'Yfory, gobeithio. Mae'n rhaid inni chwilio am rywle i guddio. Mi wna' i geisio cyrraedd yn hwyr yn y bore. Lle wnawn ni gyfarfod?'

'Mi chwilia' i amdanat ti yn y seler bob hanner awr ar ôl un ar ddeg o'r gloch. Bydd y drws yn agored. Mi fydd pawb yn yr eglwys.'

'Reit. Paid â phoeni, Megan. Mi fyddwn ni gyda'n gilydd yn fuan, ac am byth.' Cusanodd Danny Megan eto. Doedd o ddim eisiau ei gadael. Cerddodd yn gyflym ar hyd y lôn gan droi a chodi ei law sawl gwaith tan iddo gyrraedd y gornel.

Oedd hi'n saff iddo aros ar y ffordd? Byddai ambell was fferm o gwmpas erbyn hyn. Rhedodd ar hyd y ffordd. Byddai'n mynd dros y caeau ymhen milltir. Wedyn i lawr y rhiw bob cam i Fodelwyddan. Rownd y gornel nesaf roedd 'na ffordd wastad. Tasai hi'n glir mi fasai o'n cyrraedd mewn pryd. Rhedodd yn gyflym rownd y gornel a rhewi. Bum canllath o'i flaen roedd dau ddyn yn siarad gyda'i gilydd y tu allan i fwthyn. Roedd ceffyl a chert yn llawn o ganiau llefrith ar ganol y ffordd. Tad Megan oedd y dyn llefrith – y person olaf yn y byd roedd Danny eisiau ei weld.

Geiriau newydd

allor – *altar*
arwain – *to lead*
bendith – *blessing*
breuddwyd – *dream*
celwydd – *lie*
cofrestr – *register*
cuddio – *to hide*
cyfoethog – *rich*
diflannu – *to disappear*
gwas fferm – *farm worker*
gwastad – *flat*
holi – *to enquire*
llofnodi – *to sign*
llwncdestun – *toast*
llwyd – *grey*
mentro – *to venture, risk*
Pabydd – *Roman Catholic*
yn syn – *surprised*

Pennod 3

Roedd Danny eisiau bod ar ochr arall y ffordd. Cerddodd yn ôl yn araf rownd y gornel a chroesi'r ffordd. Roedd y gwrych yn rhy uchel iddo fedru mynd drosto. Rhedodd ganllath yn ôl. Dringodd dros giât a dilyn y gwrych rownd y gornel eto. Roedd yn rhaid iddo fynd i lawr y rhiw ar draws cae heb goed ynddo. Tasai un o'r dynion yn troi mi fasai o'n gweld Danny. Rhedodd ar draws y cae heb edrych yn ôl. Roedd y rhiw yn serth ac yn fuan roedd Danny'n colli rheolaeth. Yn sydyn, llithrodd ar dail gwartheg a syrthio ar ei gefn. Gorweddodd ar y cae wedi colli ei wynt. Trodd ei ben tuag at y dynion ar y ffordd. Roedden nhw'n rhy bell i fedru ei weld. Arhosodd am ychydig funudau a chychwyn eto.

Roedd Robert Wyn Jones, tad Megan, yn casáu Danny. Roedd yn gas ganddo bob milwr o Ganada. Gwelodd Danny Megan am y tro cyntaf yn ystod yr epidemig ffliw oedd wedi lledu drwy Ewrop ar ôl y rhyfel. Roedd cannoedd o ddynion wedi marw yn y gwersyll ond roedd Danny'n lwcus. Ar ôl iddo wella, cynigiodd helpu i roi cyrff mewn eirch yn yr ysbyty. Doedd o ddim yn waith pleserus ond roedd Danny eisiau bod yn ymyl Megan. Pan glywodd Robert Wyn Jones fod Danny a Megan yn ffrindiau, dwedodd wrth feddyg yn ysbyty'r gwersyll. Rhoddodd y meddyg rybudd i Megan i beidio â gweld Danny, a dwedodd un o swyddogion *(m)* Montreal yr un peth wrth Danny.

Dyn annifyr oedd Robert Wyn Jones. Roedd o'n edrych yn fudr bob amser, er ei fod o wedi gwneud pres drwy werthu llefrith i'r gwersyll yn ystod y rhyfel. Dyna sut oedd pethau yn y rhyfel, meddyliodd Danny. Roedd rhai pobl wedi gwneud pres a rhai pobl wedi dod yn arwyr, ond roedd llawer mwy wedi marw.

Roedd Robert Wyn Jones yn ffrindiau mawr efo'r cigydd, Albert Griffiths. Doedd Danny ddim yn ymddiried ynddyn nhw o gwbl. Roedden nhw'n sleifio o gwmpas *Tin Town*, casgliad blêr o siopau oedd y bobl leol wedi eu gosod y tu allan i brif giât y gwersyll. Roedd hi'n bosib cael unrhyw beth yn *Tin Town*, am bris. Roedd Danny'n siŵr fod rhywfaint o'r pres yn mynd i bocedi Robert ac Albert. Pan fyddai'r terfysg *(m)* yn dechrau, byddai'r milwyr yn dial ar ladron *Tin Town*.

Roedd côt Danny'n dechrau drewi. Sut fedrai o esbonio hynny yn y gwersyll? Doedd 'na ddim gwartheg yn y fan honno. Ond dyna'r lleiaf o'i broblemau. Mynd i mewn i'r gwersyll oedd ei broblem fwyaf. Cyrhaeddodd goedwig Hen Wern a sleifio tuag at y ffens. Byddai pobl o gwmpas erbyn hyn a ddylai Danny ddim bod yng ngwersyll British Columbia. Gwasgodd drwy'r ffens. Roedd yn rhaid iddo gyrraedd stablau'r cafalri mor fuan â phosib. Dechreuodd gerdded drwy ganol gwersyll B.C. Rhegodd yn ddistaw wrth i swyddog B.C. ddod tuag ato. Edrychodd y swyddog ar y tabiau ar ei ysgwydd.

'Tabiau Montreal, filwr! Be 'dach chi'n ei wneud yma?'

'Syr!' Saliwtiodd Danny. 'Dwi'n chwilio am y fet, syr. Mae 'na gaseg wael iawn yn stablau'r cafalri, syr.'

'Ydach chi'n dwp, filwr? Does dim fets yng ngwersyll B.C. Sais ydy'r fet. Ewch o 'ma cyn i mi ddwyn cyhuddiad *(m)* yn eich erbyn.'

'Mae'n ddrwg iawn gen i, syr. Diolch yn fawr, syr.' Saliwtiodd Danny eto. Daliodd Danny lygad y dyn arall am eiliad. Roedd ofn ar y swyddog. Trodd Danny a brasgamu i ffwrdd yn gyflym. Roedd o wedi mynd dros ben llestri efo'r holl 'syr'. Doedd y swyddogion ddim yn arfer cael cymaint o barch y dyddiau hyn. Gwenodd Danny. Ym mhob gwersyll, roedd disgyblaeth yn mynd yn waeth bob dydd ac roedd y swyddogion yn amau pob milwr. Roedd bywyd yn y gwersyll yn oer, yn anghysurus, ac yn ddiflas. Roedd y dynion yn cwyno am brinder blancedi, prinder glo, y bwyd ofnadwy, cytiau gorlawn, ac am yr oedi oedd yn eu cadw nhw rhag mynd adref. Y swyddogion oedd ar fai am bopeth, meddai'r dynion. Y prif swyddogion yn Llundain a Chanada oedd ar fai, meddai'r swyddogion. Roedden nhw'n gwybod bod 'na helynt ar droed ond doedd hyd yn oed y milwyr ddim yn gwybod o ble byddai'r helynt yn codi.

Wnaeth neb arall stopio Danny ar ei ffordd i'r stablau. Rhuthrodd i mewn i'r stabl. Roedd y gaseg wedi marw. Roedd y fet yn eistedd yn ei hymyl efo'i ben yn ei ddwylo. Yn gyflym, rhoddodd Danny ei law ar y gaseg. Roedd hi'n oer.

'Syr!' meddai Danny. 'Dwi wedi bod yn chwilio

amdanoch chi.' Cododd y fet ei ben.

Roedd hi'n amlwg bod gan y fet ben mawr.

'Dyn da, Evans. Oeddech chi efo hi ar y diwedd?'

'Oeddwn, syr.'

'Pryd buodd hi farw, Evans?'

'Tua phedwar o'r gloch, syr.'

'Wir?' Doedd o ddim yn credu Danny, ond roedd gan y fet rywbeth i'w guddio hefyd. Doedd o ddim wedi bod efo'r gaseg chwaith.

'Wel, Evans, gawn ni ddweud ein bod ni yma gyda'n gilydd?'

'Iawn, syr! Syr, mi gollais i'r cofrestru y bore 'ma. Wnewch chi siarad â fy swyddog i, syr?'

'Siŵr iawn, Evans. A rŵan, dwi angen paned o de. Ewch yn ôl i'ch gwersyll, filwr.'

Geiriau newydd

amau – *to suspect*
ar fai – *to blame*
arwr – *hero*
blêr – *untidy*
brasgamu – *to stride*
budr – *dirty*
dial – *revenge*
disgyblaeth – *discipline*
drewi – *to stink*
dringo – *to climb*
eirch – *coffins*
gorlawn – *overcrowded*
gwartheg – *cattle*
gwrych – *hedge*
lladron – *robbers*
lledu – *to spread*
llithro – *to slip*
parch – *respect*
pen mawr – *hangover*
prinder – *shortage*
rhegi – *to swear*
rheolaeth – *control*
rhybudd – *warning*
serth – *steep*
tail gwartheg – *cowpat*

Pennod 4

Brwsiodd Danny ei gôt efo'r brwsh a'r dŵr oedd ar gyfer y ceffylau y tu allan i'r stablau. Roedd ei gynlluniau'n mynd yn iawn. Roedd o wedi priodi, yn ôl yn y gwersyll yn saff ac roedd ei alibi yn ei le. Byddai'n cymryd y ffordd hiraf yn ôl i Montreal a cheisio chwilio am arwyddion o helynt ar y ffordd. Cerddodd heibio i'r gwersyll agosaf. Gwersyll bach o Saeson oedd hwn. Fydden nhw ddim yn codi twrw, ond efallai bydden nhw'n darged. Aeth heibio i'r ddau wersyll nesaf hefyd. Roedd Nova Scotia a Western Ontario mor nerfus â'r Saeson. Trodd yn ôl at wersyll New Brunswick gan obeithio y byddai o'n gweld rhywun roedd o'n ei adnabod. Roedd y milwyr yn sefyll y tu allan i'w cytiau mewn grwpiau bach, yn smocio ac yn siarad yn dawel, eu paciau cefn ar y glaswellt a'r awyrgylch yn llawn tyndra. Roedd corporal yn mynd o gwmpas gan geisio eu perswadio nhw i fynd ar daith hyfforddi *(m)*.

Gwelodd Danny wyneb cyfarwydd ac ymuno â'i grŵp. Cynigiodd sigarennau i bawb a gofyn, 'Be sy'n digwydd yma?'

Chwarddodd un o'r grŵp, 'Dim byd o gwbl, bydi.'

Gwaeddodd y milwr yn uchel i gyfeiriad y corporal, ''Dan ni'n aros am long i fynd adref.'

''Dan ni'n gwrthod mynd ar daith hyfforddi fel protest,' meddai'r dyn oedd Danny'n ei adnabod. Arhosodd Danny i gael sgwrs am dipyn. Wrth iddo adael roedd y corporal yn cynghori un o'r swyddogion i anghofio am y daith hyfforddi.

Yn y gwersyll nesaf – Alberta – doedd 'na ddim swyddogion yn y golwg, dim ond grwpiau o filwyr yn siarad â'i gilydd. Gwelodd Danni Bronski. Byddai'n chwarae gêm o gardiau efo fo'n aml. Ymunodd Danny â grŵp Bronski. Roedd y milwyr eraill yn y grŵp yn edrych yn amheus ar Danny. Roedden nhw'n cynnal parti preifat a doedd Danny ddim ar restr y gwesteion.

'Evans, Montreal,' cyflwynodd Bronski Danny. 'Mae o'n iawn. Efallai bydd o'n lledu'r gair i Fontreal.' Roedden nhw'n siarad am Gyrnol Thackeray. Gan nad oedd yr *Haverford* wedi cael hwylio ar Chwefror 25ain, roedd carfan o filwyr wedi gofyn am gyfarfod efo'r Cyrnol. Roedd Thackeray wedi trin y garfan yn wael a chynyddu dicter y dynion oedd yn ddigon dig yn barod. Unwaith eto, roedd y swyddogion wedi siomi'r dynion.

'Dwi'n dweud y dylen ni ymosod *(m)* ar y cantinau yn gyntaf,' meddai un o'r dynion.

'Wneith hynny ddim gweithio os na fydd pob gwersyll yn gwneud yr un peth. Mi fydd hi'n hawdd iddyn nhw stopio terfysg mewn un gwersyll, ond yn amhosib os bydd 'na helynt ym mhob un.'

'Oes gynnon ni gefnogaeth ym Montreal, Evans?'

'Mi wna' i ofyn i'r hogiau yno. Pryd mae'r cyrch *(m)* i fod?'

'Mi wnawn ni roi gwybod i chi.'

'Iawn.' Gadawodd Danny. Doedd o ddim yn bwriadu codi twrw yng ngwersyll Montreal. Dim ond eisiau gwybod pryd fyddai'r terfysg yn dechrau oedd o. Roedd Danny a Jackson yn cynllunio i ddianc o Wersyll Parc Cinmel yn ystod y terfysg. Byddai Jackson yn mynd i Lundain a byddai Danny'n mynd i'r bryniau i guddio tan i fyddin Canada adael y wlad. Tasen nhw'n cael eu dal mi fasen nhw'n cael eu saethu am eu bod yn encilwyr. Tasen nhw'n llwyddo, mi fasen nhw'n ddynion rhydd. Roedd rhesymau arbennig pam nad oedden nhw eisiau mynd yn ôl i Ganada.

Ar ei ffordd i Fontreal, sylwodd Danny ar grwpiau bach o ddynion yn symud i'r un cyfeiriad. Dilynodd Danny nhw i wersyll 4, rhan o wersyll Manitoba. Y tu allan i'r YMCA roedd Drake, codwr twrw adnabyddus, yn sefyll ar focs yn siarad â thyrfa o tua chant o filwyr. Roedd Drake yn un o'r garfan oedd wedi gweld Cyrnol Thackeray.

'Maen nhw wedi torri'r addewid "y cyntaf allan – y cyntaf adref". Mae rhai ohonon ni wedi bod yn Fflandrys am dair blynedd ond 'dan ni wedi gweld hogiau fuodd yn brwydro *(m)* am ddim ond chwe mis yn cael mynd adref.'

Roedd y dyrfa'n tyfu ac roedd llawer o bobl yn gweiddi eu cefnogaeth. 'Beth am yr *Haverford*?' gwaeddodd rhywun.

'Mae'r *Haverford* wedi cael ei chanslo am y pedwerydd tro,' atebodd Drake. 'Addewid arall sy' wedi cael ei dorri.'

'Beth am y *Mauretania*, yr *Aquitania* a'r *Olympic*?' gwaeddodd rhywun arall. Roedd y llongau hyn wedi cael eu llogi ar gyfer y Canadiaid hefyd ond roedden nhw wedi cael eu defnyddio i fynd â'r milwyr o America adref.

'Yn hollol,' gwaeddodd Drake. 'Yr olaf i ymuno â'r rhyfel yw'r cyntaf i fynd adref, a 'dan ni yma o hyd.' Aeth y dyrfa'n wyllt. Roedd y dynion yn casáu'r Americanwyr. Siaradodd wedyn am y sefyllfa yng Nghanada. 'Pan gyrhaeddwn ni adref fydd 'na ddim gwaith. Mi fydd y milwyr ar y strydoedd.' Roedd hynny'n rhywbeth oedd yn poeni llawer ohonyn nhw. Yng Nghanada, roedd diweithdra'n cynyddu'n gyflym a'r olaf i fynd adref fyddai'r olaf i gael gwaith. Roedd y dyrfa'n ddig iawn, ond yn y diwedd penderfynon nhw ofyn am gyfarfod arall efo Thackeray. Roedd Danny'n siomedig.

Gwelodd Danny Jackson yn y dyrfa. Aeth draw ato. Roedd un o'r swyddogion ar ymylon y dyrfa yn mynd i ddweud wrth Thackeray beth oedd yn digwydd. Dechreuodd y dyrfa grwydro i ffwrdd.

'Dim terfysg heddiw, Danny,' sibrydodd Jackson. 'Does gan Ganadiaid ddim stumog am derfysg. Maen nhw'n dal i gredu mai siarad efo Thackeray ydy'r ateb.'

Soniodd Danny wrth Jackson am y briodas, a siaradodd y ddau am beth roedden nhw wedi ei ddarganfod o gwmpas y gwersylloedd. Aethon nhw at y brif giât. Roedd Danny eisiau bod ar wyliadwriaeth *(m)* y noson honno er mwyn bod yn rhydd ddydd Sul. Edrychodd ar y rhestr enwau. Gwelodd enw un o filwyr Montreal arni!

'Gwych!' meddai Danny, 'Awn ni i gael cinio, Jacks?'

Geiriau newydd

adnabyddus – *well known*
amheus – *suspicious*
awyrgylch – *atmosphere*
carfan – *party*
cefnogaeth – *support*
codi twrw – *to make trouble*
crwydro – *to wander*
cyfarwydd – *familiar*
cynghori – *to advise*
cynnal – *to hold*
cynnig – *to offer*
cynyddu – *to increase*
dicter – *anger*
diweithdra – *unemployment*
llogi – *to hire*
sefyllfa – *situation*
trin – *to treat*
tyndra – *tension*
tyrfa – *crowd*
ymylon – *fringes*

Pennod 5

Dros ginio, eisteddodd Danny a Jackson wrth ymyl Larsen, y milwr oedd â'i enw ar y rhestr wyliadwriaeth. Roedd Larsen yn ddigalon achos roedd o'n hoffi mynd i'r Rhyl bob nos Sadwrn. Roedd y milwyr eraill wedi dechrau siarad am eu noson allan yn y Rhyl. Ddwedodd Danny ddim byd.

'Be sy' o'i le, Evans?' gofynnodd un o'r dynion. 'Dwyt ti ddim yn dod i'r Rhyl?'

'Nac ydw,' meddai Danny'n ddigalon. 'Does gen i ddim pres. Collais i ormod yn y gêm gardiau neithiwr.' Dechreuodd pawb gwyno am bres – roedd eu cyflogau'n hwyr unwaith eto. Trodd y sgwrs at ladron *Tin Town*, yr oerfel, y swyddogion gwael a phopeth arall oedd o'i le yn y gwersyll. Trodd Danny y sgwrs yn ôl at nos Sadwrn. Erbyn diwedd y pryd, roedd Larsen wedi perswadio Danny, am bris wrth gwrs, i gymryd ei le ar wyliadwriaeth y noson honno.

Roedd Danny wedi blino. 'Be sy'n digwydd y pnawn 'ma?' gofynnodd i'r lleill.

'Symud glo, mwy na thebyg,' atebodd rhywun. Aeth Danny i weld y corporal. Esboniodd ei fod wedi bod yn effro drwy'r nos efo'r gaseg ac y byddai o ar wyliadwriaeth y noson honno. Gofynnodd os oedd hi'n iawn iddo fynd i gysgu am y prynhawn.

Roedd y corporal yn fodlon. Problem y corporals i gyd oedd dod o hyd i waith i'r dynion. Os byddai Danny'n cysgu, dyna un dyn yn llai i boeni amdano.

'Fydda i ddim yn disgwyl eich gweld chi yfory chwaith, Evans.' Roedd pob milwr yn cael diwrnod rhydd ar ôl bod ar wyliadwriaeth.

'Reit, corp. Diolch.' Aeth Danny i'w gwt. O'r diwedd, tynnodd ei esgidiau a mynd i gysgu'n syth.

Roedd nos Sadwrn yn brysur wrth y brif giât. Pan gyrhaeddodd Danny, dwedodd wrth y swyddog, 'Evans yn lle Larson, syr.' Doedd dim ots gan y swyddog pwy oedd yn gwneud y gwaith. Edrych ar ôl ei niferoedd oedd yn bwysig iddo fo. Roedd y rhan fwyaf o'r milwyr yn mynd i'r Rhyl ar drên y gwersyll, ond roedd 'na ddigon o draffig yn mynd a dod drwy'r giât. Swydd Danny oedd cadw pobl rhag cael lifft ar gerbydau swyddogol, ond byddai'r gwarchodwr *(m)* yn cau ei lygaid am ychydig o sigarennau neu dipyn o bres. Y gyrwyr fasai'n dioddef tasai'r heddlu milwrol *(m)* yn eu dal nhw.

Roedd ffilm Charlie Chaplin yn cael ei dangos yn y YMCA ar gyfer y dynion oedd yn aros yn y gwersyll, ac roedd y cantinau gwlyb *(m)* yn paratoi am noson brysur arall.

Roedd hi'n brysur eto pan ddaeth pawb yn ôl o'r Rhyl. Fel arfer, collodd rhai milwyr y trên a sleifio yn ôl yn y cerbydau swyddogol. Ar ôl canol nos, cyrhaeddodd lorïau'r heddlu milwrol yn llawn o filwyr meddw oedd wedi cael eu codi o strydoedd y Rhyl. Roedd tŷ gwarchod *(m)* gwersyll 9 yn ymyl y brif giât yn llawn bob nos Sadwrn. Jîpiau a moduron y swyddogion gyrhaeddodd olaf. Roedd y swyddogion wedi treulio'r noson yn y clybiau yn Llandudno. Cafodd Danny wybod pa gerbydau oedd yn mynd allan fore dydd Sul a threfnodd lifft i Abergele efo un o'r gyrwyr ambiwlans. Roedd Larsen wedi dod â phastai gig iddo fo o'r Rhyl. Trefnodd fod y gwarchodwr arall yn sefyll tu allan i'r bwth gwarchodwr *(m)* ac aeth yntau i mewn, bwyta'r bastai a mynd i gysgu am awr.

Drannoeth, ar ôl brecwast, aeth Danny i ysbyty'r gwersyll i geisio dod o hyd i'w ambiwlans. Benthycodd feic, am bris, oddi wrth un o'r staff sifil *(m)* oedd yn gweithio yn yr ysbyty. Cuddiodd efo'r beic o dan flanced yn yr ambiwlans gwag. Gadawodd Danny'r ambiwlans y tu allan i Abergele cyn i'r gyrrwr ddechrau codi gweithwyr sifil y gwersyll. Ar y ffordd i'r bryniau, meddyliodd Danny'n galed am ei guddfan. Doedd o ddim eisiau cael ei saethu am fod o'n enciliwr. Roedd o'n cofio milwr ifanc oedd wedi colli'i blwc yn llwyr yn Fflandrys. Pan ddaeth y gorchymyn *(m)* iddo fynd at ymyl y ffos *(m)*, taflodd yr hogyn ei bac a'i wn ar y llawr a rhedeg i ffwrdd. Saethodd yr heddlu milwrol o ar unwaith. 'Lladdwyd mewn brwydr' *(m)* meddai'r llythyr at ei rieni.

Roedd gan Megan stori am Gymro lleol oedd wedi ceisio encilio hefyd. Roedd ei fam wedi ei guddio mewn hen gwt bugail yng nghanol nunlle. Daeth yr heddlu milwrol o hyd iddo ac ychydig wythnosau wedyn, cafodd ei fam lythyr – 'Lladdwyd mewn brwydr'.

'Bechod oedd hynny, yntê?' meddai Megan. Cytunodd Danny heb ddweud y gwir wrthi. Roedd o'n poeni am y stori. Roedd hi'n amlwg nad oedd merched Cymru mor glyfar â'r heddlu milwrol. Dim cytiau bugail, hen ysguboriau, na beudai iddo fo.

Cyrhaeddodd Danny'r ficerdy am hanner awr wedi un ar ddeg. Edrychodd i fyny'r bryn ar Gefn Carreg, fferm teulu Megan. Byddai'n rhaid iddo osgoi Robert Wyn Jones. Doedd neb o gwmpas y ficerdy. Cadwodd y beic yn y seler. Roedd Megan yn ei ddisgwyl. Rhuthrodd i'w freichiau ac ar ôl llawer o gofleidio a chusanu, dechreuodd y ddau drafod cuddfan Danny. Gwrthododd Danny hyd yn oed edrych ar gytiau bugail, hen ysguboriau a beudai. Roedd Megan yn ddigalon.

'Wel, Danny, mae 'na ystafell ddirgel yma.'

'Yma, yn y seler? Mae hynny dipyn bach yn amlwg tydi?'

'Does neb yn gwybod amdani, dim ond Mam a'r ficer. Cafodd ei chloi fwy nag ugain mlynedd yn ôl.' Cafodd Danny ei siomi yn Megan. Roedd hi'n edrych yn bryderus.

'Iawn, cariad,' meddai Danny er mwyn cadw Megan yn hapus. 'Gawn ni fynd i weld yr ystafell ddirgel?' Roedden nhw'n gwastraffu eu hamser, meddyliodd Danny. Goleuodd Megan lamp olew ac arwain y ffordd i'r ystafell ddirgel.

Geiriau newydd

benthyg – *to borrow*
beudy – *cowshed*
bugail – *shepherd*
cerbyd – *vehicle*
cloi – *to lock*
cuddfan – *hiding place*
dioddef – *to suffer*
dirgel – *secret*
meddw – *drunk*
nifer – *number*
pryderus – *worried*
trefnu – *to arrange*
ysgubor – *barn*

Pennod 6

Roedd y seler yn anferth. Dilynodd Danny Megan
drwy'r coridor y tu ôl i'r wal ym mhen draw'r seler.
Ond nid dyma'r pen draw. Roedd tair neu bedair o
ystafelloedd heb ddrysau y tu ôl i'r wal. Edrychodd
Danny i mewn iddyn nhw. Gwelodd fod un ohonyn
nhw'n llawn dodrefn a hen seddau'r eglwys. Roedd
un arall yn llawn llyfrau a phapurau ac un arall yn
wag. Roedd yr ystafell olaf yn llawn darnau o hen
welyau a matresi.

'Dydy'r ystafelloedd hyn ddim yn ddirgel,
Megan. Byddai'r heddlu milwrol yn dod o hyd i mi
mewn pum munud yma.'

'Aros!' meddai Megan. Rhoddodd y lamp ar hen
ffrâm gwely.

'Helpa fi i dynnu'r matresi yma.' Symudodd y
ddau o leiaf chwe matres oddi wrth y wal. Roedd
drws y tu ôl i'r matresi.

'Dyna fo,' meddai Megan. 'Ceisia agor y drws.'
Roedd hen oriad haearn yn y drws ond fedrai
Danny mo'i symud o.

'Oes 'na olew yma'n rhywle?' gofynnodd.

'Efo'r pethau garddio yn y seler fawr. Mi a' i i'w
nôl o.' Aeth Megan â'r lamp efo hi. Roedd hi'n
dywyll fel bol buwch heb olau'r lamp. Dychwelodd
Megan efo olew a rhoddodd Danny beth ar oriad y

drws ac ar y colfachau.

'Dydyn nhw ddim yn rhydlyd iawn,' meddai Danny. 'Pam tybed?'

'Mae hi'n ystafell gynnes. Dyna pam does neb yn ei defnyddio hi. Yn yr hen ddyddiau, seler win oedd hi, ond pan symudodd teulu'r ficer i Blas Newydd, mi fuodd y tŷ'n wag tan i'r ficer yma ddod. Doedd y ficer ddim eisiau llawer o win, a beth bynnag, efo'r gwres canolog mae hi'n rhy gynnes i gadw gwin yma.'

O'r diwedd, symudodd y drws ac yn sydyn, agorodd. Syrthiodd Danny i lawr gris i mewn i'r ystafell. Daeth Megan i mewn efo'r lamp.

'Fues i ddim yma o'r blaen,' meddai'n gynhyrfus.

Rhoddodd Megan y lamp i Danny ac edrychodd Danny o'i gwmpas. Roedd gwe pry cop ym mhobman. Tynnodd Danny rai ohonyn nhw i lawr a symud drwy'r ystafell. Roedd hi'n fawr, ar siâp L, a'r rhan gyferbyn â'r drws tua wyth troedfedd o led efo sinc yn y gornel, a rownd y gornel honno roedd hi tua deuddeg troedfedd o hyd ac wyth troedfedd o led efo silffoedd llechi ar gyfer y gwin.

'Mae 'na ddigon o le i fatres yma, Danny,' meddai Megan. 'Taset ti i mewn yma, mi faswn i'n medru rhoi'r matresi eraill yn ôl yn erbyn y wal ac ni fasai neb yn gwybod bod 'na ystafell yma wedyn.'

'Efallai dy fod ti'n iawn. Wyt ti'n siŵr nad oes neb yn dod yma?'

'Ydw, achos does neb yn hoffi . . . ' stopiodd Megan yn sydyn.

'Does neb yn hoffi beth, Megs?'

'Dim byd, Danny. Wnân nhw mo dy boeni di.'

'Megan, os oes 'na broblem efo'r seler, dwi am

gael gwybod. Be sy' o'i le?'

'Tyrd, mi ddangosa' i i ti.'

Dilynodd Danny Megan yn ôl i brif ystafell y seler. Aeth Megan i'r gornel y tu ôl i'r boeler. Pwyntiodd at ddrws bach pren yn y wal.

'Be ydy hwn?' gofynnodd Danny.

'Hen dwll glo. Maen nhw'n byw yno.'

'Pwy, Megan?' Roedd Danny'n dechrau mynd yn flin. Beth oedd y peth ofnadwy oedd yn byw yn y twll glo?

'Ystlumod. Dyna pam does neb yn hoffi dod i lawr yma. Dim ond weithiau maen nhw'n dod i mewn i'r seler ond wnan nhw ddim drwg i neb Danny.'

'Ystlumod?' Doedd Danny ddim yn siŵr o'r gair. 'Bats?'

Nodiodd Megan ei phen. 'Oes arnat ti ofn ystlumod?'

'Dwi ddim yn gwybod. Dwi ddim wedi cyfarfod llawer ohonyn nhw. Pa fath o ystlumod? Ydyn nhw'n fawr?' Ar ôl y llygod Ffrengig yn y ffosydd yn Fflandrys, doedd Danny ddim yn meddwl y byddai ystlumod yn ei boeni.

'Nac ydyn. Rhai bach iawn ydyn nhw. *Pipistrelles* yn ôl y ficer. Y ficer a fi ydy'r unig bobl sy'n eu hoffi nhw. Dydy'r morynion byth yn dod yma, na Mam chwaith. Fi sy'n gorfod rhoi'r dillad ar y lein pan fydd hi'n bwrw glaw.'

Trodd Danny at ganol y seler. Roedd leiniau'n hongian o'r nenfwd efo polion yn eu dal nhw yn eu lle. Roedd bwrdd y brecwast priodas wrth ochr yr ystafell efo basgedi dillad arno.

'Mae 'na ddigon o olau yma,' meddai Danny gan

gerdded ar draws yr ystafell. Medrai weld yr ardd drwy'r ffenestri. Roedd dodrefn gardd, seddau a byrddau bambŵ wrth y drws mawr.

'Cafodd y ffenestri eu gosod yn lle hen ddrysau'r tŷ coets. Mae 'na storfa i'r pethau garddio yma hefyd.' Arweiniodd Danny i ystafell fach arall yn ymyl y drws mawr. 'Mae 'na ddrws bach i fynd i mewn i'r storfa. Mae Edgar y garddwr yn ei ddefnyddio fo.'

'Edgar? Morynion? Faint o bobl sy'n gweithio yma?'

'Dim ond dwywaith yr wythnos mae Edgar yn gweithio. Mae'r morynion yn dod pan fydd ar Mam eu hangen nhw. Maen nhw'n gweithio yng Nghefn Carreg hefyd. Danny, mae'n rhaid imi fynd yn fuan i roi cinio i Dad. Mae Mam yn gwneud cinio i westeion y ficer heddiw. Wyt ti eisiau gweld y seler win eto?'

'Pam lai.' Pan gyrhaeddon nhw'r ystafell oedd yn llawn matresi, meddai Danny, 'Pryd wyt ti'n gorfod mynd, Megs?'

'Yn fuan. Pam?'

''Dan ni'n briod rŵan, Megan. Gawn ni ddathlu?'

Tynnodd Danny ei wraig i lawr ar un o'r matresi. Chwarddodd Megan. 'O Danny, dwi mor hapus.'

Geiriau newydd

anferth – *huge*
colfachau – *hinges*
dathlu – *to celebrate*
dodrefn – *furniture*
goriad – *key*
gris – *step*
gwag – *empty*
gwe pry cop – *cobwebs*
gwesteion – *guests*
haearn – *iron*
llechi – *slate*
lled – *wide*
llygod Ffrengig – *rats*
morwyn/morynion – *maid(s)*
nenfwd – *ceiling*
rhydlyd – *rusty*
syrthio – *to fall*
twll glo – *coal hole*
ystlumod – *bats*

Pennod 7

Ar ôl i Megan adael, cymerodd Danny frws o'r seler fawr a dechrau tynnu'r gwe pry cop i lawr o'r nenfwd. Roedd y seler win yn sych ac yn ddigon cynnes. Efo matresi yn erbyn y wal yn y seler arall, fyddai neb yn gwybod ei fod o yno. Efallai byddai hyn yn gweithio, ond ni fyddai'n rhaid iddo fod yno'n hir. Yn fuan, byddai'r heddlu milwrol yn darganfod cysylltiad rhwng Danny a Megan efallai.

Dychwelodd Megan efo plataid o fwyd, gweddill-ion cinio'r ficer, a photaid o de. Cafodd Danny ginio ardderchog yn y seler fawr. Sylwodd Megan ei fod o wedi dechrau glanhau'r seler win.

'Beth wyt ti'n feddwl o'r seler, Danny? Fydd hi'n iawn?'

'Bydd, dwi'n meddwl,' meddai Danny â llond ei geg o gig oen. 'Fedri di roi'r matresi'n ôl yn eu lle ar dy ben dy hun?'

Chwarddodd Megan. 'Dwi ddim yn siwgr a sbeis Danny! Merch fferm gref ydw i.'

'Ond os wyt ti'n feichiog . . . ? Pryd gawn ni wybod?'

'Mewn wythnos neu ddwy. Ti fydd y cyntaf i gael gwybod.' Rhoddodd Megan gusan i Danny. 'Wyt ti eisiau dod â phethau yma o'r gwersyll? Wyt ti'n gwybod pryd fydd yr helynt yn dechrau?'

'Nac ydw. Does gen i ddim llawer o bethau,

Megan. Esgidiau sbâr, fflachlamp ac ati. Mi wna' i roi ychydig o bethau i ti yfory. Wyt ti'n gweithio yn yr ysbyty yfory?'

'Ydw, mi wna' i ddod â bag mawr hefo fi. Dwi'n gorffen am bedwar o'r gloch.'

'Iawn. Mi wela' i di yn ystod y dydd rywsut. Ydy dy dad yn amau unrhyw beth?'

'Dim o gwbl. Dydy o'n meddwl am ddim byd ond cyfri ei bres ar ddydd Sul, a chysgu.'

Yn ôl yn y gwersyll, gofynnodd Danny i Jackson a oedd rhywbeth wedi digwydd.

'Rwyt ti wedi colli ffrae fawr, Danny boi.'

'Ffrae fawr? Ydy'r helynt wedi cychwyn?' Roedd Danny'n poeni. Doedd o ddim eisiau clywed bod popeth wedi digwydd pan oedd o i ffwrdd o'r gwersyll.

'Ydy wir, trwbl mawr,' meddai Jackson. 'Roedd rhai pobl eisiau chwarae pêl-droed a'r lleill eisiau chwarae pêl-fas. Roedd hi'n frwydr ofnadwy!'

Pwnsiodd Danny ei ffrind a syrthio ar ei wely. 'Dwi wedi blino'n lân. Mi fedrwn i gysgu am wythnos.'

'Tyrd am ddiod, Danny. Efallai medrwn ni ddechrau terfysg.'

'Dwi'n rhy flinedig heno. Gofynna iddyn nhw ddechrau hebddo i.' Gadawodd Jackson a rhai o'r lleill i fynd i'r cantîn gwlyb.

Dechreuodd Danny feddwl am bethau i fynd efo fo i'w guddfan. Byddai'n dwyn ychydig o'r gwersyll yfory. Dim ond un swfenîr oedd ganddo o'r rhyfel – gwn Luger y swyddog Almaenig roedd Danny wedi ei ladd ym mrwydr Ypres.

Tynnodd lun o'i boced. Dyna ei unig swfenîr o

Ganada. Edrychodd ar y llun o'r diwrnod pan adawodd y fferm hefo'i dad. Naw oed oedd Danny ar y pryd. Roedd ei nain, brodyr ei dad a'u gwragedd a'u plant yn edrych yn hapus. Roedd ei dad, Danny Mawr, yn gwenu, ond roedd Danny Bach yn edrych yn ofnus. Cafodd Danny Mawr arian gan y brodyr i fynd i Montreal i ddechrau bywyd newydd. Doedd Danny Bach ddim eisiau bywyd newydd. Roedd o'n hoffi bod ar y fferm efo'i dad.

Doedd ganddo ddim llun o'i fam. Roedd hi wedi marw wrth roi genedigaeth i Danny. Cafodd ei fagu gan ei nain a'i dad. Pabyddes o Iwerddon oedd ei fam. Roedd ei dad wedi addo magu Danny yn Babydd ond doedd ei nain ddim yn hoffi hynny. Cymraes o ogledd Cymru oedd ei nain yn wreiddiol. Roedd hi'n siarad Cymraeg efo Danny Bach, er bod ei phlant ei hun yn dweud bod yr hen iaith yn ddiwerth. Cyn iddo briodi, roedd Danny Mawr wedi gadael y fferm a mynd i weithio i wersyll torri coed. Ar ôl marwolaeth ei wraig, mam Danny, doedd o ddim yn medru setlo'n ôl ar y fferm. Roedd o'n meddwi'n aml a phan oedd y wisgi'n siarad, roedd o'n dweud storïau wrth Danny ynglŷn â'i anturiaethau efo'r coedwigwyr yn y gwersyll. Fedrai Danny Mawr ddim cadw trefn ar ei fywyd heb ei wraig ac roedd o'n gwrthod cymryd gwraig arall. Yn y diwedd, penderfynodd fynd i Montreal i chwilio am waith yn y dociau.

Llwyddodd Danny Mawr ym Montreal a daeth yn gaffer ar y gweithwyr. Priododd â phabyddes arall o Iwerddon hefyd. Bob blwyddyn, roedd babi newydd yn cyrraedd a doedd llysfam newydd Danny ddim yn hoffi cael ei hatgoffa o wraig gyntaf ei gŵr, mam Danny. Felly, aeth Danny i fyw efo teulu un o'i ffrindiau ysgol. Ffrancwr bach ac unig blentyn oedd Pierre Duchesne. Roedd gan M a Mme Duchesne fecws llwyddiannus ac roedden nhw'n falch iawn o gael hogyn arall yn y tŷ a'r becws. Wrth gwrs, Ffrangeg oedden nhw'n siarad bob amser, fel llawer o bobl ym Montreal, ac yn fuan roedd Danny'n medru siarad Ffrangeg yn rhugl.

Fedrai Danny ddim cofio pryd ddechreuodd o a Pierre ddwyn pethau. Afalau o'r farchnad ar y dechrau efallai, i'w gwerthu ar gornel y stryd, ac wedyn pethau o'r dociau oedd wedi cael eu dwyn yn barod gan y gweithwyr yno. Erbyn ei fod yn bymtheg oed, medrai Danny gael gafael ar unrhyw beth am bris ac roedd ganddo enw da ymhlith y mân droseddwyr ym Montreal. Roedd o wedi dweud wrth Megan mai dyn busnes oedd o, ond bod yn ffermwr oedd ei freuddwyd. Roedd rhai Cymry Cymraeg eisiau mynd i Ganada, ond eisiau mynd y ffordd arall oedd Danny – adref i Gymru. Rhoddodd y llun yn ôl yn ei boced ac aeth i gysgu.

Geiriau newydd

antur – *adventure*
becws – *bakery*
cael gafael ar – *to get hold of*
coedwigwr – *lumberjack*
cyfrif – *to count*
cysylltiad – *connection*
dwyn – *to steal*
ffrae – *row*
genedigaeth – *birth*
gweddillion – *remains*
gwersyll torri coed – *lumber camp*
llwyddo – *to succeed*
llysfam – *step mother*
rhugl – *fluent*
mân droseddwr – *petty criminal*

Pennod 8

Y bore dydd Llun canlynol yng ngwersylloedd Toronto ac Ontario, aeth carfan o ddynion at eu swyddogion eu hunain i ofyn pam nad oedden nhw'n cael hwylio adref. Aeth y dynion yno mewn heddwch ond daethon nhw'n ôl yn ddig iawn. Roedd un o'r capteniaid wedi eu trin nhw'n swta, a gadawodd y garfan gan ddweud y bydden nhw'n dechrau terfysg os nad oedd sôn am long adref erbyn hanner awr wedi deg drannoeth.

Ar y ffordd i'r ysbyty, clywodd Danny fod yr un math o gyfarfodydd yn cael eu cynnal mewn sawl gwersyll. Gadawodd ei barsel y tu allan i ddrws cefn yr ysbyty a phan aeth Megan i'w nôl o yn ystod ei hegwyl, cododd Danny ei law arni o'r pellter. Gwyliodd Danny Megan yn darllen ei nodyn: 'Gadawa ddrws y seler yn agored bob nos yr wythnos yma.' Nodiodd hi.

Drwy'r dydd, roedd pawb wedi bod yn siarad am y terfysg. Roedden nhw'n dweud bod 'na faneri coch wrth law yn barod mewn rhai gwersylloedd. Ar ôl te, aeth Danny at y brif giât i wneud yn siŵr fod Megan wedi medru gadael yr ysbyty heb gael ei dal.

Dros y ffordd, roedd tyrfa o filwyr yn gweiddi'n sarhaus ar siopwyr *Tin Town*. Brysiodd y siopwyr i gau eu siopau a rhedeg i ffwrdd fel llygod i'w tyllau. Roedd hi'n amlwg i Danny nad oedd gan y dyrfa arweinydd. Efallai eu bod nhw'n ceisio dangos eu cryfder. Yn y cantinau y noson honno roedd pawb yn siarad am yr un peth. Tasai'r newyddion o Lundain yn ddrwg yn y bore, mi fasai terfysg.

Bore dydd Mawrth, roedd y milwyr ledled y gwersylloedd yn gwrthod mynd ar barêd nac ar daith hyfforddi. Cafodd y dynion o Barti Hwylio 21 eu perswadio i fynd i gyfarfod â Major Cooper, swyddog o'r pencadlys, am hanner awr wedi naw. Pan orffennodd y cyfarfod heb drafferth, roedd Major Cooper yn credu bod y dynion yn fodlon ac aeth i'r Rhyl i drefnu adloniant yn y YMCA y noson honno. Am hanner awr wedi deg, doedd 'na ddim ateb wedi dod o Lundain i'r dynion yng ngwersylloedd Toronto ac Ontario. Dechreuon nhw brotestio am y bwyd, ond doedd dim sôn am derfysg.

Yn y prynhawn, roedd dynion yn mynd o gwmpas y gwersylloedd yn ceisio mesur maint y gefnogaeth. Byddai cyfarfod protest am naw o'r gloch y noson honno, medden nhw. Gorffennodd Danny a Jackson drafod eu cynlluniau. Gyda'i gilydd aeth y ddau â'u beiciau at y ffens derfyn – un beic at y ffens ger ffordd Lerpwl a'r llall at y ffens ger ffordd Abergele. Cuddiodd Jackson ei ddillad sifil mewn lle arall, rhag ofn byddai rhywun yn dwyn ei feic. Doedd Danny ddim yn poeni am ddillad sifil, roedd ganddo weddill ei fywyd i feddwl am bethau felly. Rhoddodd Danny ei ddisg enw *(m)* i Jackson. Efallai byddai hi'n ddefnyddiol iddo gael dewis o ddau enw, ac ni fyddai ar Danny angen disg enw yn ei fywyd newydd.

'Mi fydda i'n iawn yn Llundain,' meddai

Jackson. 'Bydd pawb yn cael ceir yn fuan, a does dim llawer o bobl yn medru eu trwsio na'u gyrru nhw. Mi fydd 'na lawer o waith ar gael.'

Un o'r pethau ddysgodd y ddau yn y fyddin oedd sut i yrru a pheth arall oedd sut i aros yn fyw.

'Pob lwc efo'r ffermio, Danny,' meddai Jackson. 'Wyt ti'n siŵr na fyddi di'n colli bywyd o droseddu ym Montreal?'

'Dim perygl,' chwarddodd Danny. Doedd o ddim eisiau dweud beth fyddai Jackson yn ei golli yng Nghanada. Roedd o wedi priodi cyn iddo adael am Ffrainc a'r flwyddyn wedyn roedd ei wraig wedi cael babi. Doedd Jackson ddim eisiau ei gweld hi eto. Roedd ei deulu'n dod o Lundain yn wreiddiol ac roedd o'n meddwl amdano'i hun fel Cockney.

Ar ôl swper, cafodd Danny a Jackson ddiod yng nghantîn gwlyb Montreal ac am naw o'r gloch, fel arfer, caeodd yr heddlu milwrol y bar. Roedd hi fel aros am orchymyn i fynd 'dros y top' yn y ffosydd, ond y tro yma roedd ganddyn nhw ddewis. Pwy fyddai'n mynd? Gadawodd tua ugain o ddynion wersyll Montreal i fynd i chwilio am y cyfarfod protest. Mi fedren nhw glywed y sŵn cyn iddyn nhw gyrraedd priffordd y gwersyll. Ar y briffordd, cawson nhw eu dal mewn tyrfa o fwy na chant o filwyr oedd yn rhuthro rhwng gwersylloedd 7 a 6. Rhedodd Danny a Jackson efo nhw.

'Beth sy'n digwydd?' gwaeddodd Jackson ar un o'r milwyr.

'Rydan ni wedi ymosod ar gantîn gwersyll 7. Gwersyll 6 fydd nesaf.'

Rhuthrodd y dyn ymlaen. Roedd y terfysg wedi dechrau. Byddai Danny a Jackson yn rhydd yn fuan.

Geiriau newydd

adloniant – *entertainment*
arweinydd – *leader*
bywyd troseddwr – *criminal life*
cryfder – *strength*
dewis – *choice*
egwyl – *break*
heddwch – *peace*
pellter – *distance*
pencadlys – *headquarters*
rhuthro – *to rush*
sarhaus – *insultingly*
swta – *abrupt*
trwsio – *to repair*

Pennod 9

Yng nghantîn gwersyll 6, roedd hi'n amlwg mai nod y milwyr oedd yfed cymaint â phosibl. Torrwyd byrddau a seddau yn y rhuthr swnllyd at y bar. Roedd Jackson wedi dwyn potelaid o wisgi o rywle ac roedd o'n fodlon ei rhannu hi efo'i ffrind gorau. Cymeron nhw lymaid neu ddau. Roedd rhai o'r milwyr yn gweiddi 'Tin Town nesaf!' a gadawodd hanner y dyrfa gantîn 6 gan weiddi am waed.

'Cantîn y swyddogion!' gwaeddodd rhywun arall. Cytunodd Danny a Jackson y byddai pethau gwell i'w dwyn yng nghantîn y swyddogion. Neidiodd Danny dros far y cantîn, ond roedd rhywun arall wrth y til o'i flaen. Roedd Danny a Jackson yn siomedig.

'Mae rhyw fastad wedi dwyn y pres yn barod,' gwaeddodd y milwr meddw gan edrych fel tasai o'n mynd i grio.

'Fedrwch chi ddim ymddiried yn neb y dyddiau hyn,' meddai Danny gan ei helpu ei hun i botelaid o wisgi. Ble roedd Jackson efo'r botel arall? Roedd pawb yn ymladd a chafodd Danny ei daro gan rywun. Ymladdodd ei ffordd allan gan daflu ei ddyrnau i bob cyfeiriad. Yn yr awyr iach, roedd popeth yn ferw gwyllt a sylweddolodd Danny ei fod o wedi colli Jackson. Cymerodd lymaid arall cyn edrych o'i gwmpas. Roedd yr heddlu milwrol yn ceisio cael cefnogaeth grŵp o filwyr nad oedd wedi dewis un ochr na'r llall.

"Dan ni'n ceisio amddiffyn *Tin Town*,' esboniodd un o'r plismyn.

'*Tin Town*? Dim gobaith caneri!' gwaeddodd y milwyr a rhedeg i ffwrdd. Roedden nhw wedi penderfynu pa ochr i'w chefnogi. Clywodd Danny fod yr heddlu milwrol wedi cael gorchymyn i wagio'r casgenni cwrw ym mhob cantîn.

Trwy niwl y wisgi, roedd Danny'n meddwl ei bod hi'n bwysig iawn iddo ffarwelio â Jackson. Efallai ei fod o wedi mynd i *Tin Town*. Cymerodd lymaid arall cyn rhedeg efo'r dyrfa. Yn sydyn, gwelodd Danny Jackson. Roedd o'n cael ei arestio gan blismon milwrol. Rhuthrodd Danny at y plismon a'i daro ar ei ben efo potel wisgi. Ar unwaith, roedd rhywun yn tynnu ei ddwylo y tu ôl i'w gefn.

"Dach chi i gyd yn cael eich arestio,' meddai'r plismon tu ôl i Danny. Dechreuodd Danny regi a gweiddi. Roedd popeth yn mynd o chwith.

Edrychodd ar Jackson. Roedd o wedi dychryn. Roedden nhw'n garcharorion a chafodd y ddau eu rhoi yn nhŷ gwarchod gwersyll 9 efo chwe milwr arall.

'Dwi'n ddieuog,' nadodd un ohonyn nhw.

'Be ydy'r cyhuddiad?' gwaeddodd Danny.

'Mi feddyliwn ni am rywbeth,' gwaeddodd y plismon gan roi clep i'r drws. Gwrandawodd y milwyr mewn anobaith ar sŵn y terfysg.

"Dan ni wedi gwneud llanast llwyr o hyn,' meddai Jackson. Tynnodd botelaid o wisgi o'i siaced a'i phasio i'r lleill. Roedd un o'r dynion yn dechrau cwyno.

'Dwi'n ochri efo'r heddlu. Maen nhw wedi gwneud camgymeriad.'

'Cau dy geg,' meddai Jackson gan dynnu ei botel yn ôl. Chwarter awr wedyn, roedd sŵn gwahanol y tu allan. Roedd rhywun yn gweiddi, 'Rhyddhewch y carcharorion!' Ymhen pum munud, roedd y terfysgwyr wedi torri'r drws ac roedd Jackson, Danny a'r lleill yn cael eu codi ar ysgwyddau grŵp o filwyr oedd yn chwifio baneri coch. Yn fuan, aeth eu ffrindiau newydd i chwilio am gêm arall a gadael i Danny a Jackson ddod i lawr.

'Mae'n rhaid inni ddianc rŵan, Jacks,' meddai Danny. Roedd y ddau ohonyn nhw'n feddw. Rhedon nhw i nôl dillad Jackson. Roedd ei ddillad yn dal i fod yno ond pan chwilion nhw am y beic, roedd o ar goll. 'Dos â fy meic i, Jacks.'

Daeth y ddau wyneb yn wyneb â dau blismon milwrol. 'Lle 'dach chi'n mynd?' gofynnodd un o'r plismyn.

''Dan ni ar eich ochr chi – 'dan ni eisiau eich helpu chi,' gwaeddodd Danny. 'Oes rhywbeth fedrwn ni wneud?'

'Dynion da,' meddai'r plismon. 'Rydan ni wedi galw am fwy o heddlu o'r Rhyl ond does neb ar gael i'w nôl nhw. Oes un ohonoch chi'n medru gyrru?'

'Fi!' meddai Jackson. Pwyntiodd y plismon at jîp a rhoi'r goriad i Jackson. Gwaeddodd gyfarwyddiadau ynglŷn â lle i godi pobl yn y Rhyl. Trodd Danny ddolen gychwyn y jîp a chododd ei law wrth i'w ffrind yrru i ffwrdd.

'Be fedra' i wneud?' gofynnodd Danny gan

edrych yn obeithiol ar feic modur.

'Mae prinder tai gwarchod i garcharorion. Ewch i wersyll Nova Scotia a gofyn oes 'na le yn eu tŷ gwarchod nhw. Dewch yn ôl i dŷ gwarchod 6 i ddweud faint o le sy' 'na.'

'Iawn.' Rhoddodd Danny saliwt am y tro olaf a rhedeg i wersyll Nova Scotia. Dyna lle roedd o wedi cuddio'i feic.

Geiriau newydd

amddiffyn – *to defend*
anobaith – *despair*
carcharorion – *prisoners*
casgenni – *barrels*
cyfarwyddiadau – *instructions*
dieuog – *innocent*
dolen gychwyn – *starting handle*
dyrnau – *fists*
gweiddi – *to shout*
llymaid – *swig*
mynd o chwith – *to go wrong*
nadu – *to whine*
neidio – *to jump*
nod – *aim*
rhannu – *to share*
wedi dychryn – *horrified*
yn ferw gwyllt – *uproar*
ysgwydd – *shoulder*

Pennod 10

Wrth i Danny adael canol y terfysg, roedd y gwersylloedd eraill yn dawelach. Pan gyrhaeddodd wersyll Nova Scotia roedd grŵp o filwyr yn sefyll wrth y giât. Doedd neb arall o gwmpas. Roedden nhw'n cuddio y tu mewn i'w cytiau mwy na thebyg. Edrychodd y dynion ar Danny'n amheus. 'Be wyt ti eisiau? Wyt ti'n chwilio am helynt?'

'Nac ydw. Dwi ddim yn un i godi twrw. Ydy'r sarjant o gwmpas?'

'Pam?' Pwy sy' eisiau gwybod?'

'Mae'r heddlu milwrol yn chwilio am ddynion ffyddlon i'w helpu nhw.'

'I ymladd yn erbyn Canadiaid eraill?'

'Wrth gwrs. Maen nhw'n derfysgwyr.'

'Dydan ni ddim wedi clywed sŵn saethu. Pwy sy'n ennill?'

'Neb a dweud y gwir. Mae hi'n dipyn o lanast. Mae llawer o ddynion yn rhedeg yn wyllt ac yn ysbeilio, ac mae'r heddlu milwrol yn arestio'r bobl feddw. Edrychwch, does dim ots gen i os 'dach chi'n dod neu beidio. Ewch i ofyn i'r sarjant. Mi arhosa' i yma.' Cerddodd y milwyr yn araf tuag at y cytiau. Cyn gynted ag y diflannon nhw, rhedodd Danny i gefn y gwersyll i chwilio am ei feic.

Gwthiodd Danny y beic dros y caeau at ffordd

fach oedd yn mynd i'r bryniau. Yna, aeth ar gefn y beic i fyny'r bryn. Ar ben y bryn, disgynnodd oddi ar ei feic i edrych ar olau'r gwersyll. Mae'n rhaid ei bod hi wedi hanner nos, meddyliodd. Yn sydyn, diffoddodd goleuadau'r gwersyll. Am syniad gwych! Roedd o'n falch nad oedd neb wedi meddwl am hynny pan oedd o yn y gwersyll. Dyna'r ffordd i ddod â phopeth i ben. Roedd o'n gobeithio bod Jackson yn bell o'r ardal erbyn hyn.

Aeth i lawr y bryn gan ganu un o ganeuon y rhyfel: *'Oh I don't want to leave you but you know I have to go.'* Dechreuodd chwerthin a chollodd ei reolaeth ar y beic. Welodd o mo'r bont yn y tywyllwch ac yn sydyn, roedd o ar wastad ei gefn ar y ffordd. Sylweddolodd ei fod o'n dal i fod dipyn bach yn feddw. Tynnodd y fflachlamp o'i boced. Roedd y beic yn gorwedd yng nghanol y ffordd efo'i olwyn yn mynd rownd a rownd. Clywodd sŵn dŵr yn llifo a dringodd dros wal y bont ac i lawr at yr afon. Tynnodd ei gap a thaflu dŵr dros ei wyneb. Ysgydwodd ei ben. Roedd y dŵr fel rhew.

Rhyw filltir o'r ficerdy, sylweddolodd Danny fod y beic yn broblem. Efallai byddai rhywun yn sylwi ei fod o wedi diflannu. Roedd hi'n bwysig nad oedd neb yn dod o hyd i'r beic ger y ficerdy. Ar ben y bryn nesaf, agorodd Danny giât a chroesi'r cae. Pan glywodd sŵn yr afon, gwthiodd y beic i lawr y bryn. Clywodd sblash wrth i'r beic daro'r dŵr. Roedd o'n sobr erbyn iddo gyrraedd y ficerdy. Sleifiodd drwy ddrws y seler a thynnu ei fflachlamp o'i boced. Symudodd y matresi a mynd i mewn i'r seler win.

Roedd Megan wedi rhoi matres ar y llawr a gwneud gwely iddo, a rhoi cadair a bwrdd bambŵ ger y sinc. Roedd 'na lamp olew ar y bwrdd. Taniodd Danny hi. Roedd Megan wedi ysgrifennu nodyn: 'Mi wna' i chwilio amdanat ti bob bore am hanner awr wedi chwech.' Byddai'n gwybod ei fod o yno wrth weld bod y matresi wedi cael eu symud. Tynnodd Danny ei esgidiau a'i gôt a gorwedd ar y gwely. Breuddwydiodd am yr heddlu milwrol. Roedden nhw'n ei hela, yn ei ddal, ac yn ei saethu. Pan gyrhaeddodd Megan am hanner awr wedi chwech, roedd Danny'n cuddio y tu ôl i'r drws ac yn pwyntio'r Luger ati. Rhoddodd ei law dros ei cheg i'w chadw hi rhag sgrechian. Roedd hi'n crynu fel deilen. Gwasgodd Danny hi.

'Megan! Diolch i Dduw.'

'O, Danny, wyt ti'n iawn? Beth ddigwyddodd yn y gwersyll?'

Yn gyflym, dwedodd Danny wrthi am y terfysg.

'Danny, mae'n ddrwg gen i, mae'n rhaid imi ddal yr ambiwlans ar y gornel am saith o'r gloch. Wyt ti eisiau bwyd?'

'Ydw plis Megan, os oes gen ti amser.' Aeth Megan i'r gegin a dychwelyd efo torth, caws, cig oer, llefrith a chacen.

'Does gen i ddim amser i wneud te, Danny, ac mae'n rhaid imi roi'r matresi'n ôl yn eu lle. Ceisia gysgu heddiw ac mi wela' i di heno.'

'Sut bydda i'n gwybod mai ti fydd yna?'

'Mi wna' i guro ddwywaith ar y drws. Ta ta rŵan, cariad.' Cusanodd Megan Danny. Roedd hi'n edrych yn bryderus ac yn welw. Gwrandawodd Danny ar sŵn Megan yn symud y matresi, wedyn aeth popeth yn dawel.

Geiriau newydd

crynu – *to shake*
curo – *to beat/knock*
chwerthin – *to laugh*
deilen – *leaf*
diffodd – *to put out*
disgyn – *to get down, descend*
dychwelyd – *to return*
ffyddlon – *faithful*
gwelw – *pale*
hela – *to chase*
llifo – *to flow*
mwy na thebyg – *more than likely*
ysbeilio – *to loot*

Pennod 11

Fel arfer, fedrai gyrrwr yr ambiwlans ddim ymuno â'r sgwrs ar y daith i'r gwersyll am fod pawb yn siarad Cymraeg, ond y bore hwnnw cafodd sylw mawr gan y staff sifil. Roedd pawb eisiau gwybod hanes y terfysg. Fel y gweithwyr eraill, roedd Megan yn awyddus i wybod popeth, ond roedd yr ambiwlans yn stopio ar bob cornel a'r gyrrwr yn dechrau'r stori eto ac eto. Chafodd o ddim cyfle i orffen dweud yr hanes i gyd cyn cyrraedd y gwersyll.

'Fuodd 'na ddim saethu, a does neb wedi marw,' meddai'r dyn, 'ac mae popeth dan reolaeth rŵan. Mi fydd 'na ddigon o waith yn yr ysbyty y bore 'ma beth bynnag, Nyrs Jones,' meddai wrth i Megan adael yr ambiwlans.

Roedd yr ysbyty'n llawn o filwyr efo briwiau a llawer ohonyn nhw'n dioddef o effeithiau yfed gormod hefyd. Roedd Megan yn pacio bandeisiau i'w hanfon i safle'r groes goch yn y gwersylloedd. Mae'n debyg nad oedd rhai o'r milwyr eisiau dod i'r ysbyty rhag ofn iddyn nhw gael eu harestio fel terfysgwyr, ond roedd gyrrwr yr ambiwlans wedi cael un peth yn anghywir – doedd popeth ddim dan reolaeth.

Daeth dynion newydd i'r ysbyty o un o'r tai gwarchod. Roedd carfan o filwyr wedi dechrau ymosod ar y tŷ gwarchod hwnnw ac roedd yr heddlu milwrol wedi rhyddhau'r carcharorion. Roedd y terfysg yn dechrau eto, y tro yma mewn gwersylloedd oedd wedi bod yn dawel o'r blaen. Roedd dau o'r dynion cafalri yn dweud storïau am ymosodiad ar wersyll y Saeson a brwydr rhwng y cafalri a thri chant o derfysgwyr oedd yn cario baneri coch. Roedd dynion y cafalri'n gwaedu.

'Roedden nhw'n taflu cerrig aton ni,' esboniodd un ohonyn nhw.

Daeth swyddog i chwilio am yrrwr i fynd â'r staff sifil adref, ond doedd y nyrsys ddim yn cael mynd – roedd eu hangen nhw ar y cleifion, a beth bynnag, byddai'r ysbyty yn saff. Yn ystod y prynhawn, cynyddodd nifer y dynion clwyfedig. Roedd pawb yn dweud bod y terfysg yn waeth na therfysg y noson cynt. Roedd hi'n amhosib i'r nyrsys ddweud y gwahaniaeth rhwng terfysgwyr ac amddiffynwyr. Roedden nhw i gyd eisiau help. Ond roedd y dynion yn gwybod yn iawn pwy oedd pwy, ac roedd brwydrau bach yn dechrau y tu mewn i'r ysbyty tan i'r prif feddyg fygwth cau'r ysbyty. Daeth dau ddyn i mewn yn cario milwr clwyfedig. Fo oedd y cyntaf i farw. Y nesaf oedd milwr efo clwyfau i'w ben. Byddai tri dyn arall yn marw cyn diwedd y dydd. Tua hanner awr wedi tri, cyrhaeddodd yr heddlu milwrol i chwilio am garcharorion. Roedd y frwydr olaf wedi cael ei chynnal yng ngwersyll 20, a rŵan roedd y milwyr yn crwydro'n ôl i'w gwersylloedd eu hunain.

Roedd Megan yn teimlo'n sâl ac aeth i gantîn yr ysbyty i eistedd. Daeth Nyrs McCann, un o'r nyrsys o Ganada, draw i wneud yn siŵr ei bod hi'n iawn.

'Dach chi eisiau sigarèt, Jones?' gofynnodd McCann. Doedd Megan ddim yn ysmygu ond cymerodd sigarèt â'i dwylo crynedig. Roedd Nyrs McCann ei hun wedi cynhyrfu.

'Mae hi fel bod yn ôl ar y ffrynt yn Fflandrys eto,' meddai. 'Dydyn nhw ddim wedi cael digon ar ymladd?'

'Beth fydd yn digwydd i'r terfysgwyr?' gofynnodd Megan.

'Wn i ddim,' meddai McCann. 'Tasai hyn wedi digwydd yn ystod y rhyfel, mi fasen nhw i gyd yn cael eu saethu fel encilwyr.'

Yn sydyn, neidiodd Megan ar ei thraed. 'Esgusodwch fi,' meddai, a rhuthro i'r toiledau.

Dilynodd Nyrs McCann hi. Ar ôl i Megan gyfogi ac ymolchi ei hwyneb, meddai'r nyrs, ''Dach chi'n edrych yn ofnadwy, Jones. Mi ddylech chi fynd adre. Mae 'na lori'n gadael y gwersyll mewn hanner awr. Mi wna' i'n siŵr eich bod chi'n mynd arni.'

Pan gyrhaeddodd Megan y fferm roedd ei mam gartref.

'Rwyt ti'n edrych yn sâl Megan. Be sy'n bod?' Dwedodd Megan wrthi am y terfysg. 'Ond beth am Danny?' gofynnodd Myfanwy.

Esboniodd Megan fod Danny'n saff yn y seler ac y byddai o'n aros yno tan i fyddin Canada fynd adref. Roedd y ddau ohonyn nhw wedi cytuno y dylai mam Megan gael gwybod. Bydden nhw eisiau ei help. Roedd Myfanwy yn falch iawn o gael bod yn rhan o'r gyfrinach.

'A phan fydd Danny'n dod allan, mi fedrwn ni ddweud wrth bawb am y briodas.'

'Mi fydd yn rhaid inni ddweud rhywbeth cyn hynny Mam,' meddai Megan yn ddistaw.

Edrychodd Myfanwy Jones ar ei merch yn ofalus. Gafaelodd yn llaw Megan.

'Wyt ti'n feichiog, Megan?'

'Ydw, dwi'n meddwl.'

Geiriau newydd

awyddus – *keen*
bandeisiau – *bandages*
briwiau – *wounds*
bygwth – *to threaten*
cleifion – *patients*
clwyfedig – *wounded*
cyfogi – *to vomit*
cyfrinach – *secret*
cynyddu – to increase
gwaedu – *to bleed*
gwahaniaeth – *difference*

Pennod 12

Dechreuodd Megan grio. Cofleidiodd Myfanwy ei merch. Medrai Myfanwy gofio'n glir iawn beth oedd wedi digwydd pan ddwedodd hi'r un peth wrth ei mam ei hun un mlynedd ar hugain yn ôl. Hyd yn oed rŵan, mi fedrai hi deimlo sioc y bonclust ar ei hwyneb. Efallai ei bod hi'n amser iddi ddweud y gwir wrth Megan.

'Paid â phoeni Megan fach, mi fydd popeth yn iawn.' Ar ôl paned o de, roedd Megan wedi tawelu.

'Wel, Megan,' meddai Myfanwy, 'mae'n rhaid imi orffen paratoi swper y ficer. Os wyt ti eisiau dod efo fi, dwi am fynd i weld fy mab-yng-nghyfraith yn ei gartref newydd.'

Gwenodd Megan. 'Fydd 'na dipyn bach o swper ar ôl ar gyfer Danny?'

'Bydd siŵr,' atebodd Myfanwy.

Ar ôl i Megan wneud yn siŵr nad oedd 'na ystlumod o gwmpas, archwiliodd Myfanwy seler Danny. Roedd hi'n falch iawn o'r trefniadau ond roedd Danny eisiau gwybod beth oedd wedi digwydd yn y gwersyll.

'Mi adawa' i chi ar eich pennau eich hunain, 'ta,' meddai Myfanwy, ond roedd yn rhaid i Megan fynd â'i mam allan o'r seler. 'Ddaw'r milwyr byth i lawr yma,' meddai Myfanwy. 'Mae ar bawb ofn ystlumod.' Roedd Megan yn gobeithio ei bod hi'n iawn.

Roedd Danny'n siŵr y byddai rhywun wedi sylwi ei fod o wedi diflannu erbyn trannoeth. 'Paid â rhoi'r matresi'n ôl yn eu lle heno, Megs,' meddai. 'Dwi eisiau mynd allan i gael awyr iach am hanner awr.' Roedd Megan yn poeni, ond mynnodd Danny.

Yn ôl ar y fferm, rhoddodd Megan swper i'w thad a cheisiodd fwyta tipyn bach pan ddaeth ei mam yn ôl o'r ficerdy. Aeth Robert Wyn Jones i'w wely am naw o'r gloch fel arfer, a buodd ei wraig a'i ferch yn siarad yn dawel yn y gegin tan hanner nos.

Drannoeth, roedd gan Megan bethau i'w gwneud cyn iddi fynd i'r gwersyll. Aeth i'r ficerdy a rhoi digon o fwyd am ddau neu dri diwrnod i Danny. Rhoddodd y matresi yn ôl yn eu lle a chododd y drws bach pren uwchben y boeler. Roedd yr ystlumod yn cysgu a sibrydodd Megan, 'Cysgwch yn dda ystlumod bach, ond cofiwch – mae'n gynnes a braf yn ymyl y boeler.'

Roedd llawer o bethau'n digwydd yn y gwersyll. Roedd chwe deg o garcharorion ac ychydig o ysbeilwyr sifil wedi cael mynd i Lerpwl. Byddai'r difrod i'r gwersyll yn costio miloedd o bunnoedd ac roedd y milwyr wedi dechrau clirio'r llanast. Cyrhaeddodd cadfridog *(m)* o Lundain ac aeth o gwmpas y gwersylloedd i ddweud y byddai'r *SS Celtica* yn hwylio am Ganada ar Fawrth y degfed. Roedd gohebyddion papurau newydd wrth brif giât y gwersyll ond roedd pawb wedi cael gorchymyn i beidio â siarad â nhw.

Am bedwar o'r gloch, daeth Nyrs McCann i'r ward i chwilio am Megan.

'Mae rhywun eisiau siarad efo chi, Nyrs Jones. Dewch efo fi.'

Geiriau newydd

archwilio – *to inspect*
bonclust – *clout*
difrod – *damage*
gohebydd – *reporter*
mynnu – *to insist*

Pennod 13

Roedd swyddog a sarjant o'r heddlu milwrol yn swyddfa'r prif swyddog meddygol.

'Eisteddwch, Nyrs Jones,' meddai'r meddyg. 'Arhoswch y tu allan, Nyrs McCann.' Trodd at y plismyn. 'Ewch ymlaen.'

"Dan ni'n deall eich bod chi'n ffrind i Preifat Evans o wersyll Montreal,' meddai un o'r plismyn, yn Saesneg wrth gwrs.

'Oes rhywbeth wedi digwydd iddo?' gofynnodd Megan.

'Mae o ar goll. 'Dan ni'n credu ei fod o wedi encilio efo'i ffrind – Preifat Jackson. 'Dach chi'n gwybod lle maen nhw?'

Cododd Megan ei llaw at ei cheg a dechrau siarad Cymraeg. 'Na, na, fedrai o ddim, wnâi o ddim.'

'Yn Saesneg, os gwelwch yn dda.'

Ailadroddodd Megan beth roedd hi wedi ei ddweud yn Saesneg. Roedd yn rhaid iddi eu perswadio nhw bod Danny wedi ei gadael hi.

'Os oeddech chi mor hoff o Preifat Evans, efallai eich bod chi wedi ei helpu o i ddianc.'

'Tasai o wedi gofyn i mi ei helpu o, mi faswn i wedi gwneud hynny. Ond os ydy o wedi eich gadael chi, mae o wedi fy ngadael i hefyd.' Dechreuodd

Megan grio yn uchel.

'A beth am ei ffrind – Jackson? 'Dach chi'n ei nabod o hefyd?'

'Dwi erioed wedi clywed amdano fo,' meddai Megan drwy ei dagrau.

'Pryd oedd y tro olaf i chi weld Evans?'

Chwythodd Megan ei thrwyn yn swnllyd. 'Dydd Sadwrn.'

'Nos Sadwrn?'

'Bore dydd Sadwrn.'

'Dyna beth rhyfedd. Beth wnaethoch chi efo Evans fore dydd Sadwrn?'

'Mi wnaethon ni briodi,' llefodd Megan.

Edrychodd y ddau blismon ar ei gilydd gan wenu. Roedden nhw wedi clywed storïau tebyg o'r blaen. Milwr o Ganada, merch leol, tipyn o hwyl ac yn sydyn roedd y milwr yn rhywle arall.

'Mae gynnoch chi ddychymyg byw, Jones, ond mae'n rhaid i chi wneud yn well na hynna. Dydy hi ddim yn bosib i filwr o Ganada gael caniatâd i briodi merch leol.'

'Dyna pam wnaeth o ddim gofyn,' meddai Megan gan lefain eto.

Torrodd y prif swyddog meddygol ar ei thraws. 'Mi fydd hi'n hawdd cael gwybod beth wnaeth Evans fore dydd Sadwrn.'

Trodd y dynion eu cefnau ar Megan i gael sgwrs. Safodd y meddyg ar ei draed ac aeth yr heddlu milwrol allan. Agorodd y meddyg y drws. 'Nyrs McCann! Cadwch Jones yn yr ystafell ochr tan inni ei galw hi eto.' Sylwodd Megan ei bod hi wedi colli ei theitl 'nyrs' yn barod. Roedd Nyrs McCann yn awyddus i wybod beth oedd yn digwydd. Doedd

Megan ddim yn ymddiried yn McCann. Roedd hi'n medru troi o fod yn neis i fod yn gas mewn eiliad ar y ward. Sychodd Megan ei llygaid. Doedd ganddi hi ddim llawer o ddagrau ar ôl beth bynnag, a dwedodd ei stori wrth McCann. Roedd hi'n amlwg nad oedd McCann yn ei chredu hi.

'Os dach chi'n briod, bydd cofnod yn rhywle. Mi ofynnan nhw yn y swyddfa gofrestru.'

Meddyliodd Megan yn gyflym. Roedden nhw wedi ei chysylltu hi â Danny. Mi fydden nhw'n dod i chwilio amdano'n hwyr neu'n hwyrach. Tasai hi'n feichiog, mi fasai hi'n bwysig iawn i bawb wybod ei bod hi'n briod. Roedd yn rhaid i'r babi gael enw ei dad. Byddai hi'n dweud wrthyn nhw.

'Dydy'r cofnod ddim yn y swyddfa gofrestru – yng nghofrestr yr eglwys mae o.'

'Pa eglwys?'

'Sant Elidir.' Dechreuodd Megan grio eto. Dyna'r wybodaeth oedd McCann ei heisiau.

'Caewch eich ceg ac arhoswch yma,' meddai'r nyrs yn swta. Gadawodd y drws ar agor a churo ar ddrws swyddfa'r meddyg. Wnaeth Megan ddim gwrando ar y sgwrs, ond roedd hi'n nerfus iawn.

Daeth yr heddlu milwrol yn eu holau ar ôl sgwrs efo'r prif swyddog meddygol.

'Ewch i nôl ei phethau, McCann,' meddai'r meddyg yn flinedig. Roedd o wedi cael llond bol ar Wersyll Parc Cinmel. Byddai'n gwneud yn siŵr ei fod o ar y *Celtica* ymhen wythnos.

Aeth y sarjant a Megan i gefn lori efo dau blismon milwrol arall. Eisteddodd y swyddog yn y ffrynt efo'r gyrrwr. Dechreuodd y sarjant ofyn cwestiynau eto, ond roedd Megan yn poeni. Efallai ei bod hi wedi dweud gormod yn barod. Doedd hi ddim yn mynd i ddweud rhagor. Gwrthododd siarad Saesneg eto. Dwedodd y sarjant na fyddai hynny'n broblem – roedden nhw wedi gofyn am help yr heddlu lleol efo'r ymchwiliad. Roedd Megan yn meddwl am Danny yn y seler, felly cafodd sioc pan drodd y lori i mewn i iard y fferm. Sylweddolodd fod yn rhaid iddi fod yn ofalus iawn.

Rhuthrodd y cŵn defaid at y lori gan gyfarth a mynd yn wyllt pan ddringodd y milwyr allan. Ciciodd un o'r milwyr un o'r cŵn ac ar unwaith, brathodd y ci arall ei goes. Daeth Myfanwy allan o'r gegin. Yn gyflym, dwedodd Megan wrthi beth oedd wedi digwydd, yn Gymraeg wrth gwrs.

'Stop that!' cyfarthodd y swyddog.

Anwybyddodd Myfanwy o. 'Gawn ni fynd ymlaen efo'r busnes yma a chael gwared â nhw 'ta,' meddai.

'They're going to hide behind that damned barbarian language of theirs,' meddai'r swyddog yn flin.

'Reinforcements on the way, sir,' meddai un o'r milwyr. Trodd pawb i weld dau blismon lleol yn cerdded i fyny lôn y fferm.

Geiriau newydd

ailadrodd – *to repeat*
anwybyddu – *to ignore*
brathu – *to bite*
cofnod – *record*
cyfarth – *to bark*
chwythu – *to blow*
dagrau – *tears*
dychymyg – *imagination*
llefain – *to wail*
sychu – *to dry*
uchel – *loud*
ymchwiliad – *enquiry*

Pennod 14

Roedd Sarjant Gwilym Roberts wedi drysu. Roedd o'n gwybod bod Myfanwy Jones yn ddraig o ddynes, ond fyddai hi ddim yn torri'r gyfraith. Cyflwynodd ei hun a PC Pritchard i'r Canadiaid. Eglurodd y swyddog ei fod o eisiau cyfieithydd.

'Tell them we want to search the house and outbuildings at once.'

Doedd Sarjant Roberts ddim yn gwybod beth oedd gêm Myfanwy. Roedd hi'n medru siarad Saesneg yn well na fo.

'Mae'n ddrwg gen i, Myfanwy, mae'n rhaid i ni eu helpu nhw. 'Dach chi'n gwybod beth mae o'n ei ofyn?'

'Ydw, Gwil. Nid chi sydd ar fai a 'dan ni ddim wedi gwneud dim byd. Dwedwch wrthyn nhw am gadw eu 'sgidiau budr oddi ar fy llawr glân i. Dwi eisiau gweld cefnau'r estroniaid hyn mor fuan ag sy'n bosib.'

Trodd Sarjant Roberts at y Canadiaid. 'Mrs Jones says she has done nothing wrong and will co-operate fully with your enquiries, and asks if your men will please wipe their feet as they go into her home.'

Ddaethon nhw o hyd i ddim byd ar y fferm, ond daeth dau o'r heddlu milwrol o'r beudy efo Twm a'i fab.

'*Found these two in the cowshed, sir. They don't seem to speak English.*'

Griddfanodd y lefftenant. '*Stupid yokels.*' Gyda help y Sarjant Roberts, cafodd y lefftenant wybod nad oedd Twm a'i fab yn gwybod dim am filwr o Ganada, dim am y briodas, dim byd o gwbl am ddim byd.

'*We'd better see this crazy vicar who's supposed to have married them. Where is he?*' Gwrthododd Myfanwy a Megan fynd yn y lori. Cerddodd y ddwy i'r ficerdy dan ofal Gwilym Roberts a PC Pritchard. Curodd y lefftenant ar ddrws y ficerdy, er bod Sarjant Roberts yn gwybod bod gan Myfanwy oriad. Agorodd Huw Rees Davies y drws.

'Myfanwy! Be sy'n digwydd?' meddai'r ficer yn syn. Dechreuodd Myfanwy ddweud wrtho yn Gymraeg.

'*That's enough Welsh,*' meddai'r lefftenant. '*I assume you speak English, sir, or would you like Sergeant Roberts to translate?*'

'*I am perfectly articulate in English young man, now what is the meaning of this intrusion?*'

Eglurodd y swyddog fod Danny wedi diflannu. Ni ddangosodd Huw Rees Davies unrhyw emosiwn o gwbl. Holodd y lefftenant y ficer am y briodas.

'*You know, I suppose, that it is against Army regulations for a Canadian to marry a local girl?*'

'*I am not accountable to the Canadian Army,*' atebodd y ficer yn oeraidd. Ar ôl sgwrs fach, aeth y ddau ohonyn nhw i festri'r eglwys i edrych ar y gofrestr. Pan ddychwelon nhw, mynnodd y lefftenant chwilio'r ficerdy.

'You may search wherever you like, no-one here has anything to hide.' Edrychodd y lefftenant yn ofalus ar Megan am gliwiau. Dechreuodd Megan siarad yn gyflym â'i mam pan gyrhaeddon nhw'r llofft.

'Be sy'n bod arnat ti, Megan? Rwyt ti'n bihafio fel plentyn,' meddai'r ficer. Roedd o'n ddig iawn.

'Do not be distressed, Megan,' cyfieithodd Sarjant Roberts. Roedd o'n mynnu cyfieithu pob gair.

'Peidiwch â chwarae gêmau, Gwilym,' meddai'r ficer yn flin.

Dechreuodd Megan grio. Ceisiodd Myfanwy ei chysuro.

'Oh my poor baby, there there now, my poor baby,' cyfieithodd Sarjant Roberts mewn llais fflat.

'Alright sergeant, I don't care about that rubbish. The girl speaks English perfectly well, she's a hostile witness. Can't you make her speak English, padre?'

'Young man,' meddai'r ficer yn swta. 'Mrs Evans has a perfect right to speak her own language in her own country. As a guest in our small nation I must ask you to respect that.'

Daeth y milwyr i lawr o'r llofft yn llwch o'u corun i'w sawdl.

'No-one's been up there for years, sir.'

'As I have already told you,' meddai'r ficer.

Yn y gegin, gwelodd y lefftenant ddrws y seler.

'Where does that go?' Edrychodd Megan drwy ffenest y gegin. Roedd hi bron â thywyllu rŵan. Dechreuodd Megan weddïo'n dawel. Aeth yr holl griw i lawr y grisiau i'r seler. Cyneuodd pawb eu fflachlampau a dechrau chwilio. Yn sydyn, roedd 'na sŵn curo yn yr awyr.

'What the hell's that noise?' meddai'r lefftenant. Fflachiodd ei olau at y to.

'Ystlumod!' sgrechiodd Myfanwy a rhuthro at y grisiau.

'Bats!' gwaeddodd un o'r milwyr. 'Oh my God!'

'Pritchard, stay with that woman!' gwaeddodd y lefftenant tra oedd ei ddynion yn dechrau dawnsio o gwmpas y seler i geisio osgoi'r ystlumod.

Edrychodd y ficer ar Megan yn galed. Trodd Megan ei phen. Roedd y milwyr mewn panig ac roedd y lefftenant yn neidio i fyny ac i lawr gan geisio rheoli'r sefyllfa.

'Can't you make them go away,' gwaeddodd ar y ficer.

'They are God's wild creatures, lieutenant, not household pets. I am sure they are more afraid of you than you are of them.'

'I'm not afraid of bats!' gwaeddodd y lefftenant gan blygu'i ben. 'Put the torches out!'

'Sir, there's nothing here – can we go now?' Daeth llais nerfus drwy'r tywyllwch.

'Is there any more of this cellar?' gofynnodd y lefftenant i'r ficer.

'A few small rooms behind that wall where I keep old books and church furniture,' meddai'r ficer. 'Follow me, please.' Roedd y milwyr ar eu pengliniau rŵan, a sleifiodd pawb ar ôl y ficer.

'I hate bats, give me a trench rat any day,' sibrydodd un o'r milwyr.

'Let's have some light here!' gorchmynnodd y lefftenant. Hedfanodd dau ystlum ar hyd y coridor.

Rhuthrodd y lefftenant yn ôl i'r seler fawr gan weiddi, *'I want a thorough search of those rooms.'* Roedd yr ymchwil ar ben mewn ychydig funudau ac aeth y milwyr i fyny'r grisiau yn gyflym.

'Any signs of recent activity down there?' gofynnodd y lefftenant.

'Nothing at all, sir, it was just as the padre said, furniture, books and matresses.'

Aeth y lefftenant a Sarjant Roberts allan am gyfarfod swyddogol. Yn y gegin, roedd pawb yn dawel.

Geiriau newydd

cyfieithydd – *translator*
cyfraith – *law*
cynnau – *to switch on*
cysuro – *to comfort*
drysu – *to puzzle*
estroniaid – *foreigners*
griddfan – *to groan*
hedfan – *to fly*
llwch – *dust*
oeraidd – *cold*
o'u corun i'w sawdl – *from head to toe*
pen-glin – *knee*
plygu – *to duck*

Pennod 15

Pan ddaeth y ddau swyddog yn ôl, meddai Sarjant Roberts wrth y ficer, 'Mae'r Canadiaid eisiau dod yn ôl yfory i chwilio am yr enciliwr yng nghaeau'r ardal.'

'Dydy hynny'n ddim byd i'w wneud efo fi,' meddai'r ficer. 'Ewch â nhw o 'ma, Gwilym, mor fuan ag sy'n bosibl.'

'I'll be reporting this matter to your cardinal, padre,' meddai'r lefftenant.

'By all means, lieutenant, but I doubt the Church of England will appreciate the interference of the Canadian army in the execution of their offices. Goodbye.' Agorodd y ficer y drws a gadawodd y criw chwilio.

Yn y gegin, edrychodd Myfanwy, Megan a'r ficer ar ei gilydd.

'Megan,' meddai'r ficer yn oeraidd. 'Dwi'n ddig iawn efo ti. Wn i ddim be sy'n bod arnat ti a dwi ddim eisiau gwybod. Dwi ddim yn hoffi cael y fyddin a'r heddlu yn cerdded o gwmpas fy nhŷ i, ac mae'r ystlumod wedi gwneud llanast ofnadwy yn y seler. Dwi am i ti ei lanhau o yn y bore. Wna' i ddim sôn am y peth eto. Dos adre rŵan.' Trodd at Myfanwy. 'Myfanwy! Dwi eisiau gair efo ti.'

Roedd Megan eisiau mynd i weld Danny ond

doedd hi ddim yn meiddio, rhag ofn i'r ficer ei dal hi. Gwelodd ei thad yn cyrraedd y fferm wrth iddi adael llwybr y ficerdy. Rhuthrodd yn ôl at ddrws cefn y ficerdy i aros am ei mam. Fedrai hi ddim wynebu Robert Wyn Jones ar ei phen ei hun. Ymhen hanner awr wedyn, daeth ei mam allan. Roedd hi wedi bod yn crio a chafodd sioc o weld Megan.

'Mam! Be sy'n bod? Oedd y ficer yn ddig iawn? Wnaethoch chi ddweud wrtho fo am Danny?'

Gafaelodd Myfanwy ym mraich ei merch.

'Naddo. Paid â phoeni, Megan, dydy o ddim yn ddig. Mae o'n drist ynglŷn â'r hyn sy'n digwydd. Ddwedais i ddim byd am Danny yn y seler. Fedrai Huw ddim dweud celwydd, felly mae'n well peidio dweud wrtho. Beth bynnag, be wyt ti'n ei wneud yma?'

'Mae Dad wedi dod adre a dwi ddim eisiau ei weld o hebddoch chi.'

'Reit. Wel, dwi'n siŵr ei fod o wedi clywed rhywbeth erbyn hyn. Mi wnawn ni ei wynebu o efo'n gilydd.'

Roedd y ffrae efo Robert Wyn Jones yn ofnadwy. Roedd o'n gweiddi ac yn rhegi ar Danny a'r cywilydd ar enw'r teulu. Trawodd Robert Megan. Yna, rhoddodd Myfanwy fonclust iddo.

'Cofia pwy wyt ti, Robert Jones!' gwaeddodd Myfanwy. Roedd hynny'n brifo ac aeth Robert yn wyllt. Pan wrthododd Myfanwy anfon Megan i ffwrdd, dwedodd Robert os na fyddai Megan yn mynd, yna byddai o'n mynd. Aeth â'i swper i'r parlwr ffrynt a gwrthod siarad â nhw eto.

'Ddylwn i ddim fod wedi dweud "Cofia pwy wyt

ti",' meddai Myfanwy yn y gegin. 'Doedd hynny ddim yn deg.'

'Chwarae teg, Mam, dwi erioed wedi eich clywed chi'n dweud hynny o'r blaen, a beth bynnag, mae pawb yn gwybod.'

'Robert druan,' meddai Myfanwy a dechrau crio'n dawel.

'Robert druan?! Ar ôl beth ddwedodd o?' Edrychodd Megan yn syn.

Roedd Megan yn dweud y gwir. Roedd pawb yn gwybod mai Myfanwy oedd perchennog y fferm. Roedd Robert wedi bod yn was ar y fferm ac ar ôl i ddau frawd Myfanwy farw, un ar ôl y llall, meddyliodd ei thad y byddai Robert, gweithiwr caled o deulu tlawd ond parchus, yn gwneud gŵr addas i'w unig ferch. Ond roedd pawb yn gwybod mai Myfanwy oedd y bos.

Flynyddoedd yn ôl, roedd tad Myfanwy wedi achub bywyd mab hynaf Syr Mansel Rees Davies, yr hen sgweiar. Roedd tad Myfanwy yn was stabl ar y pryd ac mi fuodd o'n gloff am weddill ei fywyd ar ôl ei daflu ei hun o flaen y ceffyl oedd yn sathru Pedr ifanc, mab Syr Mansel. Rhoddodd Syr Mansel denantiaeth fferm Cefn Carreg iddo, a phan fu farw yr hen sgweiar, gadawodd y fferm i dad Myfanwy.

Roedd Syr Mansel yn meddwl y byd o Myfanwy, ac roedd hi wedi cael gwersi efo Pedr a Huw, ei feibion. Medrai Myfanwy siarad ac ysgrifennu Saesneg ers pan oedd hi'n un ar ddeg oed. Pedr fyddai'n etifeddu'r teitl a byddai Huw, yr ail fab, yn mynd i'r fyddin neu i'r eglwys. Roedd Myfanwy a Huw yn ffrindiau mawr tan i Huw fynd i Rydychen i astudio.

Roedd teulu Myfanwy wedi gweithio i deulu Rees Davies am flynyddoedd, ond pan briododd Syr Pedr, roedd ei wraig, Saesnes, eisiau byw yn nes at Loegr ac roedden nhw wedi symud i'w stad ger yr Wyddgrug a gwerthu Plas Newydd i sgweiar newydd, Major Evans. Ond pan ddaeth Huw yn ôl i'r ardal yn ficer, roedd hi'n naturiol i Myfanwy fynd yn ôl i'w helpu o.

Aeth Myfanwy â phaned o de i Robert a cheisio cymodi. Gwrthododd Robert siarad â hi. Yn y gegin, golchodd y ddwy ddynes y llestri tan iddyn nhw glywed Robert yn mynd i'w wely.

'Dwi'n mynd i'r gwely hefyd, Mam. Dwi wedi blino'n lân,' meddai Megan gan agor ei cheg.

'Eistedda am funud, Megan,' meddai ei mam. 'Mae'r ficer a fi wedi cael sgwrs fach. Mae 'na rywbeth dwi eisiau ei ddweud wrthot ti.'

Geiriau newydd

agor ceg – *to yawn*
cloff – *lame*
cymodi – *to reconcile*
cywilydd – *shame*
etifeddu – *to inherit*
gafael yn – *to hold*
gwas – *servant*
gwers – *lesson*
meiddio – *to dare*
parchus – *respectable*
perchennog – *proprietor*
Rhydychen – *Oxford*
sathru – *to trample*
stad – *estate*
tenantiaeth – *tenancy*
tlawd – *poor*

Pennod 16

Drannoeth, deffrodd Megan gan deimlo fel dynes wahanol. Rhuthrodd at y drych i astudio ei hwyneb. Roedd hi wedi cael sioc pan ddwedodd ei mam mai Huw Rees Davies oedd ei thad go iawn. Cyn i Huw fynd i Rydychen, roedd o wedi dweud wrth ei deulu ei fod o eisiau priodi Myfanwy. Roedd y teulu wedi dychryn a gwrthod rhoi caniatâd. Yn syth ar ôl i Huw adael, sylweddolodd Myfanwy ei bod hi'n feichiog. Pan gyrhaeddodd Huw adref am wyliau Nadolig, roedd Myfanwy wedi priodi Robert Wyn Jones.

Wrth gwrs, doedd Robert Wyn Jones ddim yn gwybod y gwir, ond rŵan medrai Megan weld pam roedd hi a'i thad mor wahanol i'w gilydd. A dyna pam roedd y ficer wedi cymryd diddordeb ynddi drwy ei bywyd. Roedd hi wedi addo i'w mam na fyddai hi'n sôn am y peth wrth neb – ddim wrth y ficer na Danny – neb. Penderfynodd fod ganddi drwyn y teulu Rees Davies.

Arhosodd Megan tan i Robert Wyn Jones adael y fferm ac yn gyflym, sleifiodd i'r ficerdy i weld Danny. Cuddiodd y tu ôl i'r gwrych pan welodd y ficer yn mynd i'r eglwys. Gwnaeth botaid o de a mynd â fo i Danny. Symudodd y matresi a churo ddwywaith ar ddrws y seler win. Roedd 'na arogl ofnadwy yn y seler a theimlodd Megan yn sâl. Roedd yn rhaid iddi wagio bwced Danny.

Dwedodd Megan bopeth wrtho am y diwrnod cynt. Roedd Danny wedi clywed synau ond doedd ganddo fo ddim syniad beth oedd yn digwydd. Chwarddodd yn uchel pan glywodd stori'r ystlumod.

'Wyt ti'n meddwl y dôn nhw'n ôl, Megs?' gofynnodd.

'Maen nhw'n dweud eu bod nhw'n bwriadu chwilio'r ardal heddiw, ond ddôn nhw ddim yma dwi'n siŵr. Dwi wedi colli fy swydd, felly mi gadwa' i lygad arnyn nhw o'r fferm.'

'Dwi eisiau awyr iach, Megs. Oes 'na rywun o gwmpas?'

'Mi ddaw'r ficer yn ôl o'r eglwys cyn bo hir, ac mae Elias yn cyrraedd am wyth o'r gloch. Dwi'n meddwl ei bod hi'n saff am bum munud.'

Gafaelodd Danny yn ei fwced a mynd i'r ardd. Cliriodd Megan y llestri budr. Roedd ganddo ddigon o fwyd am ddiwrnod arall. Pan ddaeth Danny'n ôl, cusanodd Megan o ac addo dod i'w weld y noson honno. Rhoddodd Megan y matresi'n ôl yn eu lle eto ac aeth i fyny'r grisiau i wneud brecwast i'r ficer.

Buodd yr heddlu milwrol a'r heddlu lleol yn chwilio'r ardal drwy'r dydd ac am bump o'r gloch, cyrhaeddodd Gwilym Roberts y fferm i ddweud nad oedden nhw wedi dod o hyd i ddim byd.

'Maen nhw wedi dod o hyd i jîp y fyddin ger Mostyn. Mae'n debyg fod y ddau enciliwr wedi dianc ynddo. Mae'n ddrwg iawn gen i am hyn i gyd Myfanwy, mae'n fusnes trist. Ro'n i'n meddwl bod gan Megan fwy o synnwyr.'

'Diolch, Gwil. Dwi'n siomedig iawn yn y dyn ifanc, wrth gwrs, ond mae'n rhaid i fywyd gario 'mlaen.'

Byddai pawb yn cael gwybod yn ddigon buan bod Megan yn feichiog a bod Robert eisiau ei hanfon hi i ffwrdd. Yn ystod yr wythnos ganlynol roedd Megan yn mynd â swper i Danny bob nos, ac wedyn roedd Danny'n mynd allan pan oedd hi'n dywyll. Ar ôl iddi roi brecwast i Danny, byddai Megan yn rhoi'r matresi'n ôl yn eu lle am y diwrnod.

Roedd y papurau newydd yn llawn hanesion am y terfysg. Darllenodd y ficer y *Times* yn uchel i Myfanwy a Megan.

'*VC officer trampled to death and 25 killed in the riot.*'

'Am lol!' meddai Megan.

'Mi fydd achos y terfysgwyr yn Lerpwl yn fuan,' darllenodd y ficer.

Ar y degfed o Fawrth, hwyliodd y *Celtica* o Lerpwl i Ganada yn llawn o filwyr. Roedd oes Gwersyll Parc Cinmel yn dirwyn i ben. Roedd Danny'n ddigon bodlon treulio dau neu dri mis yn y seler. Darllenodd y *Times* a'r *Liverpool Courier* ychydig ddyddiau ar ôl i'r ficer orffen efo nhw, gan chwilio am newyddion am longau o Lerpwl.

Bythefnos ar ôl chwilio'r ardal, roedd Megan ar iard y fferm pan gyrhaeddodd Gwilym Roberts a lefftenant yr heddlu milwrol eto. Rhuthrodd i mewn i'r llaethdy i nôl ei mam. Edrychodd Myfanwy ar wyneb Gwilym a gofyn, 'Newyddion drwg, Gwil?'

'Maen nhw wedi dod o hyd i'ch gŵr, Megan.'

Taflodd y lefftenant rywbeth ar fwrdd y gegin.

'This was found on a body washed up on the side of the Dee. You're husband's dead, Mrs Evans.'

Geiriau newydd

achos – *trial*
arogl – *smell*
canlynol – *following*
dirwyn i ben – *to draw to a close*
drych – *mirror*
oes – *lifetime*
synau – *sounds*
synnwyr – *sense*
taflu – *to throw*
trannoeth – *the next day*

Pennod 17

Doedd Megan ddim yn gwybod beth i'w ddweud. Roedd hi wedi gweld Danny ddwyawr yn ôl. Clywodd rywun yn chwerthin yn hysteraidd. Hi oedd o. Aeth Myfanwy ati a'i hysgwyd.

'Paid, Megan. Paid!'

'Look at the tag please, Mrs Evans.'

'Dwi ddim eisiau edrych ar y tag. 'Dach chi wedi gwneud camgymeriad. Mae Danny wedi dianc. Mi ddaw o'n ôl ata' i,' sgrechiodd Megan. Cyfieithodd Sarjant Roberts.

Griddfanodd y lefftenant. *'There's no mistake – and I'm sick of this language business. Tell her what happened Sergeant and what we want.'*

'Mae'n ddrwg iawn gen i, Megan. Daethon nhw o hyd i gorff yn gwisgo'r ddisg yma yn afon Dyfrdwy ger Hoylake. Wedyn, daethon nhw o hyd i gwch bach ger New Brighton. Roedd y cwch wedi cael ei ddwyn o Fostyn ac maen nhw'n meddwl bod eich gŵr wedi ceisio croesi afon Dyfrdwy. Roedd y llif yn gryf iawn yn yr aber yno, a phan drodd y llif, mae'n debyg fod y cwch wedi troi drosodd a'r milwr wedi boddi.' Petrusodd Sarjant Roberts.

'Are you finished?' gofynnodd y lefftenant.

'Dim eto, y . . . y . . . *not yet,*' atebodd y sarjant.

'Beth arall?' gofynnodd Myfanwy. Roedd Megan

yn gafael yng nghefn cadair ac yn edrych drwy'r ffenest. Sut ddylai hi fihafio?

'Dwi'n siŵr na wnewch chi hoffi hyn Myfanwy, ond maen nhw eisiau mynd â Megan i Lerpwl i adnabod y corff.'

Edrychodd Megan arno'n syn. Tasai hi'n actio'n wallgof efallai basen nhw'n mynd i ffwrdd. Roedd hi wedi gweld *Hamlet* unwaith. Roedd pawb wedi osgoi Ophelia. Dechreuodd Megan grwydro o gwmpas y gegin gan ganu 'Dafydd y Garreg Wen'. Roedd Ophelia wedi canu cân drist hefyd.

Edrychodd Sarjant Roberts yn anghysurus. 'Be sy' o'i le arni hi, Myfanwy? Mae'n rhaid inni gael ateb.'

Peidiodd Megan â chanu. Mewn llais breuddwydiol, dwedodd, 'Dwi ddim yn mynd i Lerpwl, Sarjant Roberts. Nid Danny ydy'r corff. Dwi ddim yn credu ei fod o wedi marw. Mi ddaw o'n ôl ata' i.' Ailadroddodd hyn sawl gwaith.

'What's going on?' gofynnodd y lefftenant yn flin.

Eglurodd Sarjant Roberts. Dechreuodd Megan grwydro a chanu eto.

'Get the handcuffs out and arrest her – she's coming to Liverpool with me.'

'I'm afraid I can't do that, sir. Mrs Evans has not broken the law.' Trodd at Myfanwy, 'Tybed ydy'r sioc wedi cael effaith ar feddwl Megan?'

Roedd y lefftenant yn dechrau colli ei amynedd.

'Damned foreigners, you're impossible to deal with! At least with the Bosch we knew who the enemy was!'

'Ewch i'ch gwlad eich hun 'ta, a gadewch lonydd

i ni,' meddai Myfanwy yn ddistaw.

'What was that?'

'Mrs Jones says it must be very hard for you poor soldiers being away from home so long.'

Edrychodd y lefftenant yn amheus.

'Tell them – no don't bother – they understand. I'll be back in the morning with an armed guard to take the girl to Liverpool.'

Pan oedd pawb wedi mynd, cytunodd Megan a Myfanwy fod mynd yn wallgo'n syniad da. Byddai Megan yn waeth erbyn yfory. Aeth Myfanwy i'r ficerdy i baratoi cinio ar gyfer y ficer ac i ddweud wrtho beth oedd wedi digwydd.

Geiriau newydd

anghysurus – *uncomfortable*
boddi – *to drown*
breuddwydiol – *dreamy*
gwallgof – *mad*
llif – *tide*
llonydd – *peace*
troi drosodd – *to overturn*

Pennod 18

Aeth Megan i'w gwely cyn i Robert Wyn Jones gyrraedd adref. Roedd hi'n sâl wedi'r cyfan. Wnaeth Robert ddim ceisio cuddio'r ffaith ei fod o'n falch iawn o glywed bod Danny wedi marw. Ar ôl i Robert fynd i'w wely, sleifiodd Megan allan o'r tŷ i weld Danny yn y seler. Doedd him ddim yn siŵr a oedd marwolaeth Danny yn gwneud pethau'n hawdd neu beidio, ond roedd Danny'n siŵr.

Ar y dechrau, fedrai Danny ddim meddwl am ddim byd ond y corff. Pwy oedd o? Teimlodd Megan yn euog. Doedd hi ddim wedi meddwl am y milwr marw o gwbl.

'Mae'n rhaid mai Patrick Jackson ydy o,' meddai Danny'n ddigalon.

'Efallai ei fod o wedi rhoi'r ddisg i rywun arall,' awgrymodd Megan.

'Ond pam? Daethon nhw o hyd i'r jîp ger Mostyn, ac roedd y cwch yn dod o Fostyn.'

'Ond roedd Jackson eisiau mynd i Lundain,' meddai Megan.

'Oedd y corff yn gwisgo dillad sifil neu wisg filwrol?'

'Wn i ddim, ond mae'n amlwg nad oedd disg arall ar y corff. Roedd gan Jackson ddwy ddisg.'

'Efallai dylet ti fynd i Lerpwl i weld os mai corff

Jackson ydy o.'

'Na Danny! Paid â gofyn imi wneud hynny!'

Edrychodd Danny ar ei wraig. Roedd o'n gofyn gormod. Roedd o wedi gweld cyrff oedd wedi bod mewn dŵr am gyfnod.

'Rwyt ti'n iawn. Dydy hynny ddim yn syniad da.'

'Ond beth wnawn ni rŵan, Danny? Os wyt ti'n farw, wnân nhw ddim chwilio amdanat ti eto.'

'Siŵr iawn. Ond mewn tri mis, fedra' i ddim cerdded i fyny'r ffordd a dweud 'Helo cariad, dwi gartref!'

'Dwi'n gweld.' Doedd Megan ddim wedi meddwl am hynny. 'Efallai medret ti fynd i ffwrdd a dod yn ôl fel rhywun arall.'

'A be nesa? "Ga' i waith ar eich fferm, Mr a Mrs Jones, a ga' i syrthio mewn cariad efo eich merch eto?" Dim diolch! Dwi ddim eisiau bod yn Robert Wyn Jones yr ail.'

Cusanodd y ddau a gafaelodd Danny'n dynn yn Megan. Dechreuodd Danny siarad am Jackson eto. Gwrandawodd Megan yn dawel. Roedd yn rhaid iddi roi amser iddo alaru am Jackson.

Drannoeth, roedd pwyllgor croeso yn yr iard pan gyrhaeddodd y lefftenant a'i griw y fferm. Roedd Myfanwy, y Parch Rees Davies, ei hen ffrind Dr Williams, Sarjant Roberts a PC Pritchard yn sefyll yno gyda'i gilydd. Roedd Twm a'i fab yn gwylio o gornel yr iard ac roedd Rol y bugail yno hefyd. Wnaeth o ddim ymdrech o gwbl i dawelu'r cŵn. Dr Williams siaradodd gyntaf. Gwrthododd adael i'r lefftenant weld Megan.

'Mae hi'n rhy sâl i deithio,' meddai. Cyfieithodd Sarjant Roberts.

'*Don't you speak English?*' gofynnodd y Canadiad.

'*You are a guest in our country, sir, and I must ask . . .*'

'*OK! OK! I've heard it all before,*' gwaeddodd y lefftenant.

Ar ôl llawer o weiddi ar ran y lefftenant, ac atebion cwrtais ond pendant ar ran y Cymry, penderfynodd y ficer fod yn garedig.

'*Surely the solution is in your own hands, lieutenant. I doubt if any next of kin were called to identify the thousands who were slaughtered in Flanders. Identifying one more dead soldier can't be so difficult.*'

'*This is peacetime!*' gwaeddodd y lefftenant.

'Wir?' meddai'r meddyg.

'Diolch i Dduw,' meddai'r ficer.

'Mae o eisiau achosi cymaint o drafferth â phosib i Megan,' meddai Sarjant Roberts.

Dechreuodd y lefftenant ddadlau eto.

'*We will not be bullied, lieutenant,*' torrodd y ficer ar ei draws yn dawel.

'Gwil,' meddai Myfanwy, 'Dwedwch wrtho fo am adael fy nhir i ar unwaith, neu mi wna' i droi'r cŵn arno.'

'*Mrs Jones says if you don't get off her land at once she will ask me to arrest you for trespassing on private property.*'

'Gwilym!' Doedd y ficer ddim yn hoffi celwyddau. 'Peidiwch â bod yn wirion.'

Sylweddolodd y lefftenant ei fod o wedi colli.

'*Evans was a yellow-bellied coward,*' hisiodd. '*His desertion attempt went wrong and he probably*

drowned himself rather than face the firing squad.'
Roedd o'n meddwl hefyd fod Evans wedi cael dihangfa lwcus rhag ei fam-yng-nghyfraith. Syllodd y lleill arno mewn tawelwch. Yn sydyn, trodd Myfanwy ei chefn ar y lefftenant.

'Dwi wedi cael llond bol ar y mochyn Canadaidd yma. Pwy sy' eisiau paned?'

Wrth i'r ficer, y meddyg a PC Pritchard ddilyn Myfanwy i mewn i'r tŷ, meddai Sarjant Roberts, *'I'm sorry I cannot help you further, sir, without direct instructions from my superiors.'*

Roedd y lefftenant yn wyllt. *'Thanks for nothing,'* meddai gan droi at ei ddynion. *'Fall in men!'*

'Croeso o waelod calon, lefftenant!' meddai'r Sarjant yn ei gefn.

Geiriau newydd

dadlau – *to argue*
galaru – *to grieve*
syllu – *to stare*
ymdrech – *effort*

Pennod 19

Roedd yn rhaid i Megan fod yn sâl am dipyn o amser. Roedd ffrindiau a chymdogion wedi clywed am y briodas, ac am farwolaeth ei gŵr, a phawb eisiau ymweld â hi i glywed y stori o lygad y ffynnon. Dim ond pan ddechreuodd pethau dawelu y dwedodd ei bod hi'n teimlo'n well. Roedd hi'n poeni am Danny. Roedd o'n ddigalon iawn. Fedrai o ddim siarad am Jackson heb grio, na meddwl am ffordd i ddod allan o'r seler. Fedrai o ddim gwneud cynlluniau ar gyfer y dyfodol chwaith. Dyn marw oedd o, meddai, a doedd ganddo ddim dyfodol.

Rhoddodd Megan wisg filwrol Danny ar silff win yng nghefn y seler. Byddai hi'n gwau siwmper iddo i'w gwisgo efo hen drowsus y ficer. Ceisiodd ennyn ei ddiddordeb wrth siarad am y babi, ond doedd gan Danny ddim diddordeb mewn dim byd. Gwrthododd siafio hyd yn oed.

'Dydy dynion marw ddim yn siafio,' meddai. 'Mi wna' i siafio pan ddo' i allan o'r seler.'

Roedd ei locsyn yn goch fel locsyn ei dad. Cymerodd Danny y cyfle i grio am ei dad hefyd.

Ym mis Mai, darllenodd Danny adroddiadau yn y *Liverpool Courier* am achos y terfysgwyr. Roedd un ar bymtheg o ddynion wedi ymddangos yn y llys marsial. Fedrai Danny ddim gwneud na phen na chynffon o'r achos. Roedd hi'n amlwg fod pawb yn dweud celwyddau. Roedd y swyddogion yn dweud bod y Rwsiaid wedi dechrau'r terfysg, ond dim ond pedwar ohonyn nhw oedd ar brawf. Cafodd rhai o'r terfysgwyr eu dedfrydu i dri mis o garchar, ond cafodd eraill eu dedfrydu i ddeng mlynedd o lafur caled. Chafodd neb ei saethu. Efallai na fydden nhw'n saethu encilwyr chwaith. Fedrai Danny ddim bod yn siŵr.

Erbyn yr haf, roedd byddin Canada wedi gadael Gwersyll Parc Cinmel. Doedd dim ots gan Danny. Byddai'r ficer yn mynd i weld ei frawd yn yr Wyddgrug unwaith bob mis a byddai Megan yn mynd â Danny i gael bàth i fyny'r grisiau pan nad oedd neb o gwmpas. Benthycodd Danny lyfrau o lyfrgell y ficer ond ddarllenodd o mohonyn nhw.

Weithiau roedd Danny'n mynd allan yn y nos, ac un bore daeth yn ôl yn gwisgo crys smart. Roedd o wedi dwyn y crys oddi ar lein ddillad Plas Newydd. Ymddangosodd pibell a baco ryw fore arall.

'Wyt ti wedi torri i mewn i rywle, Danny?' gofynnodd Megan.

'Dyna'r unig beth dwi'n medru ei wneud yn dda,' meddai Danny. Doedd Megan ddim yn ei ddeall o.

Daeth brawd y ficer a'i deulu i aros yn y ficerdy am wythnos yn yr haf. Rhoddodd Syr Pedr barti mawr i'w hen ffrindiau lleol ar lawnt y ficerdy. Diflannodd poteleidiau o wisgi, jin a brandi o'r tŷ haf yn yr ardd. Roedd Megan yn flin a mynnodd fod Danny'n rhoi'r gorau i'r dwyn, ond wnaeth o ddim. Byddai'n dwyn ei ddiod o'r dafarn ac o Blas Newydd lle roedd Major Evans yn cadw digon o ddiod i'r ddau ohonyn nhw, ym marn Danny. Un noson, dringodd Danny goeden, efo potelaid o wisgi, i osgoi dau ddyn lleol oedd yn hela cwningod. Roedd Danny'n cadw llygad arnyn nhw rhag ofn iddyn nhw ddod o hyd i'w faglau.

Doedd y dynion ddim ar frys a gorffennodd Danny y botelaid gyfan. Syrthiodd i gysgu ac yna syrthiodd o'r goeden ar ben carreg fawr. Roedd ei ochr yn brifo'n ofnadwy. Cofiodd gael ei gicio yn ei asennau ar strydoedd Montreal unwaith ond roedd y boen yn waeth y tro yma. Cafodd drafferth i sleifio adref a phan edrychodd Megan ar ei ochr, dwedodd fod Danny wedi torri ei asennau. Doedd hi ddim yn bosib mynd â Danny at y meddyg, wrth gwrs, felly lapiodd Megan fandeisiau tynn o gwmpas ei ganol. Roedd hi'n llawn cydymdeimlad, ond a dweud y gwir, roedd hi'n falch o feddwl y byddai'r ddamwain yn atal Danny rhag dwyn. Beth bynnag, roedd gan Megan broblem arall i feddwl amdani. Roedd Danny mewn poen mawr a fedrai o ddim symud am wythnosau. Byddai Danny'n ddigalon iawn am weddill yr haf.

Geiriau newydd

adroddiadau – *reports*
ar brawf – *on trial*
asen – *rib*
cydymdeimlad – *sympathy*
cynffon – *tail*
dedfrydu – *to sentence*
ennyn – *to spark*
gwau – *to knit*
hela cwningod – *to hunt rabbits*
lawnt – *lawn*
locsyn – *beard*
llygad y ffynnon – *from the original source (idiom)*
maglau – *snares*
pibell – *pipe*
tynn – *tight*

Pennod 20

Gwnaeth Megan ei gorau glas i osgoi Robert Wyn Jones. Roedd o'n wyllt pan sylweddolodd ei bod hi'n feichiog. Fel arfer, byddai Robert yn gadael y fferm cyn y wawr efo'r llefrith ac yn dod yn ôl tua chwech o'r gloch, ond yn ystod yr haf roedd o wedi dechrau aros efo'i chwaer yn y Rhyl dros nos Sadwrn a dydd Sul. Roedd Robert yn ddyn siomedig. Doedd o erioed wedi bod yn feistr ar ei dŷ ei hun. Roedd o wedi gobeithio y byddai Megan yn priodi dyn lleol a symud allan o'r fferm, ond roedd hi'n amlwg rŵan y byddai'r fferm yn mynd yn syth i Megan a'i babi Canadaidd. Penderfynodd Robert wneud ei gynlluniau ei hun. Byddai'n dangos i Myfanwy a Megan faint roedden nhw'n dibynnu arno.

Cafodd Myfanwy sioc pan ddwedodd Robert ei fod o'n bwriadu cadw'r siop drws nesaf i siop Albert Griffiths yn y Rhyl. Roedd o'n mynd i werthu llefrith, llaeth enwyn, menyn, wyau ac ati, meddai. Byddai'n parhau i fyw efo'i chwaer drwy'r wythnos a dod yn ôl i'r fferm ar ddydd Mercher a dydd Sul i nôl cynnyrch y fferm. Fedrai neb ddweud ei fod o'n gadael ei deulu, ond roedd o eisiau bod yn ddyn busnes ac roedd ei ddyfodol yn y dref. Roedd o'n disgwyl cael ffrae gan Myfanwy, ond ddwedodd hi'r un gair. Roedd hi'n flin, ond roedd hi eisiau amser i feddwl am ei symudiad nesaf.

'A be am bres, Robert?' gofynnodd.

'Paid â phoeni, Myfanwy,' meddai'n hunan-fodlon. 'Mi wnes i gasglu digon o bres yng Ngwersyll Parc Cinmel i ddechrau busnes bach.'

A dyna broblem Myfanwy. Roedd y fferm yn llwyddiant, a'r busnes llefrith hefyd, ac er bod Myfanwy yn gwybod faint oedd yn y banc, roedd hi wedi gadael i Robert gadw'r cyfrifon. Yn sydyn, sylweddolodd nad oedd ganddi syniad faint o bres wnaeth Robert yn y gwersyll, na lle roedd o'n ei gadw fo. Doedd dim ots ganddi fod Robert eisiau byw yn y Rhyl – byddai hi'n falch o gael gwared arno – ond roedd hi'n poeni am y pres.

'Pryd wyt ti'n bwriadu agor dy siop, Robert?' gofynnodd.

'Tua chanol mis Tachwedd, dwi'n meddwl.' Felly, meddyliodd Myfanwy, dyna sut mae hi. Roedd Robert yn bwriadu mynd cyn i fabi Megan gael ei eni.

Dechreuodd Danny fynd allan dros nos eto yn yr hydref. Byddai'n cyfarfod hen filwyr mewn ysguboriau. Eglurodd wrth Megan mai 'boneddigion y ffordd' oedden nhw'n cael eu galw.

'Mae'r milwyr yn dweud nad oes 'na lawer o waith o gwmpas,' meddai Danny. 'Roedd rhywun yn dangos llun papur newydd i mi o hen filwyr yn gwerthu matsys ar y strydoedd yn Llundain. Dyna sut maen nhw'n diolch i ni.'

Roedd o wedi cael gwybod beth oedd yn digwydd i encilwyr hefyd. Roedd rhai o 'foneddigion y ffordd' yn encilwyr.

'Mae'n dibynnu ar y gatrawd (m). Weithiau

maen nhw'n cael *dishonourable discharge* ac weithiau maen nhw'n mynd i garchar. Ond os 'dach chi'n Ganadiad neu'n Americanwr, maen nhw'n eich anfon chi adref. Maen nhw'n dweud bydd 'na amnest ar gyfer encilwyr yn fuan.' Cytunodd Megan â Danny y byddai'n syniad da i aros am yr amnest.

Un noson, cafodd Danny sioc pan geisiodd rhywun werthu medal ryfel iddo. Doedd gan Danny ddim diddordeb mewn medalau ond dwedodd y dyn fod 'na lawer o alw am bethau felly.

'Americanwr 'dach chi? Ydy eich hen ddisg enw gynnoch chi?' gofynnodd y dyn. 'Mae rhai pobl eisiau prynu disgiau enw Americanaidd neu Ganadaidd i gael mordaith i America yn rhad ac am ddim.'

Dechreuodd Danny feddwl am ei ddisg. Efallai bod Jackson wedi ei gwerthu i rywun, ac efallai mai'r dyn hwnnw foddodd yn afon Dyfrdwy? Byddai o'n hoffi cael gwybod, ond sut?

Cafodd Danny syrpreis arall pan ddwedodd Megan wrtho am gynlluniau Robert Wyn Jones.

'Ond mae Mam yn poeni am y pres. Dydy hi ddim yn gwybod sut i gadw'r cyfrifon.' Roedd hi'n amlwg fod Megan yn poeni hefyd.

'Os bydd hi eisiau help, dwi'n gwybod tipyn bach am gyfrifon.'

Roedd hynny'n wir. Er nad oedd 'na gyfrifon ar gyfer ei fusnes nwyddau wedi'u dwyn, roedd Danny wedi cadw cyfrifon ar gyfer M. Duchesne yn y becws pan oedd o'n ddeuddeg oed.

Roedd Myfanwy'n falch iawn o gael mab-yng-nghyfraith oedd yn medru cadw cyfrifon ac roedd

Danny'n falch iawn o gael swydd go iawn.

Ond rŵan, roedd Robert Wyn Jones yn poeni. Doedd Myfanwy ddim wedi protestio o gwbl am y siop newydd. Daeth i'r Rhyl i'r agoriad hyd yn oed, er mwyn i bawb fedru gweld bod y siop yn cael sêl ei bendith a bod popeth yn iawn efo'r teulu Jones.

Geiriau newydd

boneddigion – *gentlemen*
cyfrifon – *accounts*
cynnyrch – *produce*
gwawr – *dawn*
hunanfodlon – *smug*
llaeth enwyn – *buttermilk*
llwyddiant – *success*
mordaith – *passage*
nwyddau – *goods*
sêl – *seal*

Pennod 21

Doedd dim croeso i Megan yn siop Robert yn y Rhyl. Roedd y babi yn cyrraedd mewn mis a doedd Robert ddim eisiau i bobl weld Megan mor feichiog. Doedd Robert ddim yn bwriadu bod gartref pan fyddai'r babi yn cyrraedd chwaith.

Roedd Megan, Myfanwy a Danny wedi trafod eu cynlluniau ynglŷn â sut i roi gwybod i Danny pan fyddai'r babi'n cael ei eni. Roedd 'na dipyn o broblem am nad oedd Myfanwy eisiau mynd i'r seler ar ei phen ei hun. Erbyn hyn, roedd ystafelloedd y ficerdy yn gyfarwydd iawn i Danny. Roedd o'n hoffi chwarae efo'r clychau ym mhob ystafell oedd yn canu mewn bocs ar y wal yn y gegin. Roedd Danny wedi astudio sut roedd y system yn gweithio, a phenderfynodd greu system i'r seler. Wrth i Myfanwy'n dynnu rhaff yn y gegin, byddai cloch yn canu'n y seler win.

Yn rhyfedd iawn, dechreuodd poenau esgor Megan yn y seler pan oedd hi'n cael swper efo Danny. Aeth Danny â Megan i fyny'r grisiau i'r gegin. Roedden nhw'n medru clywed lleisiau yn y gegin. Roedd Betsan yno.

'Mae'n rhaid iti fynd o 'ma Danny, mae'n ddrwg gen i. Mi ddaw Mam i ddweud wrthot ti pan gyrhaeddith y babi.'

Cusanodd Danny hi. 'Pob lwc, Megs cariad.'

Aeth yn ôl i'r seler gan deimlo'n drist. Hwn oedd
digwyddiad pwysicaf ei fywyd ac nid oedd o'n
medru bod yno. Byddai Betsan yn mynd ar gefn ei
beic rŵan, i nôl y fydwraig o rywle ger Llanfair
Talhaearn.

Arhosodd Danny am ddwy awr ond doedd y
gloch ddim wedi canu. Doedd o ddim yn medru
aros mwy. Aeth allan drwy ddrws yr ardd ac i'r
fferm. Roedd hi'n bwrw glaw yn ofnadwy ac roedd
o'n wlyb domen pan gyrhaeddodd dan ffenest
Megan yng nghefn y ffermdy. Chwiliodd am ysgol
yn yr ysgubor a'i rhoi hi'n erbyn y wal heb wneud
sŵn. Dringodd yr ysgol. Fyddai neb yn clywed dim
byd yn y glaw. Cyrhaeddodd y ffenest, ond roedd y
llenni ar gau. Rhegodd yn ddistaw. Gwrandawodd
yn ofalus. Clywodd fabi'n crio a lleisiau gwragedd.

Doedd dim lle i ddynion yno ond roedd o eisiau
gweld ei blentyn. Dringodd i lawr yr ysgol. Roedd
yn rhaid iddo guddio y tu ôl i wal gefn y tŷ tan i'r
fydwraig fynd. Yn fuan, clywodd lais Myfanwy wrth
ddrws y gegin yn dweud, 'Diolch yn fawr, Mrs
Williams. Mae hi'n noson ofnadwy. Mae croeso
ichi aros.'

Na! meddyliodd Danny.

'Dim diolch,' meddai'r fydwraig. 'Dwi wedi bod
allan mewn tywydd gwaeth na hyn.'

Gwyliodd Danny wrth i'r fydwraig fynd ar gefn ei
beic. Roedd Betsan yn dal i fod yn y gegin. Pryd
fyddai hi'n mynd i'w gwely? O'r diwedd, diffoddodd
golau'r gegin. Dringodd Danny'r ysgol eto. Curodd
yn ddistaw ar y ffenest. Tynnodd Myfanwy y
llenni'n ôl a neidio mewn dychryn pan welodd hi
Danny. Yn gyflym, agorodd y ffenest a dringodd

Danny i mewn. Rhoddodd Myfanwy ei bys ar ei gwefus. 'Ust!' sibrydodd. Roedd Megan wrth ei bodd pan welodd hi o, ond fedrai Danny wneud dim byd ond syllu ar ei wraig a'i fabi. Meddyliodd ei fod yn mynd i grio.

"Dach chi'n wlyb domen, Danny bach,' sibrydodd Myfanwy gan roi tywel iddo. 'Tynnwch eich côt cyn i chi gyffwrdd â'ch mab.'

Tynnodd Danny ei gôt ac yna, fel un mewn breuddwyd, cerddodd yn araf at y gwely. Cusanodd Megan. Estynnodd Megan y babi iddo.

'Wyt ti eisiau gafael yn dy fab?'

'Mae o mor fach!' sibrydodd Danny gan godi'r babi. Roedd 'na lwmp anferth yn ei wddf ac roedd rhywbeth yn ei lygaid hefyd. Llyncodd yn galed.

'Mi wna' i baned i chi'ch dau,' meddai Myfanwy, a gadawodd yr ystafell.

'Beth wyt ti eisiau ei alw fo, Danny?'

'Patrick,' atebodd Danny ar unwaith.

'O!' Swniodd Megan yn siomedig. 'Roeddwn i'n gobeithio cael enw Cymraeg.'

'Siŵr iawn,' meddai Danny'n gyflym, 'Ond beth?'

Awgrymodd Megan ddwsinau o enwau Cymraeg, ac enwau o'r Beibl, ond doedd Danny ddim yn hoffi'r un ohonyn nhw. Daeth Myfanwy'n ôl efo potaid o de a brechdanau i Danny.

'Mae croeso i chi aros, Danny, ond mae'n well i chi fynd cyn y wawr. Mi fydd Betsan yn codi am chwech o'r gloch a dwi'n siŵr bydd hi eisiau gweld Megan a'r babi ar unwaith.'

Roedd Megan wedi blino'n lân. Gwyliodd Danny ei wraig a'r babi dros nos gan feddwl am enwau.

Am hanner awr wedi pump, cusanodd Danny y ddau a gadael nodyn ar grud y babi: 'Bryn Patrick Evans'.

Geiriau newydd

bydwraig – *midwife*
clychau – *bells*
cyffwrdd – *to touch*
digwyddiad – *event*
gwddf – *throat*
gwlyb domen – *soaking wet (idiom)*
llyncu – *to swallow*
poenau esgor – *labour pains*
rhaff – *rope*
ysgol – *ladder*

Pennod 22

Wrth gwrs, fedrai Danny ddim mynd i fedydd Bryn, ond byddai Megan yn mynd â'r babi i'w weld o pryd bynnag medrai hi. Ar y dyddiau pan na fyddai Elias yn gweithio, pan nad oedd morwyn y gegin a morwyn y tŷ o gwmpas, pan oedd y ficer i ffwrdd, pan nad oedd Betsan yn mynd â'r babi am dro, dyna pryd roedd Danny'n cael gweld ei fab. Roedd Danny'n teimlo bod pawb arall yn gweld mwy o Bryn na fo. Roedd gormod o bobl yn cymryd diddordeb yn y babi di-dad i blesio Danny. Roedd hi'n haws i Megan ymweld â Danny heb y babi. Unwaith, gadawodd Megan y babi efo Danny am dipyn a phan gyrhaeddodd y gegin hebddo fo roedd Betsan mewn panig gan feddwl bod y babi ar ei ben ei hun yn y seler efo'r ystlumod. Roedd yn rhaid i Megan fod yn ofalus.

Ond ar y cyfan, roedd Danny'n fodlon ar ei fywyd rhyfedd. Fel arfer, byddai'n mynd allan gyda'r nos a dod yn ôl cyn y wawr. Roedd o'n dod i adnabod yr ardal yn dda ac roedd ganddo dipyn o gig yn ei boced bob amser i'w roi i'r cŵn lleol, i'w cadw nhw rhag cyfarth. Roedd o'n boblogaidd iawn efo cŵn yr ardal. Yn y bore, byddai Danny'n cysgu ac os oedd popeth yn iawn, byddai Megan yn dod draw ato efo Bryn yn y prynhawn. Ambell ddiwrnod, byddai Danny'n gweithio ar gyfrifon y fferm. Roedd Myfanwy'n hoffi cadw rhai cyfrinachau rhag Danny ond roedd o'n amau ei bod hi wedi rhoi pres i Robert ddechrau'r siop. Roedd 'na dipyn o ddirgelwch ynglŷn â Robert a faint roedd o'n ei dalu am y pethau roedd o'n eu cymryd o laethdy'r fferm. Rhoddodd Danny rybudd i Myfanwy ei bod hi'n creu problemau at y dyfodol, ond gwrthododd hi drafod y peth.

Pan ddaeth mis Mawrth, dechreuodd Danny fynd i wylio'r defaid yn ystod y nos. Doedd gan Megan a Myfanwy ddim digon o ddynion i gadw gwyliadwriaeth ar y defaid drwy'r nos ac fel arfer, bydden nhw'n colli llawer o ŵyn. Yn fuan, roedd Rol y bugail yn dweud wrth bawb bod Cefn Carreg yn colli llai o ŵyn eleni. Pan oedd gan Danny amser, byddai'n ymweld â ffermydd eraill hefyd i warchod y defaid. Soniodd am ei waith wrth un o foneddigion y ffordd un noson, pan gymerodd egwyl mewn ysgubor. Ar ôl hynny, roedd pawb yn siarad am dramp dirgel oedd yn achub ŵyn o gwmpas yr ardal. Rhoddodd y bobl leol enw iddo – Ffrind y Ffermwr, ond doedd neb wedi ei weld.

Roedd cymdeithas y trampiau yn hoffi sôn am Ffrind y Ffermwr. Roedd y stori'n rhoi enw da iddyn nhw, ond roedd storïau eraill yn dod o rosydd Dinbych. Roedd lladron yn dwyn ŵyn y ffermwyr yno ac roedd rhai ohonyn nhw'n amau'r trampiaid. Doedd Danny ddim yn credu'r storïau.

'Mae'r trampiaid yn hoffi teithio'n ysgafn. Fydden nhw ddim eisau cario ŵyn o gwmpas,' meddai wrth Megan.

'Sipsiwn, mae'n debyg,' meddai Megan. 'Does 'na ddim ffensys na waliau ar y rhosydd. 'Dan ni'n saff yn yr ardal yma.'

Roedd Megan wrth ei bodd efo gwaith dirgel Danny, ond roedd hi'n poeni hefyd.

'Cymer ofal, Danny, mae llawer o bobl eisiau gwybod pwy ydy Ffrind y Ffermwr. Bydd rhywun yn ceisio dy ddal di rhyw noson.'

Ond roedd gan Danny gynllun arall ar y gweill. Roedd gan Megan gaseg o'r enw Sandi yn un o'r caeau uchaf. Doedd hi ddim yn hoffi dynion. Roedd Danny'n benderfynol o'i marchogaeth ac yn araf roedd o'n magu ei hyder hi. Doedd hi ddim yn bosib dod â chyfrwy bob nos, ond fel arfer roedd Danny'n cario'r awenau a'r ffrwyn efo fo. Roedd y tymor wyna'n dod i ben. Doedd 'na ddim ond ychydig ar ôl i gael eu geni. Cychwynnodd Danny am y caeau uchaf un noson. Roedd o'n gobeithio bod Sandi'n barod i drotian o'r diwedd.

Geiriau newydd

ar y gweill – *on the go (idiom)*
awenau – *reins*
bedydd – *christening*
cyfrwy – *saddle*
dirgelwch – *mystery*
ffrwyn – *bridle*
hyder – *confidence*
marchogaeth – *to ride*
penderfynol – *determined*
rhosydd – *moors*
ŵyn – *lambs*

Pennod 23

Roedd y lleuad yn cuddio y tu ôl i'r cymylau pan aeth Danny i weld Sandi. Croesodd y ffordd i'r caeau uchaf. Dyna beth rhyfedd – roedd y giât yn agored. Fyddai Rol ddim yn gadael giât yn agored. Beth oedd o'i le? Safodd Danny yn stond a gwrando. Roedd o'n medru clywed sŵn y defaid a'r ŵyn yn brefu ar ei gilydd ac roedd 'na arogl anarferol. Beth oedd o? Tynnodd ei fflachlamp o'i boced. Efallai bod clicied y giât wedi torri. Na, roedd y glicied yn iawn, ond sylwodd Danny ar farciau teiars ar y glaswellt. Beic modur Rol mwy na thebyg. Edrychodd ar y marciau eto. Roedd dwy res ohonyn nhw, fel teiars car neu fan. Ond pwy fyddai'n dod â modur i'r cae? Dyna fo, arogl petrol oedd o.

Dilynodd Danny'r wal i fyny'r bryn ar ochr y cae. Yn y cae agosaf at Sandi roedd y defaid yn gwneud llawer o sŵn. Roedd arogl petrol yn dal i fod yn yr awyr ac roedd giât y cae nesaf yn agored hefyd. Yn sydyn, gwelodd Danny olau yng nghanol y cae. Diffoddodd y golau mewn eiliad ond roedd Danny wedi gweld siâp cerbyd o ryw fath. Sleifiodd yn nes. Dyna'r golau eto, a rŵan medrai glywed sŵn lleisiau dynion. Edrychodd Danny ar y cymylau. Byddai'r lleuad yn dod allan mewn munud. Gorweddodd ar y ddaear. Yng ngolau'r lleuad gwelodd bopeth. Roedd dau ddyn yn rhoi ŵyn mewn hen ambiwlans byddin.

'Dyna ddigon,' meddai un ohonyn nhw. Clepiodd ddrws cefn yr ambiwlans. Cychwynnodd y modur a chlepiodd drws arall.

Beth fedrai o wneud? Tasai Danny'n ceisio stopio'r ambiwlans, basen nhw'n ei daro. Mi ddylai o eu dilyn nhw. Aeth yr ambiwlans heibio iddo, yna rhedodd i gae Sandi. Rhoddodd foronen iddi'n gyflym gan siarad yn ddistaw â hi. Rhoddodd yr awenau a'r ffrwyn arni. Protestiodd y gaseg fel arfer, ond dwedodd Danny'n bendant, 'Nid dyma'r amser i wneud ffŷs, Sandi. Mae gynnon ni waith i'w wneud.'

Dringodd ar gefn y gaseg, ond gwrthododd Sandi symud. Tarodd Danny ei hystlys a rhedodd yn wyllt yn syth. Arhosodd Danny ar ei chefn rywsut. Basen nhw'n dal yr ambiwlans tasai hi'n rhedeg mor gyflym â hyn. Marchogodd Danny o gwmpas y cae ddwy waith tan i Sandi dawelu. Mwythodd ei gwddf. 'Hogan dda,' meddai a throi ei phen tuag at y ffordd.

Roedd yr ambiwlans wedi troi i gyfeiriad Abergele. Roedd o'n symud yn araf a rhwng sŵn yr injan a brefu'r ŵyn, go brin eu bod nhw'n medru clywed y gaseg. Cadwodd Danny ei bellter oddi wrthyn nhw. Trodd yr ambiwlans dair neu bedair gwaith, ond erbyn hyn roedd Danny'n gwybod lle roedd o. Ond lle roedd y dynion yn mynd? Doedd 'na ddim tai ar y ffordd o gwbl, ac roedd y ffermdai yn bell o'r ffordd yn yr ardal yma. Ar ôl tua phedair milltir, trodd yr ambiwlans ar hyd llwybr cul. Dilynodd Danny'n araf. Arhosodd yr ambiwlans mewn iard fach gerllaw bwthyn ar fryn serth. Penderfynodd Danny gerdded, felly arweiniodd Sandy i waelod y lôn a'i chlymu wrth goeden. Rhoddodd foronen arall iddi a sibrwd, 'Paid â gwneud sŵn.' Gweryrodd y gaseg. 'Cau dy geg,' meddai Danny.

Daeth hen wraig efo lamp allan o'r bwthyn. Cuddiodd Danny y tu ôl i'r wal yn ymyl mynedfa'r iard.

'Faint sy' gynnoch chi?' gofynnodd y wraig.

'Tua dwsin, Mam,' atebodd un o'r dynion. Dechreuon nhw symud yr ŵyn i gwt bach yn yr iard.

'Mae'n well i chi fynd â'r ambiwlans yn ôl cyn iddyn nhw sylweddoli ei fod wedi diflannu,' meddai'r wraig. 'Mi a' i i wneud paned.'

Trodd un o'r dynion yr ambiwlans i wynebu'r bryn. Yna, meddai'r llall, 'Gawn ni adael y fan am awr neu ddwy? Dwi eisiau bwyd.'

'Iawn. Dwi eisiau cysgu am dipyn hefyd.'

Aeth y ddau ohonyn nhw i mewn i'r tŷ. Beth fedrai Danny wneud? Ddylai o fynd yn ôl i Gefn Carreg i ddweud wrth Megan beth oedd wedi digwydd? Doedd Danny ddim yn gwybod os oedd yr ŵyn wedi cael eu marcio eto. Heb farciau byddai'n anodd profi mai ŵyn Cefn Carreg oedden nhw, ac os oedd yr ambiwlans wedi diflannu, Danny, y dyn marw, oedd yr unig un oedd wedi gweld y lladron.

Diffoddodd y golau y tu mewn i'r bwthyn. Roedd yr ŵyn yn dal i frefu'n swnllyd. Penderfynodd Danny beth i'w wneud. Roedd y dynion wedi dwyn ŵyn Danny ac felly, byddai Danny'n dwyn yr ŵyn yn ôl.

Geiriau newydd

brefu – *to low, bleat*
clicied – *catch*
clymu – *to tie*
cul – *narrow*
cymylau – *clouds*
glaswellt – *grass*
gweryru – *to whinny*
lleuad – *moon*
sefyll yn stond – *to stand still*
ystlys – *flank*

Pennod 24

Sleifiodd Danny yn dawel at yr ambiwlans. Roedd y cerbyd yn wynebu i lawr y bryn ac roedd y ddolen gychwyn ar y sedd ffrynt. Agorodd ddrws y cwt bach a drws cefn yr ambiwlans. Symudodd yr ŵyn yn ôl i'r ambiwlans, un ar ôl y llall. Roedd yr ŵyn wedi dychryn, felly roedd yn rhaid i Danny gau drws yr ambiwlans bob tro rhag ofn iddyn nhw ddianc. Roedd y dynion wedi dwyn un ar ddeg oen. Caeodd Danny ddrws yr ambiwlans yn ddistaw. Gollyngodd frêc y cerbyd a'i symud dipyn bach. Aeth Danny allan a rhoi ei ysgwydd ar gefn yr ambiwlans a'i wthio. Roedd o'n drwm iawn, ond roedd Danny wedi gwthio ambiwlans byddin o'r blaen. Defnyddiodd ei holl nerth i symud y cerbyd, ond pan ddechreuodd yr olwynion droi roedd yn rhaid iddo redeg i ddringo i sedd y gyrrwr. Doedd 'na ddim amser i gau'r drws – roedd yr ambiwlans yn cyflymu. Trwy ddefnyddio'r brêc, gyrrodd Danny yn araf i lawr y bryn. Roedd ei broblem nesaf yn aros ar y gwaelod.

Gweryrodd Sandi wrth groesawu Danny ond roedd yn rhaid iddo fynd â'r ambiwlans ar y ffordd. Stopiodd ar ben bryn bach ac aeth i nôl Sandi. Fedrai o ddim gadael y gaseg yno, roedd hi'n rhy werthfawr. Mwythodd hi.

'Wyt ti'n cofio'r gân: *"My old man said follow the van"* Sandi? Wel, dyma beth wyt ti'n mynd i'w wneud.' Safodd Sandi yn ofnus wrth i Danny gychwyn yr injan. Doedd hi ddim yn hoffi sŵn yr injan a symudodd i ffwrdd yn gyflym. Daliodd Danny hi. Gafaelodd yn yr awenau ac aeth i mewn i'r ambiwlans. Eisteddodd am funud. Roedd hi'n amhosib arwain y gaseg a gyrru'r ambiwlans ar yr un pryd. Roedd o'n gobeithio y byddai hi'n dilyn y cerbyd.

Cychwynnodd Danny ond safodd Sandi yn stond. Ganllath yn nes ymlaen, arhosodd Danny ac aeth i nôl y gaseg. Tynnodd foronen o'i boced a'i chwifio o dan drwyn Sandi. 'Tyrd ymlaen, hogan, tyrd ymlaen,' meddai'n ddistaw. Dilynodd Sandi y foronen. Pan gyrhaeddon nhw'r ambiwlans, tynnodd Danny ei siaced a'i hongian hi drwy'r ffenest agored a'r foronen yn gwthio allan o'i boced. Dechreuodd symud yr ambiwlans yn araf. Dechreuodd Sandi ddilyn y foronen. Hanner milltir ar hyd y ffordd, rhoddodd Danny y foronen iddi. Doedd 'na ddim ond dwy foronen ar ôl. Cerddodd Sandi yn ddistaw wrth ochr yr ambiwlans. Roedd hi'n fodlon ymuno â gêm Danny ond doedd hi ddim ar frys, felly roedd yn rhaid i Danny yrru mewn gêr isel yr holl ffordd adref. A dyna sut y cyrhaeddon nhw eu tir eu hunain, ddwy awr yn ddiweddarach.

Yn gyflym, rhoddodd Danny Sandi a'r ŵyn yn ôl yn y cae. Byddai'r defaid yn dod o hyd iddynt yn ddigon buan. Ond rŵan, roedd yn rhaid iddo gael gwared ar yr ambiwlans. Doedd o ddim eisiau i neb gysylltu Cefn Carreg â Ffrind y Ffermwr. Byddai'r wawr yn torri mewn awr. Pwy oedd biau'r ambiwlans? Roedd y lladron wedi dwyn y cerbyd, siŵr o fod. Ysgrifennodd nodyn a gyrru'r ambiwlans i Lanfair Talhaearn. Roedd o wedi bod yn Llanfair yn ystod y nos o'r blaen. Roedd 'na blismon yn byw yno. Parciodd yr ambiwlans ar ganol y bont ar y ffordd i'r pentref a gadael nodyn dan garreg ar y sedd ffrynt. Cerddodd yn ôl i'r fferm ac roedd y wawr ar dorri pan gurodd ar ffenest Megan i ddweud, 'Tyrd i'r seler yn gyflym.' Pan ddwedodd Danny wrthi beth oedd wedi digwydd, atebodd Megan,

'Sipsiwn o Iwerddon – teulu'r Lovells ydyn nhw.'

Drannoeth, daeth y plismon o hyd i'r ambiwlans mewn cyflwr ofnadwy a'r nodyn, 'Mae'r teulu sy'n byw ym Meudy Newydd yn lladron ŵyn. Dwi wedi mynd â'r ŵyn yn ôl i'w fferm. Edrychwch yn y cwt yn yr iard am dystiolaeth. FF y FF.'

Roedd yr ambiwlans yn llawn o faw defaid a deallodd y plismon yn syth beth oedd ystyr y nodyn. Daeth y plismon o hyd i'r brodyr Lovell yn glanhau'r cwt, ond roedd y dystiolaeth yn dal i fod yno ac roedd pawb yn gwybod nad oedd gan y teulu ddefaid eu hunain. Roedd can o betrol yno hefyd, a marciau teiars, ond protestiodd y brodyr fod rhywun wedi defnyddio eu hiard er mwyn i bethau edrych yn ddrwg arnyn nhw. Doedden nhw'n gwybod dim byd am y peth, medden nhw.

Gadawodd y plismon gan wenu. Roedd yr hogiau Lovell wedi dychryn. Doedd 'na ddim llawer o bobl a fedrai ddychryn y brodyr Lovell. Byddai'r plismon yn hoffi cyfarfod Ffrind y Ffermwr.

Geiriau newydd

baw defaid – *sheep droppings*
biau – *to own*
cyflwr – *condition*
diweddarach – *later*
gollwng – *to drop/release*
gwerthfawr – *valuable*
nerth – *strength*
tystiolaeth – *evidence*

Pennod 25

Yn y cyfamser, roedd Rol y bugail yn poeni. Aeth i'r ffermdy i ddweud wrth Megan bod rhywbeth rhyfedd wedi digwydd. Roedd yr ŵyn a'r defaid efo Sandi yn y cae anghywir. Roedd rhywun wedi marchogaeth Sandi. Roedd 'na farciau teiars ar y ddaear ond doedd dim byd ar goll. Cytunodd Megan fod rhywbeth rhyfedd wedi digwydd.

Amser cinio, cyrhaeddodd plismon y pentref ar gefn ei feic. Dangosodd y nodyn oddi wrth Ffrind y Ffermwr iddyn nhw.

'Wrth gwrs, fedra' i wneud dim byd ynglŷn â'r Lovells, ond tybed gafodd unrhyw un o'r ffermwyr drafferth neithiwr?'

Roedd yn well gan Megan gadw'n ddistaw am y peth, ond roedd Rol yn hoffi meddwl bod gan Ffrind y Ffermwr ddiddordeb arbennig yng Nghefn Carreg. Dwedodd Rol wrth y plismon beth oedd o wedi ei ddarganfod y bore hwnnw, ac aeth y ddau ddyn i weld y marciau teiars. Wedyn, dros baned yn y ffermdy, penderfynodd y ddau y dylen nhw gadw golwg am Ffrind y Ffermwr y noson honno.

Ar ôl i'r ficer gael ei swper, aeth Megan i rybuddio Danny.

'Paid â mynd allan am ychydig nosweithiau, Danny.'

'Siŵr iawn, cariad,' meddai Danny'n ufudd, ond doedd o ddim yn bwriadu aros i mewn. Roedd o'n mwynhau ei nosweithiau allan. Penderfynodd fynd i gyfeiriad Dinbych am newid. Roedd Rol a PC Pritchard yn siomedig. Mi welon nhw ddau neu dri o bobl y noson honno. Roedden nhw i gyd yn gwneud yr un peth – roedd pawb eisiau cyfarfod Ffrind y Ffermwr. Doedd y trampiaid erioed wedi bod mor boblogaidd ac roedd llawer ohonyn nhw'n dweud eu bod nhw'n gwybod pwy oedd Ffrind y Ffermwr, ond roedden nhw eisiau cadw eu cyfrinach. Mewn ysgubor ger Henllan, gofynnodd hen filwr i Danny, 'Pwy ydy'r dyn yma? 'Dach chi wedi ei weld o?'

'Dwi wedi ei gyfarfod o unwaith, bythefnos yn ôl,' meddai Danny. 'Dwi ddim yn gwybod ei enw, ond hen filwr ydy o.'

Yr wythnos ganlynol, aeth Danny'n ôl i'w domen ei hun a chafodd sioc. Byddai Danny'n symud fel cysgod yn y nos, ond roedd y rhan fwyaf o bobl yn gwneud sŵn ofnadwy. Clywodd leisiau a gweld golau wrth derfyn tir Cefn Carreg a'r fferm nesaf. Sleifiodd yn nes. Dau hogyn oedd yno yn siarad am Ffrind y Ffermwr. Arhosodd Danny tan eu bod nhw wedi blino ac yna dilynodd nhw adref i fwthyn Rol.

Drannoeth, gofynnodd Danny i Megan, 'Beth ydy enwau meibion Rol, Megs?'

'Hefin ac Edwin – pam?' Chwarddodd Megan pan ddwedodd Danny beth oedd wedi digwydd.

'Mae hi fel *Piccadilly Circus* yn y caeau y nosweithiau hyn,' cwynodd Danny. 'Dwi'n meddwl ei bod hi'n amser i Ffrind y Ffermwr ddiflannu.'

Y noson wedyn, aeth Danny i fwthyn Rol. Roedd cŵn Rol yn adnabod Danny'n iawn. Daethon nhw ar hyd y lôn i'w gyfarfod gan siglo eu cynffonnau a gwthio eu trwynau i'w bocedi i chwilio am gig. Gadawodd Danny nodyn ar garreg y drws: 'Hefin ac Edwin. Dwi'n gadael yr ardal heno i chwilio am waith yn ne Cymru. Diolch am eich diddordeb. FF y FF.' Aeth Danny adref gan deimlo fel brenin y nos.

Roedd Hefin ac Edwin yn gynhyrfus iawn. Sut oedd Ffrind y Ffermwr yn gwybod beth oedd eu henwau? Dyn hud oedd o, yn wir. Ymhen ychydig ddyddiau roedd pawb yn gwybod bod Ffrind y Ffermwr wedi mynd. Daeth yn chwedl ar unwaith a'i anturiaethau'n chwyddo bob tro roedd rhywun yn eu hadrodd.

Geiriau newydd

ar ei domen ei hun – *on home ground (idiom)*
chwedl – *legend*
chwyddo – *to swell*
darganfod – *to discover*
hud – *magic*
siglo – *to wag*
ufudd – *obedient*

Pennod 26

Ar ôl gwanwyn llwyddiannus, haf diflas iawn gafodd Danny. Roedd o'n helpu efo'r ŵyn a'r cyfrifon ond doedd o ddim yn mwynhau'r haf. Roedd y nosweithiau'n rhy fyr ac roedd 'felan yr haf' yn disgyn arno eto. Doedd gan Megan ddim amynedd efo fo. Roedd hi wedi blino'n lân. Rhwng y fferm, y llaethdy a'r ficerdy – heb Robert Wyn Jones – roedd Megan a'i mam yn brysur, yn rhy brysur i roi llawer o sylw i Danny. Roedd o'n treulio mwy a mwy o amser efo'r trampiaid yn yr ysguboriau a phan oedden nhw'n siarad am y dinasoedd, roedd Danny'n dechrau hiraethu am Montreal.

Daeth brawd y ficer a'i deulu am eu gwyliau haf eto, ac fel arfer, rhoddodd Syr Pedr barti ar lawnt y ficerdy. Aeth Megan yn wyllt pan ddechreuodd Danny ddwyn y diodydd eto, a phan ymddangosodd dillad a phethau pysgota Syr Pedr yn y seler, mynnodd Megan fod Danny'n eu rhoi nhw'n ôl. Dros yr haf daeth seler Danny'n 'ogof Aladdin' efo esgidiau, dillad dringo, a phabell hyd yn oed.

'Mae 'na lawer o ymwelwyr o gwmpas,' chwarddodd Danny. Roedd Megan mewn anobaith. Ym mis Medi, cyrhaeddodd ben ei thennyn pan roddodd Danny gadwyn hyfryd iddi. Roedd Mrs

Evans, Plas Newydd, wedi gwisgo'r gadwyn ym mharti Syr Pedr. Roedd Megan yn ddig iawn. Taflodd y gadwyn at Danny.

'Mae'n rhaid iti stopio hyn, Danny. Bydd yr heddlu wrth y drws unrhyw ddiwrnod rŵan.'

'Ond pam, Megan? Does 'na ddim lleidr yma. Dwi ddim yn fyw!' Roedd o'n iawn wrth gwrs, ac roedd hi'n amlwg fod Danny'n bwriadu manteisio ar y ffaith ei fod o'n 'ddyn marw'.

'Os oeddet ti'n medru torri i mewn i'r Plas i ddwyn y gadwyn, mi fedri di dorri i mewn eto a'i rhoi hi'n ôl yn ei lle. Dwi ddim yn gwybod lle rwyt ti wedi dysgu dwyn, ond fedri di mo'i wneud o yma.' Roedd Danny'n ddig hefyd.

'Does gen i ddim byd arall i'w wneud, Megan. Pa fath o fywyd ydy hwn i mi? Dwi'n dibynnu ar fy ngwraig am bopeth, dwi byth yn gweld fy mab a dwi ddim yn gweithio. Be arall fedra' i wneud? Iawn. Os wyt ti'n flin, mi a' i â'r gadwyn yn ôl.'

'Ac addo i mi na wnei di ddwyn eto.'

'Na wna'. Paid â dweud wrtha' i beth i'w wneud!'

'Felly, mae'r ateb yn syml. Dwi ddim eisiau bod yn briod â throseddwr. Os wyt ti eisiau bod yn lleidr, dos i Loegr i ddwyn. Mi fydd o'n fywyd anoddach na chuddio yn y seler. Tyrd yn ôl pan fyddi di wedi gwneud rhywbeth o werth.'

'Os bydda i'n mynd, ddo' i ddim yn ôl,' gwaeddodd Danny.

'Mae hynny'n iawn efo fi,' gwaeddodd Megan gan ruthro allan o'r seler.

Y noson honno, aeth Danny â'r gadwyn yn ôl. Fel arfer doedd o ddim yn dwyn pres, ond roedd y tro hwn yn wahanol. Byddai arno angen pres ar gyfer ei daith. Roedd o am fynd i Lundain i chwilio am Jackson. Doedd gan enciliwr estron ddim gobaith dod allan o'i guddfan a gwneud bywyd newydd mewn lle bach fel hwn. Byddai'n rhaid iddo wneud bywyd newydd yn rhywle arall, heb ddibynnu ar hwyl merched. Drannoeth, rhoddodd Megan frecwast iddo a cherdded o'r seler heb ddweud gair. Teimlodd Danny fel un o'r cŵn defaid. Bywyd ci oedd hwn.

Y noson honno, pan oedd y ficerdy'n dawel, aeth Danny i'r pantri a chymryd digon o fwyd am dri diwrnod. Go brin y byddai o'n cael bwyd fel pastai cyw iâr Myfanwy eto. Cerddodd i lawr y ffordd i gyfeiriad Lloegr heb edrych yn ôl. Roedd ei freuddwyd wedi dod i ben.

Geiriau newydd

cadwyn – *necklace/chain*
dig – *angry*
hwyl – *mood*
manteisio – *to take advantage*
pen ei thennyn – *the end of her tether*
taith – *journey*
y felan – *the blues*

Geirfa

achos – *trial*
adloniant – *entertainment*
adnabyddus – *well known*
adroddiadau – *reports*
addewid – *promise*
agor ceg – *to yawn*
anghysurus – *uncomfortable*
ailadrodd – *to repeat*
allor – *altar*
amau – *to suspect*
amddiffyn – *to defend*
amheus – *suspicious*
anadlu – *to breathe*
anferth – *huge*
anobaith – *despair*
antur – *adventure*
anwybyddu – *to ignore*
ar brawf – *on trial*
ar ei domen ei hun – *on home ground (idiom)*
ar fai – *to blame*
ar y gweill – *on the go (idiom)*
archwilio – *to inspect*
arogl – *smell*
arwain – *to lead*
arweinydd – *leader*
arwr – *hero*
asen – *rib*
awenau – *reins*
awyddus – *keen*
awyrgylch – *atmosphere*
bandeisiau – *bandages*
baw defaid – *sheep droppings*

becws – *bakery*
bedydd – *christening*
beichiog – *pregnant*
bendith – *blessing*
benthyg – *to borrow*
beudy – *cowshed*
biau – *to own*
blêr – *untidy*
boddi – *to drown*
bonclust – *clout*
boneddigion – *gentlemen*
brasgamu – *to stride*
brathu – *to bite*
brefu – *to low, bleat*
breuddwyd – *dream*
breuddwydiol – *dreamy*
briwiau – *wounds*
budr – *dirty*
bugail – *shepherd*
bydwraig – *midwife*
bygwth – *to threaten*
bywyd troseddwr – *criminal life*
cadwyn – *necklace/chain*
cael gafael ar – *to get hold of*
cam – *step*
canlynol – *following*
carcharorion – *prisoners*
carfan – *party*
caseg – *mare*
casgenni – *barrels*
cefnogaeth – *support*
celwydd – *lie*
cerbyd – *vehicle*
cleifion – *patients*
clicied – *catch*

cloff – *lame*
cloi – *to lock*
clwyfedig – *wounded*
clychau – *bells*
clymu – *to tie*
codi twrw – *to make trouble*
coedwigwr – *lumberjack*
cofleidio – *to hug*
cofnod – *record*
cofrestr – *register*
colfachau – *hinges*
crwydro – *to wander*
cryfder – *strength*
crynu – *to shake*
cuddfan – *hiding place*
cuddio – *to hide*
cul – *narrow*
curo – *to beat/knock*
cydymdeimlad – *sympathy*
cyfarth – *to bark*
cyfarwydd – *familiar*
cyfarwyddiadau – *instructions*
cyfieithydd – *translator*
cyflwr – *condition*
cyfoethog – *rich*
cyfogi – *to vomit*
cyfraith – *law*
cyfrif – *to count*
cyfrifon – *accounts*
cyfrinach – *secret*
cyfrwy – *saddle*
cyffwrdd – *to touch*
cynghori – *to advise*
cymodi – *to reconcile*
cymylau – *clouds*

cynffon – *tail*
cynnal – *to hold*
cynnau – *to switch on*
cynnig – *to offer*
cynnyrch – *produce*
cynyddu – *to increase*
cysgod – *shadow*
cysuro – *to comfort*
cysylltiad – *connection*
cywilydd – *shame*
chwedl – *legend*
chwerthin – *to laugh*
chwyddo – *to swell*
chwythu – *to blow*
dadlau – *to argue*
dagrau – *tears*
darganfod – *to discover*
dathlu – *to celebrate*
dedfrydu – *to sentence*
deilen – *leaf*
dewis – *choice*
dial – *revenge*
dicter – *anger*
dieuog – *innocent*
diflannu – *to disappear*
difrod – *damage*
diffodd – *to put out*
dig – *angry*
digwyddiad – *event*
dioddef – *to suffer*
dirgel – *secret*
dirgelwch – *mystery*
dirwyn i ben – *to draw to a close*
disgyblaeth – *discipline*
disgyn – *to get down, descend*

diweddarach – *later*
diweithdra – *unemployment*
dodrefn – *furniture*
dolen gychwyn – *starting handle*
drewi – *to stink*
dringo – *to climb*
drych – *mirror*
drysu – *to puzzle*
dwyn – *to steal*
dychwelyd – *to return*
dychymyg – *imagination*
dyrnau – *fists*
egwyl – *break*
eirch – *coffins*
ennyn – *to spark*
ergyd – *blow*
esgyrn – *bones*
estroniaid – *foreigners*
etifeddu – *to inherit*
ffrae – *row*
ffrwyn – *bridle*
ffyddlon – *faithful*
gafael yn – *to hold*
galaru – *to grieve*
genedigaeth – *birth*
glaswellt – *grass*
gohebydd – *reporter*
gollwng – *to drop/release*
gordd – *sledgehammer*
goriad – *key*
gorlawn – *overcrowded*
griddfan – *to groan*
gris – *step*
gwaedu – *to bleed*
gwag – *empty*

gwahaniaeth – *difference*
gwallgof – *mad*
gwartheg – *cattle*
gwas – *servant*
gwas fferm – *farm worker*
gwasgu – *to squeeze*
gwastad – *flat*
gwau – *to knit*
gwawr – *dawn*
gwddf – *throat*
gwe pry cop – *cobwebs*
gweddillion – *remains*
gweddïo – *to pray*
gweiddi – *to shout*
gwelw – *pale*
gwers – *lesson*
gwersyll torri coed – *lumber camp*
gwerthfawr – *valuable*
gweryru – *to whinny*
gwesteion – *guests*
gwisg – *dress*
gwlyb domen – *soaking wet (idiom)*
gwrych – *hedge*
haearn – *iron*
hedfan – *to fly*
heddwch – *peace*
hela – *to chase*
hela cwningod – *to hunt rabbits*
helynt – *trouble*
holi – *to enquire*
hud – *magic*
hunanfodlon – *smug*
hwyl – *mood*

hyder – *confidence*
lawnt – *lawn*
locsyn – *beard*
lladron – *robbers*
llaeth enwyn – *buttermilk*
llaith – *damp*
llechi – *slate*
lled – *wide*
lledu – *to spread*
llefain – *to wail*
lleithder – *dampness*
lleuad – *moon*
llif – *tide*
llifo – *to flow*
llithro – *to slip*
llofnodi – *to sign*
llogi – *to hire*
llonydd – *peace*
llwch – *dust*
llwncdestun – *toast*
llwyd – *grey*
llwyddiant – *success*
llwyddo – *to succeed*
llygad y ffynnon – *from the original source (idiom)*
llygod Ffrengig – *rats*
llymaid – *swig*
llyncu – *to swallow*
llysfam – *step mother*
maglau – *snares*
mân droseddwr – *petty criminal*
manteisio – *to take advantage*
marchogaeth – *to ride*
meddw – *drunk*
meiddio – *to dare*

mentro – *to venture, risk*
mordaith – *passage*
morwyn/morynion – *maid(s)*
mwy na thebyg – *more than likely*
mynd o chwith – *to go wrong*
mynnu – *to insist*
nadu – *to whine*
neidio – *to jump*
nenfwd – *ceiling*
nerth – *strength*
nifer – *number*
nod – *aim*
nwyddau – *goods*
o'u corun i'w sawdl – *from head to toe*
oeraidd – *cold*
oes – *lifetime*
Pabydd – *Roman Catholic*
parch – *respect*
parchus – *respectable*
pellter – *distance*
pen ei thennyn – *the end of her tether*
pen mawr – *hangover*
pen-glin – *knee*
pencadlys – *headquarters*
penderfynol – *determined*
perchennog – *proprietor*
pibell – *pipe*
plygu – *to duck*
poenau esgor – *labour pains*
prinder – *shortage*
priodferch – *bride*
pryderus – *worried*

rhaff – *rope*
rhannu – *to share*
rhegi – *to swear*
rheolaeth – *control*
rhes – *row*
rhosydd – *moors*
rhugl – *fluent*
rhuthro – *to rush*
rhybudd – *warning*
rhydlyd – *rusty*
Rhydychen – *Oxford*
sarhaus – *insultingly*
sathru – *to trample*
sefyll yn stond – *to stand still*
sefyllfa – *situation*
sêl – *seal*
serth – *steep*
sibrwd – *to whisper*
siglo – *to wag*
stad – *estate*
swil – *shy*
swta – *abrupt*
sychu – *to dry*
syllu – *to stare*
synau – *sounds*
synnwyr – *sense*
syrthio – *to fall*
taflu – *to throw*
tail gwartheg – *cowpat*
taith – *journey*
tenantiaeth – *tenancy*
tlawd – *poor*
trannoeth – *the next day*
trefnu – *to arrange*
trin – *to treat*

troi drosodd – *to overturn*
trwsio – *to repair*
twll glo – *coal hole*
tyndra – *tension*
tynn – *tight*
tyrfa – *crowd*
tystiolaeth – *evidence*
tywyllwch – *darkness*
uchel – *loud*
ufudd – *obedient*
wedi dychryn – *horrified*
ŵyn – *lambs*
y felan – *the blues*
ymchwiliad – *enquiry*
ymdrech – effort
ymddiried – *to trust*
ymylon – *fringes*
yn ferw gwyllt – *uproar*
yn syn – *surprised*
ysbeilio – *to loot*
ysgol – *ladder*
ysgubor – *barn*
ysgwyd – *to shake*
ysgwydd – *shoulder*
ystlumod – *bats*
ystlys – *flank*

Marcus Berkmann writes regularly for *Private Eye* and *The Oldie* and has been pop music critic for the *Spectator* for twenty-five years. His books include *Rain Men: The Madness of Cricket*, *Zimmer Men: The Trials and Tribulations of the Ageing Cricketer*, *Fatherhood: The Truth* and *A Matter of Facts: The Insider's Guide to Quizzing*.

Also by Marcus Berkmann

Rain Men: The Madness of Cricket

Zimmer Men: The Trials and Tribulations
of the Ageing Cricketer

Fatherhood: The Truth

A Matter of Facts: The Insider's Guide to Quizzing

Ashes to Ashes: 35 Years of Agony
(and About 20 Minutes of Ecstasy)
Watching England v Australia

A Shed of One's Own

MIDLIFE WITHOUT THE CRISIS

MARCUS BERKMANN

ABACUS

First published in Great Britain in 2012 by Little, Brown
Reprinted 2012 (four times)
This paperback edition published in 2013 by Abacus

A CIP catalogue record for this book
is available from the British Library.

ISBN 978-0-349-12372-1

Typeset in Bembo by M Rules
Printed and bound in Great Britain by
Clays Ltd, St Ives plc

Papers used by Abacus are from well-managed forests
and other responsible sources.

Abacus
An imprint of
Little, Brown Book Group
100 Victoria Embankment
London EC4Y 0DY

An Hachette UK Company
www.hachette.co.uk

www.littlebrown.co.uk

CONTENTS

INTRODUCTION

'You are forty. That is a critical age. Between thirty-five and forty everybody has to turn a corner in his life, or smash into a brick wall.'

Dr von Haller in Robertson Davies,
The Manticore (1972)

Some years ago, I chanced upon an interview with two of my favourite musicians, Walter Becker and Donald Fagen of Steely Dan. Then in their late forties, the pair had recently started working together again after fifteen years of floundering around in underachieving solo careers. What had they been up to? asked the interviewer. Did the fallow years constitute some sort of, well, midlife crisis?

Becker (or it might have been Fagen) snorted. Midlife crisis? he said. It's not as simple as that. You have a midlife crisis, fine, and you get over it. Then you have another one. After that there's another one and then another, and so on and so on until you die. There followed a brief pause, as the interviewer tried to remember what his next question was. Beads of sweat may have spontaneously formed on his forehead.

For some reason the exchange stayed in my memory. I hadn't yet thought of writing a book about midlife. I didn't feel the term applied to me. I was only forty or so, a mere stripling. Even so, there was something deeply convincing in the notion of the midlife crisis as a semi-permanent state, from which only death could deliver you. Around ten years later, after failing to celebrate my fiftieth birthday, and not leaving the house for nearly a fortnight, I started thinking about this book. The Becker/Fagen story came back to me. I set about tracking it down. Maybe I had torn the interview out of the magazine and put it in the drawer in my desk I reserve for magazine articles I tear out and never read again. No, I hadn't — although I did spend a happy afternoon reading these old articles, before putting them back in the drawer, possibly for ever. But everything is on the internet, isn't it? Not this article. I began to wonder whether I had imagined it. I discussed the problem with the woman I live with (also, by coincidence, the mother of my children). Has it occurred to you, she said, that it may have been an interview with completely different people in a different magazine at a different time?

No it hadn't. But thanks for that.

This sorry little tale is, of course, middle age in microcosm. When my brain was sharp and my shoes were occasionally polished, I would have been sure of my facts, and might even have remembered the next question the interviewer asked. Even if I hadn't been, the indefatigable researcher I like to think I used to be would have made calls, gone to libraries, done anything to verify the story. But now I couldn't be bothered. Was it time for tea yet?

Middle age is comedy, and also tragedy. Other people's

middle age is self-evidently ridiculous, while our own represents the collapse of all our hopes and dreams. Mel Brooks's great quote says it all: 'Tragedy is when I cut my finger. Comedy is when you walk into an open sewer and die.' Our own indignities may be intolerable, but those of our friends and our loved ones keep us sane. What we all fear, more than anything else, is turning into sitcom dads: long, droopy men in inadequate knitwear, sitting in armchairs railing against the iniquities of the modern world. The fear is understandable. Ours was the generation most blighted by the spectre of the sitcom dad, who dominated television comedy between the 1960s and the 1980s, the years when we were most open to suggestion. But where once we identified with Harold Steptoe, now we begin to see the world through the eyes of his malign, almost toothless father Albert. It's a long time since we sympathised with Bart Simpson. His father is our role model now, and that of tens of millions of men across the world. Hundreds of millions, maybe.

If we are talking about 'blight', though, there was an even more iniquitous influence on our impressionable childhoods, and an unusually tall man with glasses was mainly to blame. In the 1970s I was among millions of bored schoolchildren who sat in front of the television on dull, rainy afternoons and watched something called *Looks Familiar*. This daringly cosy panel game traded in nostalgia for the 1940s and 1950s, and its host, Denis Norden, began each show with a wry definition of middle age. (He was in his mid-fifties at the time.) 'Middle age is when, wherever you go on holiday, you pack a sweater,' he said in January 1976. The show's most dedicated viewers, who were actually older than middle-aged, crotchety and increasingly housebound, nodded their heads in approval. A ghost of a smile might even have been seen to cross their bitter, cracked lips. But we children watched in horror and fascination. There was, literally, nothing else on, and we hadn't reached an age when not watching television was a genuine option. I am firm in my belief that my generation's repugnance towards the concept of middle age is a direct consequence of our having watched too many episodes of *Looks Familiar* in our youth.

Anyway, we are all in denial on the subject, according to the British Social Attitudes Survey. Only 3 per cent of Britons in their thirties consider themselves middle-aged. They prefer terms like 'thirtysomething' (58 per cent) or even 'young' (31 per cent). No more than a third of Britons in their forties own up to middle age. There is more acceptance of the term among fiftysomethings, but here's the rub: 27 per cent of people in their seventies are still calling themselves middle-aged. How many centenarians, one wonders? It shows that you're only as young as the adjective you feel.

Curiously, we can be more precise about what makes other people middle-aged. According to research conducted at the University of Kent, Britons believe that you stop being young at thirty-five and start being old at fifty-eight. Middle age therefore lasts for twenty-three years. But this is an average: different age groups have different definitions. Young people, the fifteen to twenty-fours, say that middle age starts at twenty-eight and ends at fifty-four. Octogenarians, by contrast, say it starts at forty-two and ends at sixty-seven.

'Mr Salteena was an elderly man of forty-two,' wrote nine-year-old Daisy Ashford in *The Young Visiters*.

'I have always loved jokes,' said Tim Brooke-Taylor, of *The Goodies* and *I'm Sorry, I Haven't A Clue*. 'I loved them when I was very young and I still love them now that I'm … well, now that I'm … er … still very young.'

(If you watched *The Goodies* as a child, you must be middle-aged by now.)

Frasier Crane, in *Frasier*, had three definitions of middle age. You can no longer eat pizza after sundown. You go 'oof' when you sit down on a sofa. And I'm afraid I can't remember the third, which itself is another signifier.

Perhaps it's safe to say that middle age is in the eye of the beholder. I had schoolfriends who were middle-aged at twelve. (They haven't changed much.) When I was nineteen my girlfriend was also nineteen, and she had previously gone out with a 24-year-old called Alistair. I met him once. Methuselah might have lived to 969 and Noah to 950, but neither of them could have been as old as Alistair. He wore a tie with a short-sleeved shirt and had a briefcase. My friends and I all laughed at him behind his back, but we might as well have been laughing at death itself. We could recognise a grim portent when we saw one. We only had five years left, and then we would be … Alistair.

That said, I have known at least one man in his seventies who had an absolutely whopping midlife crisis – not his first, by any stretch – which suggests that Becker and Fagen were spot on. So – and this is not a blatant attempt to sell my book to as many people as possible – I would suggest that middle age can begin pretty much as soon as you can talk, and last until death. Youth, by comparison, is a mere passing fancy.

This book is about men in middle age. It is about humiliation, loss of dignity, crushing disappointment and aching knees. It is also about liberation, loss of fear, the abnegation of ambition and the pleasures of inactivity. Although it moans incessantly, and loses its temper once or twice, I would like to think that, at heart, it is hopeful and optimistic. For I believe there are consolations in this time of life. We may have lost our hair, our waistline or our way completely, but we have also gained self-knowledge, a certain amount of guile and what some might call 'gravitas' (and others would call weight). As Jane Fonda told an interviewer in January 2011:

'I've learned that people tend to get happier over fifty – less stressed, less anxious, less hostile. They don't know why, but scientists surmise it's because we've been there, done that, and none of it killed us. You don't make mountains out of molehills, you make lemonades out of lemons. Everything becomes more positive.'

Actually, typing in that paragraph has just made me angrier than I have been for a while. But you can see what she means. Sort of.

1

MATURE

'Nobody realises that some people expend tremendous energy merely to be normal.'

Albert Camus

There was, in my teenage years, a boy at school who was very mature. He had a larger head than most of us, and white blond hair, and large black-rimmed glasses, which he knew were a strength rather than a weakness. He went mountaineering in the school holidays, and may well have stared death in the face during one of those expeditions. He certainly stared me and my friends in the face. 'You're really immature,' he would say.

Well, we couldn't let him get away with that. In purely physical terms, he was plain wrong. My friend M, who has Greek Cypriot parentage, was infinitely hairier than him. M was also hairier than most of our teachers, hairier in fact than I am now. Maturity, in this sense, was a matter of genetic good fortune. It wasn't to be gained by scaling Welsh peaks, or adopting a superior air in school corridors. We mocked the mountaineer relentlessly. He became Mr Mature. To our consternation and dismay, he responded to our ridicule with considerable maturity. He rose above it, and us, and everything, his mind far away and several thousand feet above sea level. Is he still scrambling up sheer cliff-faces, breathing the clear high air of maturity? I do hope so. If he has fallen off a mountain in the meantime, I have no doubt that he tut-tutted at the absurdity of it all on the way down.

Thirty years pass, in the wink of an eye, and still we wonder about maturity. Have we acquired it yet? What is maturity anyway? Is it a good thing? And what precisely does it want from us?

The first time I wore a suit to work, it was 1984, and I was twenty-three. I looked in the mirror, marvelled at the polished shoes, admired the absence of stains on the tie, and wondered who this person was. I was young, and looked younger than my years, and I had never shown much aptitude for impersonating grown-ups. But the suit is a costume, and an ingenious one. Mine was grey, cheap and undistinguished, but it magically transformed me into someone who had a job at last. A suit's power is not unlimited. It cannot do much for the job interviewee, who looks so nervous and out of place entering the giant building in clothes he would never normally wear, carrying the briefcase he may have borrowed from Alistair. But once you have the job, the suit settles you down and takes over the general running of things. You are no longer wearing it just to impress a single individual, who has the power to give or deny you a job you don't really want because it's dreadful, boring beyond measure and probably pointless. Once you have the job, you wear the suit because you are someone who has a job that requires you to wear a suit. Without the smallest effort on your part, your suit confers on you an authority you never previously possessed. It gives you validation in your own eyes, in the eyes of your proud parents (who may have been mentally fitting you for this suit since infancy), and in the eyes of all the other people who wear suits. It also saves you having to decide what to wear every morning. It is a short cut to seriousness.

I can't believe how quickly I bought into the suit. Low was my salary, and mundane were my duties, but somehow the suit managed to nullify my youth and inexperience and, indeed, my rampant foolishness. I went to meetings and talked nonsense with the best of them. I learned that an expensive and distinctive tie could offset the cheapness of the suit, announcing you as an imaginative, even creative thinker to people who, as a rule, distrusted these qualities in others but would welcome them, if not expressed too fervently, by someone in a meeting who was wearing a cheap suit. After a while I got really daring, and bought another suit. This one was grey and cheap too, but it was of a lighter cloth, and so could be worn during summer, or when the first one became so stained and disgusting that my colleagues started to avoid me.

As I became accustomed to my new life, I saw that individuality could be expressed through tiny fluctuations in the dress code. My friend D, who worked in the basement, mostly on his first novel, had suit trousers that were slightly too short, allowing him to reveal a bohemian inch of brightly coloured sock. One of our bosses, a raffish old gentleman with an evil laugh, wore a deliberately wide pin-stripe that somehow communicated both his eminent education and his innate wideboyness. Both these men showed that they were wearing the suit: it wasn't wearing them. This was a state of grace I never quite achieved.

Indeed, after two years and four months, it had become apparent to everyone that I had no aptitude for this job whatsoever. My bosses and I discussed the situation, and we arrived at a mutual agreement that I should leave. (They decided and I couldn't disagree.) You might wonder how I had survived so long. So did I, but they explained that, while the job itself had been beyond me, I was quite good at appearing to know what I was talking about, or 'schmoozing the client', as the raffish old gentleman called it. All those years at school of trying to master content while deliberately ignoring style had come to nothing. I had 'schmooze potential' and, accordingly, a bright future.

The suits went in the wardrobe, where they stayed until taken to Oxfam years later. Subsequent jobs required no formal uniform, and for twenty years now I have been a freelance writer, gradually losing the ability to get dressed at all. I never built on my schmooze potential, if it ever existed in the first place. These days I think it may have been the suits. For me, maturity was cloth-deep. I still keep some of the ties as a reminder, or maybe a warning.

We learn early, then, that there's a wealth of difference between real maturity, whatever that is, and the appearance of maturity. For many of us, of course, the ability to fake it is all we'll ever need. Modern capitalist society – suit world, if you like – doesn't seem to require much more. Everyone needs to be able to do their job, but you will get no further if you cannot adapt your responses to the prevailing ethos. You could call this mature behaviour – and at the time I think we did. With hindsight, a more useful word might be 'expedient'. There's something faintly heartbreaking about the idea of us all, young, foolish, bursting with ambition, happily conforming to accepted norms because that's the way to get on. It never occurs to you that there might be a price to pay later on.

Corporate maturity, therefore, lies either in cutting and shaping your personality to what's required, or in pretending to do so and thus having to wear a mask for the rest of your adult life. An old friend of mine, sharp, tricky, an instinctive anarchist and piss-taker, entered suit world after university and rose quickly through the ranks, as though he knew something they didn't. I used to ask him, have you ever made any friends at work? Good God no, he'd say, I keep my home life completely separate. But can't you help it? I'd say. Every so often you're bound to meet a like-minded person. He looked at me as though I was mad.

Some years ago we started to see brief profiles of him in newspapers. He was a tough customer, they said. Disciplined, committed, highly intelligent, but rather dry, even humourless.

Hmm, we thought. Humourless?

For this character is a funny man. Not in a gentle way; in fact, his humour is needlessly provocative. (He and I have fallen out badly in the past when I thought he had gone too far and he couldn't see it at all.) But this new perspective made me realise that he had spent twenty-five years in work wearing a mask, pretending to be a version of himself, albeit a supremely effective one. No wonder that, when any of us saw him in his spare time, he would go slightly bonkers and start winding people up at random. No wonder, also, that although he found the job intellectually stimulating and fantastically lucrative – he is rich beyond imagination – he always talked about chucking it in, becoming a teacher, living a different life. None of his friends believed he would. Every time he talked about giving up, he would be offered a more senior job with an even larger pile of money. How much do you need? In suit world there's no such thing as enough. However much you have, you always need (i.e. want) more.

The danger is that, one day, you try and take off the mask, and find that it's stuck on. In an episode of the reimagined *Doctor Who*, set during World War II, gas masks became permanently attached to people's faces, and everyone turned into a zombiefied automaton. Few children seemed to find this episode particularly terrifying, but all the adults I knew were filling their trousers. At the end of the show, while men of a certain age cowered behind substantial items of furniture, the Doctor solved the mystery and saved everybody's lives. Well, everybody on screen anyway.

You have an old friend. You have known him for years. (It probably is a 'him', but I know a 'her' who qualifies as well.) You are fond of him, you see him from time to time, but when you see him, you spend most of your time waiting, waiting, waiting for a spark of whatever it was you liked about him in the first place. You are sure it's there somewhere. But these days it's cleverly concealed. After a few years of boredom and disappointment, you realise that this isn't a friendship any more, it's an echo of one, because your old friend is an echo of the person he used to be. You see him less and less often, then not at all, and one day you think, why am I sending this dreary turd a Christmas card? Waste of postage.

Then you lie in bed at four in the morning and wonder how many people feel the same way about you.

Doctors call this the Michael Fish Syndrome, after the prominent TV weatherman and raconteur. There, in front of his map of the UK, stands Michael Fish, bald, with glasses and one of those moustaches no one grows any more. He is wearing a drab jacket. His voice is a monotone. He is uncommonly pleased with himself. Try imagining this Fish as a child. It is impossible. Picture a youthful, unpompous Fish, fired with enthusiasm for isobars and scattered showers, determined to make a career in the Met Office, and emulate his heroes, Bert Foord and Jack Scott, by appearing on television in a drab jacket after the *Six O'Clock News*. You can't. The young Fish has been obliterated by the middle-aged Fish, as though it never existed.

Where does pomposity come from? Perhaps there is a genetic element. 'It's not my fault. My father was pompous, and his father before him was pompous, and his father before him was pompous. If my son isn't pompous, I shall want to know why.' Or it could be nurture rather than nature: pompous parents, talking endless self-serving drivel over dinner, hard-wiring their children to drone on and on at parties forty or fifty years later. Either way, there doesn't seem to be much you can do about it. However light and bright and funny you might be as a young person, in middle age you will be drawn inexorably to all that is grey and tedious, and nothing in the world will give you more pleasure than the sound of your own voice.

Not so long ago I was hanging around in a local bookshop, quietly seething because they didn't stock one or other of my books, when I heard a man complaining at the counter. 'You said the book would be in today.' The young female assistant was suitably apologetic, but he was getting angrier and angrier. 'I don't care about the wholesalers: you absolutely assured me it would be in today.' He had grey hair, wore a long overcoat and had a grumbly old voice. Poor old sod, I thought. You knew he really wanted to say 'Do you know who I am?', even though he knew she wouldn't know who he was, because he wasn't anybody. He turned round and I saw his face for the first time. He had been in the year above me at school. He had been quite a gentle soul then. Now, purple with rage, he stormed out of the shop. He didn't see me, let alone recognise me, which was lucky. Is this what it comes to? I thought. Is that it?

Maybe pomposity is a virus. Airborne particles infect us on public transport, or in the queue in the post office when the man in front of us discovers that it's going to cost £1.92 to send that tiny package second class. Or maybe it's just a defence mechanism, an antibody trying to protect our system from the world's indifference and hostility. A gentle, bookish fourteen-year-old becomes an angry old fool in a bookshop, defeated by someone else's very mild inefficiency.

At the heart of pomposity, though, is a loss of humour.

You can only take yourself too seriously if you have forgotten how ridiculous you are. When I get pompous – and I can feel it almost physically, as though I was calcifying from the inside out – there is almost always a sense-of-humour failure at the heart of it. When you are younger you seem to absorb failure and humiliation far more efficiently. But later on you feel you have put in the hours, you have paid your dues, and now you deserve more and better from the world. And the world doesn't give it to you. In fact it pays you no attention at all. All it asks of you is that you sod off and leave it alone. But still the minor humiliations rain down upon you, and as usual you have left your umbrella at home. They said it would be sunny today. I blame that Michael Fish. Can't he ever get it right?

There is a way of turning pomposity to your advantage, and that's called eminence. The only qualification here is unchallengeable worldly success. In the late 1990s, like many writers before and since, I made the grave mistake of trying to write a screenplay. After months working with my co-writer, stomping around his office arguing about whether a particular character really would have said that, we had several meetings with powerful film people who might or might not have seen something potentially lucrative in our feeble scribblings. One such was an Englishman who had made a good career for himself in Hollywood. So good was it, in fact, that he palpably regarded it as a comedown to be back in London stuck in a meeting with people like us. You could not catch his eye. It focused only when there was something worth focusing on.

At the end of the meeting I rolled up to him and said, 'I remember you from school. You were in the year above me.'

He raised his face, and very nearly looked at me. Can you develop a squint in middle age? I don't believe so. Briefly studying my right ear, he muttered 'Hmpflflmpfl', or some such, and then turned round and walked away. Whether or not he remembered me wasn't relevant. The point is that he was too eminent to be seen to remember me. Burnished by power to a glimmering sheen, he had passed beyond the realm of normal conversation. Or maybe he thought I was going to ask him for 10p for a cup of tea.

Eminence, for him, had become a form of self-protection. To acknowledge even the most tangential connection would have been to show weakness, but the determination not to show weakness in itself showed weakness. A minute later he was out of the office and within five minutes I am sure he had forgotten he had ever met me. Every time I see him profiled in a magazine, always adoringly, by a writer who'd love to sell him something, I think, 'You are an arsehole.' But to be mature about this for a moment, it's possible that people pretend to have been at school with him every single day of his life.

(I really was at school with him. So was the angry man in the bookshop. Or were we?)

Eminence gives you a glow. You emit light without being plugged in. There's a newspaper executive I used to know when he was number four or five on the paper, still approachable, good fun, a little bit scary but wholly recognisable as a human being. A dozen years later he is running the show and whenever he walks into a party, a respectful hush falls. He is now eminent. He exudes power. It is natural that people fawn on him. It could be a different man. All signs of youthful innocence and vulnerability are gone, or at least shielded by eminence. If he turned round to one of his minions and said 'Give me an avocado', you can guarantee that he would have one, peeled and sliced, in his hands within thirty seconds. How can that not change you?

No one really wants to be middle-aged. We would all rather be twenty-five, however awful it may have been at the time. But eminence somehow gives a purpose to the middle years. You will almost certainly be humbled one day, by old age and infirmity and younger people who want everything you have, but for now the world is yours. You have worked hard for this; you deserve it. Eminence is the ultimate reward, better even than money. Mother Teresa managed to resist its call, but she is just about the only one. She renounced worldly success, and there can be no eminence without it. Take away worldly success and we're back with the sad, angry man in the bookshop. Pomposity is eminence on a budget.

Is there maturity in any of this? Maybe, maybe not. When women talk about maturity they usually mean emotional maturity, and for many men that's always going to be a tough call. Looking inwards may not come naturally to you. You may prefer to look elsewhere. (The television, for instance.) Not everyone has the gift of introspection. Besides, do you need emotional maturity? Will it get you anywhere? Worldly success and eminence don't appear to demand it; indeed, it might even be a disadvantage. We don't look to Simon Cowell and Piers Morgan for signs of emotional maturity, just as we don't expect cats to swim. As I said, a plausible manner can take you a long way, and a psychopathic will to succeed should help you complete the journey. A thick skin is the only protection you need against the vicissitudes of life. Nothing can dent the carapace of Morgan's self-regard. No argument will ever convince Cowell that he is anything other than right.

It seems terribly unfair that society should reward the untalented but supremely confident over all others. It *is* unfair. What makes it even more galling is that by giving these people everything they want, we only reinforce their sense of self-worth, which seems to increase their certainty that they are doing the right thing. Even worse is the knowledge that if you did happen to capture them, torture them and kill them slowly and very, very painfully, other Morgans and Cowells would scuttle out from behind the wardrobe to take their place in the world. People actually want to be like Piers Morgan and Simon Cowell. They crave fame and fortune that will enable them to bypass maturity completely. It's not perpetual youth Simon Cowell seeks, but perpetual immaturity. The second is easier to buy than the first.*

Emotional maturity is an option, no more. If we so wish, we can learn nothing from life at all. The mountaineer thought that maturity was a given: he was lucky enough to have it, and we weren't. There was hope for us. We could still acquire it if we wanted it badly enough. And we tried, we really tried. At the same time you do want to retain some of your youthful *joie de vivre*, that part of you that feels like the real you. I don't want to be the man in the

* On a segment of *America's Got Talent*, Cowell, goaded by Morgan, pointed out that he had sold 150 million records. 'Well, I can remind you, then, that I have sold 2.8 billion newspapers,' was Morgan's response. Gentlemen, choose your handbags.

bookshop, or the newspaper editor, or the film executive. I certainly don't want to be Piers Morgan or Simon Cowell. But then I never wanted to be the mountaineer. My friends and I are still making the same facile jokes we made thirty years ago, some of which will turn up in this book. True maturity, whatever it is, remains just out of reach. Perhaps you only attain it when you realise you can never attain it. Mountains, I now see, could help you in this process. Maybe the mountaineer hasn't fallen off. Maybe he has jumped.

2
RAGE

'The only way I would return to my old school would be with a sub-machine gun and a fully armoured platoon.'

Robert Morley

The man in the bookshop, storming out, thwarted, powerless, humiliated. We all know what it feels like. On this occasion, though, my primary feeling was one of relief. When we see someone else overwhelmed by rage, we might feel frightened, or amused, or contemptuous, or deeply concerned that the angry person will see us and recognise us, which could make things very sticky. But we rarely feel more rage.*

* I am excepting crowd scenes from this. Once you are part of an angry crowd, you cease to be yourself in some sense, and become instead a

So a man in a bookshop loses his rag. We watch as the rage radiates from his shaking body and reddening face like waves in a ripple tank. And we feel our own underlying fury recede a little, as though the man has somehow tapped into it to replenish his own supply. That's a neat trick, we think. Can we all do that? What the man in the bookshop sees, though, is that he is the only person there who feels so angry, and everyone else's lack of anger makes him even angrier. If he were not a man in his early fifties with poor circulation and a chronic terror of lifelong imprisonment, he would tear someone apart with his bare hands. Maybe that man over there, whose face is vaguely familiar. As it is, he bangs the door on his way out and declares that he will never come back to this stupid fucking shop, at least until the next time he needs to buy a book.

The rest of us stay behind and breathe again. For a few seconds, the angry man siphoned off some of our own excess rage and we feel almost light-headed as a consequence. Sometimes you only realise you are labouring under a burden when someone momentarily takes it away from you. How much rage must we be living with every day? And why do we only notice it when, briefly, it is gone?

Rage, I have come to believe, is the dominant emotion of our times. For my parents, and probably yours too, it was fear. They lived through the war, when many didn't. They survived the Cold War, to their astonishment. And they

---

small unit of collective rage, a foot soldier of fury, if you like. When we see a riot on the television, our first response might be: that looks dangerous and frightening. And our second response might be: that looks as though it might be fun.

lived at a time when, in Britain at least, gradations of class were so tightly defined that everything you said, everything you did, identified you as lower-upper-lower-middle class or whatever. Twitch those net curtains. The port goes this way. No one says settee or serviette, unless they do. My mother, now in her seventies, delights in the recent freeing of social bounds, although, like an Alan Bennett character, she still can't say the word 'lesbian' out loud. She whispers it, while articulating it in an exaggerated manner so you know what she means. There's a part of me that wants to force her to scream the word from the rooftops, to free herself from these shackles of fear. Not that she's a lesbian, of course, although I'm quite tempted to tell her that I am.

Rage has spread. At first it seemed only to affect people in cars. Once it had been given a name, road rage multiplied like a lethal virus accidentally let out of its laboratory. Soon, men were killing other men for cutting them up on motorway slip roads. So apoplectic did drivers become that I'm sure more accidents were caused by middle-aged men having heart attacks and dying at the wheel than by simple bad driving. These accidents, by their very nature, would generate ever longer tailbacks, which would push up driver stress levels yet further. One morning the M25 could become so congested with cars driven by sedentary, slightly overweight middle-aged men with an important meeting in twelve minutes' time, that some sort of critical mass will be reached. Drivers will be dying faster than the emergency services can get to them. Bodies will have to be helicoptered out, company cars abandoned on the hard shoulder and whole swathes of middle management will be wiped out overnight. Come to think of it, maybe this has happened already. Maybe it happens all the time, and no one thinks to mention it.

Wherever you look, there is something to be angry about. Some of us are actually looking quite hard for things to be angry about. At least one newspaper we could name employs hundreds of reporters, or rage correspondents, to scour the world for stories that will make its readers kick a cat and punch holes in the wall. This newspaper is fuelled by rage. As it happens, rage is quite an efficient fuel. The more you use, the more you generate. People who woke up in the morning in a state of cruel vexation buy this newspaper to make themselves even crosser. If we could tap in to all this pent-up anger, we wouldn't need wind farms or nuclear power stations. A hundred or so people in Leatherhead, foaming at the mouth at the story on page six, could probably generate enough electricity to power a town the size of Leatherhead.

This newspaper knows its market, though. It knows its readers will be rendered furious by many of the same things. I am not sure I can make the same assumption of this book's readers. Different strokes enrage different folks. How do you feel about fortnightly rubbish collections, for instance? Famous people saying they would never have plastic surgery when they obviously have had loads? Speed bumps? Cold callers? Jeremy Clarkson's huge smug face? Here's how each one rates on my personal wrath-ometer:

- Fortnightly rubbish collections: doesn't affect me personally, yet. But willing to be furious about the possibility that they might be imposed at some point in the cost-saving future. Anticipated rage scores highly on the wrath-ometer.

- Plastic surgery: pathetic and self-deluding. But does it make me angry? No.

- Speed bumps: can just about see the purpose of them, when I'm trying to be rational.

- Cold callers: reminds me of when I was young and worked for a PR company, and had to call people who really didn't want me to call them. So while I am now as rude and unpleasant to cold callers as everyone else, I can't help pitying anyone who has to do as ghastly a job as that, because no one, surely, does it because they want to.

No, the only one of the five that makes me uncontrollably furious is Jeremy Clarkson's huge smug face. And not just the sight of it, either. The mere thought of it. Hang on a moment while I drink a glass of water and try to calm down.

We might not agree on what we are angry about: indeed, I suspect we could come to blows over it. You will have a fair idea of what will light your own touchpaper, but you can only guess what lights someone else's. It might not be Jeremy Clarkson, or misplaced apostrophes, or hot-air hand driers in public lavatories that give you second-degree burns. It could even be you.

A good way to check this out is to spend some time on the internet. Read something on a website, form an opinion and be bold enough to express it in a little box at the bottom of the page. Then come back later, read the response from others, and see your modest observations flattened by waves of bile and contumely.

There are many theories as to why people express themselves on the internet with a violence they would never contemplate in normal conversation, let alone life. One is that the closing of all the loony bins in the 1980s and the change of emphasis to 'care in the community' pushed mad people on to the streets and, thereafter, into internet cafés. Another is that people who express themselves thus simply do not realise that the people who read what they say might be hurt and upset by it. Because it's 'virtual' and at one remove from reality, they don't recognise that they have any responsibility to the feelings of others. To be in touch with your inner psychopath has never been easier.

Or maybe it's even sadder than that: that they know they hurt, but the power to hurt is the only power they have. I'm not sure any single theory can encompass all the reasons why people are beastly to each other on the interweb, but this great flowering of rage does suggest a disconnection from the rest of humanity. Which may be why the words 'online community' always make me bark with mirthless laughter. It's an oxymoron: you can't have a 'community' of solitary, solipsistic, socially inept compulsive masturbators. You see what has happened? They have made me lose my temper again. There's no escape from it.

At the root of our anger lies this sense of powerlessness. Maybe we have always been powerless as individuals, constantly at the mercy of external forces we cannot predict, let alone control. But then the cheerful forces of late-twentieth-century capitalism gave us the illusion that we did have some power after all. Mainly, they said, we had the power to choose. We could choose schools for our kids. We could take on a small debt to buy a small car or a titanic debt to buy a massive car with eleven seats that would keep us safe from carjackers and run over squirrels and small children without even a bump. We could buy organic cornflakes for double the price of identical cornflakes in a different packet, or we could buy the one with extra sugar and honey and chemicals that make your eyes leap out of your head and explode on the table in front of you. No wonder people burst into tears in supermarket aisles.

Just the other day I was in Sainsbury's (probably because of its perfectly placed apostrophe), staring at a vast display of pickled onions. 'Buy me some pickled onions,' my daughter had said that morning. She loves pickled onions. I don't like pickled onions and know nothing about them, beyond their origins as onions and their current status as pickled. I counted thirty-six different varieties. I bought some cornichons in the end. At least they were green.

The power to choose is no substitute for genuine power. Most of us would rather not choose, given the choice. There used to be a franchise of American ice cream shops called 32 Flavors, which didn't last long. Perhaps thirty-two was too many for most of us. For what do you think was the most popular of the thirty-two 'flavors'? Was it Key Lime Sherbet or Mint Chocolate Chip, or the more than averagely emetic Bubble Gum? No, by far the most popular ice cream they sold, every year, in every shop, was Vanilla. People would come in, look at all those alternatives, feel exhausted by the process, and choose the one they knew they wouldn't hate.

Are there any other powers we are supposed to have? I'm not aware of many. According to the psychologist Oliver James, the British education system is now geared to produce employees and consumers. That's what they want of us. We are to be good little boys and girls and do as we are told. Which is a little like going into 32 Flavors and finding that they only have Vanilla, and the others have sold out. So why do you call yourself 32 Flavors? Because no one would go into a shop called 1 Flavor, you fool. Do you want Vanilla or don't you? No we don't, because once the other choices we didn't want aren't there, we don't want what we'd otherwise want. We are complicated human beings, and we need to be treated with kindness and respect, and occasionally brought a nice cup of tea when we aren't expecting it.

So who has the power, then? We would like to think that the government is in charge, and governments do their best to convince us that they are too, but I think we all know it's no longer the case. Mere politicians are at the mercy of the markets, the media, a handful of monied sociopaths and transnational corporations who couldn't give less of a fuck if they tried. Deal with any large company now and you will end up feeling dirtied by the experience. 'Corporate rogering' is, I believe, the technical term. My telephone company charges me £4.50 per quarter because I want to pay by cheque rather than by direct debit, which would suit them but not me. My bank invites me to move my meagre savings to a new account that pays more interest than the old account, but six months later the new account is paying almost no interest at all, so you call them up and they talk about their new 'products' (i.e. silly names for accounts), so you move the money to yet another new account, which has excellent terms and conditions now but won't have in a fortnight's time. Train companies still call us 'customers' rather than 'passengers': an old complaint, for sure, but they still do it, and why? Because some 24-year-old in marketing who has been on a course and has his own desk thinks we prefer being called customers, when we obviously don't? Or just because turning the whole process into a transaction removes any responsibility to public service on their part, and it's best that we know that from the off? *Caveat emptor*, you poor idiots. Give us your money and bugger off.

'Responsibility' is the crucial word here. Large corporations don't need to bother with it any more. If you have suffered a corporate rogering, and fear you may never sit down again, you might try and complain, only to find that there's no one to complain to. That's why we shout at people in call centres, even though it's not their fault. Indeed, they are victims of this as much as we are. (The precisely phrased patter they are obliged to learn and repeat seems to have been designed specifically to annoy us, the 'customers', and debase them, the underpaid employees.) Companies know they don't have to bother pleasing individuals any more. They make self-congratulatory corporate ads, often claiming the precise opposite of whatever it is they do (hideous polluters show lots of footage of green fields, banks pretend to value their customers, and so on). But very gradually, these corporations are making revolutionaries of us all. When a big company went belly up thirty years ago, it was a national (or even transnational) disaster, and we all mourned. Now, it makes our day. When a merchant bank goes down, we contemplate street parties.

You would like to think that all this could be dealt with by means of a little selfless, dedicated kindness. And maybe it can, although we are all so angry we might not even notice, or so suspicious we might assume the other person was taking the mickey. Living in the city, I take a lot of buses, and most people never even acknowledge the driver as they beep their Oyster cards on the electronic beepy machine (its actual technical name, you know). Everyone needs a little human interaction in their lives, so I make a point of saying thank you to the driver as I get on. Some drivers appreciate it. One or two don't. ('What for?' said one with a snarl, and tore up the Archway Road at 55 mph, which suited me as I was late.) The oddest looks I get, though, are from some of the other passengers, who seem to believe that my courtesy to the driver is, in truth, a critical comment on their own discourtesy, as though being polite has itself become an aggressive act. And who is to say it hasn't? Ambiguities like these are among the stranger pleasures of middle age.

Rage is seasonal. Tasteless strawberries and gigantic killer mosquitoes spark it off in summer; in winter it's the wrong kind of snow. Rage is particular. You get a bill from your credit card company, and there's a little note from the Customer Experience Director. Why is he called that? How much is he being paid? Rage is irrational. For my friend Z it's vegetarians being served first on planes. Rage is endlessly renewable. Only a week passes between Jeremy Clarkson's columns, but in those seven days he has always found something else to be furious about. How long can he go on? Will all that cash he has made eventually erode the anger? Does a columnist like that start to fear the onset of warm contentment, as the rest of us fear arthritis?

Worst of all, rage can make you look ridiculous. The man in the bookshop knew he had made a fool of himself.

It's the inability to carry it through that undermines us. When my son was a baby, I used to carry him about in a sling, an arrangement that incited the admiration of women of all ages and the contempt of the local hard men. One day we were waiting at a bus stop on the main road. The road was clear, but some young arse was cycling towards me on the pavement. He expected me to get out of the way. Cyclists are routinely bullied by car and lorry drivers, but they regard pedestrians as fair game. I thought, no, I'm not moving. So I didn't. He had to swerve to miss me. 'Fucking cunt!' he shouted at me. 'Fuck off yourself, cyclist,' I shouted. But he had only turned round to shout that when he was twenty yards past me. Which was why I felt safe to shout back. Just then the bus turned up. 'Thank you,' I said to the driver, meaning it more than ever. I did try to persuade him to run the cyclist down and mash him to a pulp, but for some reason he didn't fancy it.

3

CRUMBLING

'A bald man is a desperate man; but a bald *vain* man
is a hairless Greek Tragedy.'

Spike Milligan, *Puckoon* (1963)

No one likes going to the dentist. A dentist of my acquaintance reckons even dentists don't like going to the dentist. Dentists know this, and they don't like it. Everyone wants to be loved. Being mildly dreaded isn't the same. According to the *Journal of the Canadian Dental Association*, dentists become unusually susceptible to a chronic mood disorder known as dysthymia, which is characterised by 'loss of appetite, low levels of energy, desperation, excessive anger, social withdrawal, working long hours to compensate for declining performance, troubles in concentration, guilt and suicidal thoughts'.

So that's what it's called. Dysthymia.

But as well as describing about half the people you know, dysthymia may also explain certain behaviour patterns peculiar to dentists. They say, 'Let me know if it hurts.' They drill away, and you try your damnedest not to shake with fear. Then a nerve is touched, and you yelp with pain. My own personal yelp is a modest micro-yelp that could offend no one. Nonetheless, every dentist I have ever opened my mouth to reacts to the yelp not with concern or sympathy, but with irritation, almost as though the pain is my fault. Well brought up as I am, I wonder briefly whether I should apologise. Should I have borne the pain in stoic silence? Did he actually mean 'Please don't let me know if it hurts under any circumstances, because I don't want to know'? Should I mention that I saw *Marathon Man* again recently?

Poor dentists, they can't win. Peering into mouth after mouth, dealing with cavity after cavity, they wage war against the relentless forces of decay and decline. Teeth never get better, they only get worse. We start as children with perfect, unsullied gnashers, and then we eat our first packet of Rowntree's Fruit Pastilles. As life goes on, we acquire fillings and caps and crowns and bridges and God knows what. We endure root canals and extractions with giant pliers. Our gums recede and our teeth discolour, loosen and fall out of their own accord, like the keys of an ancient pub piano. And we clean and floss and go to the dentist more and more often, trying to keep the teeth going for as long as possible, the few that remain. All we can do is to slow down the rate of decline. We cannot stop it altogether. Reversing it is a fantasy, the stuff of science fiction. Dentistry is a matter of managing decline. There's no happy ending. Sooner or later your last tooth falls out and, after a few years of puréed bananas, you die.

You never think about any of this when you are young. I am sure I am not the only person who gave up going to the dentist altogether for a few years in his late teens and early twenties. I was busy; it didn't seem important. (Also, I had seen *Marathon Man* and it had scared the willies out of me.) At seventeen, I had no fillings at all. At twenty-five, after my triumphant dentistry comeback, I had acquired a mouthful of them. Similarly, flossing. Several dentists, failing to keep the sigh out of their voices, said you really have to floss. And I did, the day before the next appointment at the dentist. After a few years of this you develop a dull ache in your gums that won't go away, and then you notice that your teeth look bigger than before. Do teeth grow as you get older, like ears? Or might the gums not be covering them as they once did? From that day on you become a frantic flosser, tugging and scraping away morning and night to forestall further damage. But it's too late. You might as well put up an umbrella in a hurricane. Not for the first time you look back at your youthful self and think, what an idiot.

Dentists have to deal every day with people who didn't listen to them when they were younger and have effectively cocked things up. 'Let me know if it hurts' means 'This is your own stupid fault, and hideous pain is all you deserve.' Teeth, though, are just the early warning system for midlife man. They are decay's front line. Where teeth lead, the rest of the body will follow. Before we realise we are alive, we are getting old. Two-thirds of men will go bald by retirement age. The median age for starting to go grey (i.e. half the population start greying before this age, half after) is thirty-four. Most professional sportsmen are knackered by this age. The former England footballer Peter Reid was recalled to international colours at the age of thirty-four, already greying. The *Sun* thought he was so old it called him 'Timelord Peter Reid'. Think back to when you were thirty-four. You were young, weren't you? Even at the time, you thought you were.

Unless you are unlucky, though, your body lets you down gently. Not many of us acquire nasty diseases and die early. Instead we get unsightly hair in our noses. It's a little like ivy on an old building: it creeps all over the brickwork until you can see nothing else, but it doesn't make the house fall down. Most of the manifestations of decay we shall consider here are inconvenient, some are faintly depressing, and one or two are disgusting, but all are trivial. Baldness, for instance, never killed anyone.*

Baldness

Unfortunately, there is only one proven way to prevent it: castration. Pliny the Elder suggested the following cure: you burned the genitals of an ass, pounded up the ashes with oil in a mortar and spread the gungy mixture over the afflicted area, to wit, the head. Patrick Stewart, Captain

---

* Unless you count the Greek tragedian Aeschylus, whose shiny dome was mistaken by a passing eagle for a rock. The eagle happened to be carrying a tortoise at the time, and dropped it on the 'rock' in order to crack its shell. The only shell it cracked was Aeschylus's.

Jean-Luc Picard in *Star Trek: The Next Generation*, went bald at nineteen and never seemed to mind at all. His predecessor as captain of the USS *Enterprise*, William Shatner, couldn't understand it. Wear a wig, he exhorted. (But it was Stewart rather than Shatner who was voted Sexiest Man on Television.) Roughly a quarter of men have started going bald by the age of thirty. Baldness is of course hereditary, and for many years it was thought that the maternal grandfather was to blame. But while a majority of baldness genes do come through the mother's side, you can get them from your father as well. (My maternal grandfather went bald in his forties; my father was bald at twenty-four; my younger brother was bald by his early thirties; I have a full head of hair.)

Baldness isn't just a human trait. Other primates suffer from it too: certain chimpanzees, stump-tailed macaques and South American uakaris. It's not known whether they have evolved far enough to adopt the combover.

Charles the Bald, younger son of Louis the Pious, was Holy Roman Emperor between 875 and 877. One of Charles's last acts before he died was to award copious lands around Barcelona to the Catalan count Wilfred the Hairy, for his assistance in a local uprising. A less broadminded bald monarch was Czar Paul I of Russia, son of Catherine the Great and Peter III. Anyone who even alluded to his hairlessness could expect to be flogged to death.

Did I mention that I have a full head of hair?

One bald friend of mine told me that one unexpected advantage of going bald was that you stopped worrying about whether or not you were going to go bald. With some younger baldies, you only realise after they have lost their hair that it had always looked somehow temporary, had only ever been there on a short lease. Before they could become too attached to their hair, they attained the state of baldness that was always going to be theirs. Baldness was their destiny, and like Captain Picard they have embraced it. You can also see them more clearly in moonlight.

Going bald in your forties may be more traumatic. Just for a moment there, you thought you had got away with it. After all, there is no moral dimension to hair loss. You don't keep it if you brush it every day and use conditioner once a week. Baldness is sheer dumb luck. But herein lies the deeper problem, because if you go bald, not only must you suffer the misery of going bald, but you must also make it known that you don't really mind. This is the domehead double whammy. To be nonchalant in the face of disaster is what being British is all about, but for many men this is asking too much. They cannot pretend they don't care.

Fortunately, or unfortunately, depending on your point of view, a multi-million-pound industry loiters just out of sight, ready for this very eventuality. The comedy syrup has been adopted by male celebrities as eminent as Paul Daniels, and Sean Connery wore an absolute corker in *Never Say Never Again*. My friend McV, who has had a few interesting jobs in her life, spent a year or so looking after the wigs of a world-famous singer-songwriter of restricted height. He was on a world tour and would wear his three rugs in strict rotation – the Just Had A Haircut, the Don't Need A Haircut Yet, and the Badly Need A Haircut Because It'll Be In My Eyes Soon. Her job was to look after the wigs when they weren't being used – feed them, water them, and so on. At the end of the tour, she decided the music business was not for her.

Did I mention that I have a full head of hair?*

Silver fox

Greying can start early too. I knew someone at university whose great shaggy mop contained telltale flecks of something white that was more than mere dandruff. Obviously we all felt sorry for him, although our publicly expressed sympathy was a mere drop of water in the Lake Windermere of relief that it was someone else and not us. No one wants to be visibly ageing before you have had a chance to be young. I saw him not so long ago. He is white-haired but otherwise unchanged, for like the premature baldies he has long since got over it. Of course he has. What's the big deal?

Personally, I would prefer to go grey rather than go bald, but then I am going grey rather than going bald, so that's convenient. It's an odd process, with a number of discrete stages that, confusingly, can happen in any order. Your hair might go grey while your beard retains its original pigment, or vice versa. You might go grey only at your temples, which would encourage people to use words like 'distinguished'. Or you might go grey in a strange quiff in the middle of the forehead, which would encourage people

* Editor's note: A recent aerial photograph of the author's crown revealed a small patch of denuded scalp about the size of a 10p piece. We shall keep you informed of its progress in subsequent editions.

to use words like 'Dickie Davies'. You could go white everywhere except for your beetling black eyebrows, like Alistair Darling. Or you could go full gun-metal grey with a strange tinge of blue, like Blake Carrington in *Dynasty*. Every imaginable variation seems to be possible.

The real nightmare is grey pubic hair. One of the defining characteristics of youth, it seems to me, is that it never occurs to you for a second that your pubes will go grey. It may be the one pigment you take wholly for granted. If you think of your pubes at all, it's with mild concern that they may grow so long you won't be able to put your pants on. Does a gentleman trim his pubic hair? I have no idea, but I suspect that a true gentleman of the old school probably has someone to trim it for him. As a non-trimmer myself, I have often been struck by my own pubic region's remarkable resemblance to a large and unruly handlebar moustache, of a type once popularised by the comedian Jimmy Edwards. If you put some wax on it, you could even go for the Salvador Dali look. Did Salvador Dali wax his pubic moustache as well as his facial one? And did he dye it once it started going grey?

Of course you may not notice it for a while. We all have busy lives, and few of us can take time out of our packed schedules to have a really close look at our pubic hair. Let's face it, we may not be able to see it even if we wanted to. If we have eaten all the pies, we may need to construct a complex arrangement of mirrors even to have a glance at it. Only when you are lying in the bath, conducting your regular audit of physical decline, and your gut floats conveniently off to one side, do you catch sight of this cherished territory, now crumbling and overgrown through disuse. And there it is: the first Dulux-white pube. It glows in the sunlight. There's something innocent, even pure, about its absolute lack of pigmentation, which makes it all the stranger that it has palpably grown out of something (and someone) neither innocent nor pure. And it's alone. All by itself. A solitary mutation, surrounded by colour and plenty. But it's not afraid. It knows it's the future. The next generation. An evangelist, keen to convert its new friends. Pigmentation? So last year. Soon a shock of white fuzz, just like Santa's, will envelop what remain of your sexual organs. The need to wear clean underpants at all times will never have seemed so pressing.

Weight gain

This one, I suppose, depends on how fit and beautiful you were as a gilded youth. Maybe you spent hours a day in the gym, running on one of those machines, or lifting heavy things on one of those other machines, toning your pectorals in order to look 'good' in a T-shirt and bulking up your calf muscles so that you could crack walnuts behind your knees. People did all that, back in the day. There was probably a good reason for it, although no one I have spoken to can remember what it was.

Still, it all matters naught in the end, because midlife punishes the pious and the impious equally. You could have been exercising all your adult life, to a peak of physical fitness that enables you to come third in the parents' sack race and pick up a telephone directory with your ears. But as soon as you stop, even for a week, you realise that your body is not a temple at all, but one of those self-inflating mattresses you'd take on a camping holiday. I knew a musclebloke who, when he reached forty-five, sat down for about half an hour and KAPOW! a fatty. Not an ordinary fatty, either, but a great wheezing mound, who now rolls from side to side on the rare occasions that he moves at all. Admittedly I hadn't seen him for about five years, so it's possible that the transformation wasn't quite as instantaneous as I would like to think. But his wife says it was pretty fast. (Ex-wife, I should now say.)*

Whereas those of us who have never done any exercise at all, other than to search the house for snacks, seem to gain weight in a more gradual, comfortable manner. Soon we begin to resemble the sofas we spend so much time sitting on. Middle-aged spread is well named. As a youth I was skinny going on weedy. My buttocks were so sharp they could slice bacon. But every few years there was a shift in the tectonic plates of my metabolism and I would gain five or six pounds, apparently overnight. A small pot belly developed. Women pretended to like it. (In my experience the only people who really like your fat tum are your children. They find it comforting.) The pot belly has gradually increased its influence, and while I can still see my penis, I know it's only a matter of time. Sometimes I think I should do something about it. Then I think of all those men on running machines and lifting machines and I break out into

---

* Gyms remain a hotbed of anxiety and insecurity for everyone. In his book *Urban Worrier*, Nick Thorpe talks about men using 'a complex towel screening system' in the changing room. Muscles are for display, but penises must always be carefully concealed.

a cold sweat. But if you're sweating then you must be losing weight, right? Just thinking about it could be enough to do the job.

It would be nice to compare notes, to discuss it over a few drinks with friends of like mind and heft. But obviously we don't. 'Does my bum look big in this?' No, I can't see it. Sure, we will josh and tease and provoke each other to the point of manslaughter. I could probably do with losing a bit of weight, but you, sunshine, are a fat bastard.* But when one of our friends piled on the pounds to such an extent that we feared for his future, none of us said a word. Then he became ill, lost the weight in a hurry and looked worryingly gaunt. We didn't know what to say then either. Only when he got better and resumed eating and drinking far too much did we all say, 'It's good to see you looking healthy again,' where 'healthy' means 'comfortingly overweight'. All this fearful obfuscation was the nearest any of us came to starting a proper conversation on the subject.

In truth, many men are proud of their stomachs. They have been working on them for years. They believe that their weight lends them authority, and believing it makes it true. No longer a skinny young person to be blown over by a high wind. Now a man of substance, under whom pavements tremble, and chairs scream for dear life.

For there are undoubted advantages to being fat. An expanded physical presence equips you for all sorts of new roles in life, because fat men are simply better than thin men for certain things. I always think fat men look better behind

---

* Australians have a good phrase for it. 'You're getting a roof over the toolshed, mate.'

the wheel of a car, for instance. Thin people can drive just
as skilfully, but they don't look as though they and the car
are one. A fat man driving along, holding the steering
wheel with his left hand, with his window fully open and
his right arm resting on the door, possibly holding a dough-
nut: there's a symmetry to that image, a sense that all is as it
should be. The car is an extension of his personality, and not
just because it takes him about ten minutes to get in and out
of it. Put it this way: we all trust a fat cab driver. Even if he
does turn out to be a homicidal maniac, we know that we'll
be able to run away from him. In fact we'll probably be able
to walk away from him.

Fat men also look at home behind enormous desks. They
are good at raising their voices and firing people. Many
prominent industrialists have been fat boys. Would Robert
Maxwell have been half as successful if he had been a puny
man? *Daily Mirror* executives lived in terror of being shouted
at, or sat on. Only when Maxwell had lost all his (and
everyone else's) money and sought to drown himself did his
weight become what you might call a millstone around his
neck. In fact, that's probably what he had to use. (Fat men
have a tendency to float.)

Fat crime bosses rarely fail to prosper. They sit in Italian
restaurants eating pasta while their skinny underlings go
outside and gun each other down. Fat men have ruled
many nations around the world, launched the Luftwaffe,
founded Evans the Outsize Shop, played Superman's father
for an enormous amount of money, and dominated international darts for decades. They make excellent nightclub
doormen, breakfast television hosts and draught excluders.
Only when required to move at all does their weight

become an impediment. But then, if they had moved at all, would they have become so fat in the first place? It's a thought worth considering, ideally over a hearty lunch.

Hair growing in odd places

Unlike Esau, I was never an hairy man. In teenage years this was hard to bear. We all wanted to have to shave, desperately. The feeblest outcrop of bumfluff was whisked off before anyone knew it was there. My friend M, who was more physically mature than the mountaineer, was so hairy at fifteen that he already had to decide each morning where his beard stopped and his chest hair began. Whereas I was the youngest in my year and had not the smallest suggestion of facial hair, unless I stuck it on with glue. (I was tempted, I have to admit.) You really don't want to have suffered through my adolescence. But then I don't want to have suffered through yours.

Countless decades later, I am still not a hairy man. I could probably just about grow a goatee, but fluffy sideburns and the full gay naval beard remain beyond me. My chest hair is sparse, like parkland grass in a heatwave. The big difference is that now I don't care. Most of my hairier contemporaries have gone bald. Even if they haven't, they have great rugs of unruly wool spreading all across their back and shoulders, and must cope with widespread cries of horror whenever they take their shirts off on the beach. The only occasionally visible bits of my bod that are genuinely hirsute are my legs, and there the hair helpfully conceals a pair of catastrophically knobbly knees. (If I wear shorts I look like a scoutmaster.) I look in the full-length mirror now and think, Well, it could be worse. Because it has been worse, much much worse.

But just as you have come to terms with your physical form, you reach your forties and odd things start to happen. One day you are idly raking around in your ear and you feel a single hair growing out of one of the folds or recesses. 'Is that a hair in there?' you say to your partner. 'Looks more like a small tree,' she says. 'I'd pull it out.' Easily said, of course, especially if you are a girl and have been ripping unwanted hairs from your body all your life. Women have a far greater tolerance of pain than we do. This allows them to give birth, and leap into bathwater the temperature of molten lava. Depilation is as nothing to them. Whereas we men are made of softer stuff. Which of us does not live in mortal fear of having to pull a sticking plaster off a hairy bit? It can be no coincidence that women tend to favour fabric plasters, which are pretty much superglued to the skin, over the lighter plastic variety, which we men prefer, and which tend to fall off of their own accord after about twenty minutes.

I toyed with that first ear hair for several weeks before, one night, after a decent slug of brandy, I finally tugged it out. It felt as though I'd pulled the entire ear off. I looked in the mirror and was amazed to see it was still there. I looked at the tugged-out ear hair, which by now had the constituency of cheese wire. I expected to see roots, maybe an inch or so long, but there were none. Still, at least it was gone now. Two weeks later it had grown back.

No one tells you about any of this. No one tells you that a small forest of pubically robust hairs will suddenly sprout from your nostrils. Do you pluck them or trim them? You need to decide quickly, or you'll be plaiting them. No one tells you that your eyebrow hairs will become thicker and longer and start growing out at 90 degrees from your head. That again, you will have to choose whether to trim or to pluck, or to accept that you are soon going to look very odd indeed. Since my eyebrows developed a will of their own, I have pulled out enough of them to stuff a chaise longue. Many now have the consistency of Velcro. Where are they coming from? What do they want with me? All the nutrition we ingest as children makes us grow and strengthens our bones and our internal organs. As young adults we maintain our bodies without apparent effort, for these finely tuned machines are still safely within the limits of their built-in obsolescence. But in middle age our bodies begin to feel as if they are falling apart. Why? Is it because all the vitamins and minerals we consume are now being directed towards our eyebrows and our ear hair? Is there anything about this thought that doesn't chill you to the bone?

Jowls

It's bad enough when you start looking like your grandfather; even worse when you start looking like your grandmother. You can already carry your shopping home in my jowls. The US President I shall increasingly resemble as I get older is Richard Nixon. I am trying to come to terms with this, but it's not easy.

The other inheritance of note from my mother's side of

the family – in place of money, which is what I really need – is a droopy wattle. So you spend your middle years slowly mutating into a turkey, and your dotage going one stage further, and turning into a pelican. Try as I might, I cannot imagine what my extreme old age will be like, but if leaping for raw fish doesn't feature somewhere, I shall be surprised.

Man-boobs

All the women I know who have breast-fed their babies complain that their boobs now dangle to the floor. But the other day I was in a changing room in a cricket pavilion with a lot of middle-aged men and it turns out that all of ours do too. What is that all about? We never breastfed anyone. Perhaps this is our punishment for turning over and going back to sleep during the 4 a.m. feeds.

It's strange, though, that we have only heard this appalling term – man-boob, or worse, 'moob' – over the past five years or so. We know that men of all ages are getting fatter, and one of the obvious consequences of increased girth is a nice bouncy pair of knockers. The men who seem most surprised by this are the ones who spent their youth building them up in the first place. All those years pumping your pectorals, and what do you get? A cleavage. The day cannot be far away when some sort of man-bra is on the market, designed to lift and separate. Maybe middle-aged men will come to be proud that they have shapelier embonpoints than their wives ever had. Just don't ask me to wear a low-cut top. Anything but that.

And don't think there's an alternative. A few years ago there was a drama series on TV about middle-aged men, starring Nigel Havers. We frequently saw him and his friends chatting in the sauna, and every single one of them had man-boobs. If Nigel Havers can't get away with it, no one can.

Child-bearing hips

No, sorry, this really has to stop, right now.

4

WORK

'It is the most shattering experience of a young man's life, when one morning he awakes, and quite reasonably says to himself, "I will never play the Dane." When that moment comes, one's ambition ceases.'

Uncle Monty in *Withnail and I* (1987)

True terror is to wake up one morning and discover that your high school class is running the country.'

Kurt Vonnegut

Waking up is just the half of it. The real challenge is to get out of bed, put on your clothes, grab some breakfast and go off to work.

To be honest, I thought I would have made my fortune

by now. Life would be easy, and money would no longer be too tight to mention. People would ask me, 'How do you fill your days?' Well, I'm up at nine, cracking my knuckles and straight into the marginally overheated pool for thirty lengths. Roll into the office just in time for elevenses. Sign some papers, take a call or two and soon it's time for lunch. After an enormous feed in an expensive restaurant with other plutocrats, it's back to the office for a short nap on the chaise longue, possibly accompanied by my ... but hold on, what business is it of yours? I'm fantastically well off: I don't need to tell you how I live my life. Sod off.

How was I going to accumulate this vast, teetering pile of currency? When I was twenty-five, I actually had a few ideas. I have a few ideas now. They are different ideas, and equally useless. At twenty-five you have ambitions, but it isn't until much later that you realise they were only dreams. In the meantime, you have spent so much time imagining what your life would be like when you were rich, you never got round to making the money.

Instead we go off to work each morning. We get up, too early of course, we eat our nutritious Oatiflakes and, chances are, we go somewhere else to do whatever it is that gives us the money to do whatever it is we would like to do in our time off but haven't got the energy even to start. We have been doing this for a quarter of a century. Surely that's enough for anyone?

Some people enjoy their work. I know a few men for whom work is a lifesaver. If they didn't have an office to go to, they would have to spend more time with their loved ones. Others have managed to find jobs that actually reward them in some way, if not financially, then intellectually or emotionally or even spiritually. If you can find fulfilment in work, you are a lucky person indeed, or you are good at making the world work for you. Let us not pretend that any employer in all history actually has our interests at heart. It's a simple equation. You turn up on time and do what is required of you, and they pay you money. You complain incessantly about everything, and they don't listen. You steal as many boxes of staples as you can carry, and they turn a blind eye. You try and open your seventh-floor window, and they tell you that you can't. You smuggle in an oxy-acetylene torch, cut a large hole in the reinforced glass window and leap to your doom, and they get the window repaired in a hurry before your replacement moves in. And they make sure your replacement knows how lucky he is to be given an office with a window. Other employees have to fall down lift shafts to get away.

In 1922 J.M. Barrie, who wrote *Peter Pan* and was very short indeed, addressed students at St Andrews University, possibly while standing on a box. 'It's not real work,' he said, 'unless you would rather be doing something else.' One can only imagine the murmurs of appreciation this elicited from his audience, many of whom would rather have been doing something else. But someone must have valued this gloomy apophthegm highly enough to write it down and record it for posterity, for eighty years on, it still regularly crops up in books of quotations. What was Barrie trying to say? Was he preparing his audience for the shock of adult life? If so, he was hardly the man to talk. By this stage in his career, Barrie had written several novels, dozens of plays and millions of words of now forgotten journalism. He was universally admired and, by the standards of the day, flush with cash. Yet he carried on scribbling. The speech he gave that day, he had presumably written beforehand, which counts as work. So perhaps he was saying: look at me, up here, talking to you. I enjoy my work. Indeed, I have found the secret of enjoying my work. And the secret is, knowing that other people aren't enjoying theirs.

I bet he got a kick out of that.

When I was a student, I hadn't the slightest idea what I was going to do for a living afterwards. The problem was, I didn't really want to do anything. Work looked like unlimited drudgery. Sure, it was a means to an end. How great was that end, though? Was it worth all the means? For me, three years as an undergraduate amounted to little more than displacement activity, the only way I could come up with of avoiding the inevitable. When it came to job interviews, I fear that prospective interviewers may have spotted this. Despite my big smile and those polished shoes, I was effectively unemployable. I went for 155 jobs, and it took me two and a half years to land one.

That was in the early 1980s. Students today are utterly geared to the workplace. Many have already decided they want to be merchant bankers and have been wearing pinstripe suits in their spare time since the age of thirteen. They are deluded. Their brains have been washed and left out to dry. They have been saddled with debts they will never be able to pay back, and will move back with their parents in a few years, lock themselves in their old rooms and listen to Joy Division and The Cure. They will discover what we suspected long ago, and have since had confirmed to us many times, that work is not the answer. It may keep you occupied, but so does chronic disease. It pays the bills, but is that the sum of human aspiration? Put it on my gravestone: 'He paid the bills.'

Work's promise is jam tomorrow. Today may be dry toast, without even a scraping of butter-style vegetable-oil spread, but if you are a good boy, the Raspberry Seedless or Thick-Cut Marmalade will be made available in modest quantities at some point down the line. Boredom and servitude are the price we must pay for the warm, lip-smacking future we are all working towards. It's a familiar theme. As a child you are told that the stuff you are learning at school may be a bit dull, a bit brown bread, but wait until 'O' level/GCSE. It gets much more interesting then. So you are doing your 'O's and they say, OK, it's still a little dull, but just wait until 'A' levels. Well, yes, 'A' levels aren't that great either, but just wait until university. Well, yes, the degree course leaves something to be desired, but your master's course will be much more fun. In the end, you realise, it's all complete shit until you get to be Regius Professor of Ecclesiastical History, by which time you have wasted your entire life.

Still, that's only one life. As Regius Professor of Ecclesiastical History, you go to church and hear the priest announce in all seriousness that, while this world may be unbearable, the next one will be so magnificent it will make all our struggles worthwhile. Then you go to the mosque and hear the imam say the same thing, with the proviso that your sojourn in the afterlife would be even more glorious if you could see your way to blowing yourself up on public transport next Tuesday during the rush hour. Work may not demand sacrifices like these, but then its rewards are designed to be enjoyed in this life, rather than the next. Greater riches, more power and bigger cars could be yours, with the ultimate recompense at the end of the process, the great carrot of retirement. When we complete our long years of toil, we shall gain entry to a quiet, prosperous, pastel world of golfing holidays and Caribbean cruises, resting our weary limbs in padded deckchairs while sexually ambiguous serving staff mix us margheritas and massage our aching feet. Paradise on earth can be ours, one day, if we work hard enough and can manage to avoid dying of a massive heart attack in the interim.

The Great Carrot of Retirement, though, was far more effective when people knew they would keep their jobs for as long as they wanted them. The end of job security has done for that. Our parents never imagined for a moment that work was the answer, but they knew they wouldn't be deprived of it at a moment's notice for something that wasn't their fault. Who loses their job nowadays because they are no good at it? That's the last reason anyone would use. As a consequence, millions of us live in perpetual, grinding fear of losing a job we never wanted anyway.

But as so often in middle age, there are unexpected consolations. All these frustrations and disappointments we endure have one significant and benign consequence: the purging of ambition. All that scurrying around we did when we were young, and where did it get us? Well, probably quite a long way, but the time for scurrying is past for most of us. We even have a different word for it now. Once we were 'ambitious': an open-sounding word, it seems to me, suggesting broad horizons, a certain fearlessness, a jutting jaw and British pluck. Whereas those of us who still show these symptoms are 'driven', suggesting single-minded obsession, narrow horizons and foam-flecked lips. Youthful ambition was natural and healthy, while being 'driven' in middle age suggests that something went severely wrong with your childhood that only unlimited power and sixteen-hour days can hope to assuage. The satirical website the Daily Mash offers Ten Quick Steps to Easy Happiness, the fifth of which is 'Give Up'. 'Having a goal in life is stressful. And annoying. No one cares if you're "successful" and neither should you.'*

In theory, then, we can ease back on the throttle, engage cruise control and coast through our remaining years of work, dreaming idly about where we'd like to stick the Great Carrot of Retirement. But if youthful ambition has left us, it still impinges upon our lives. The little bastards don't just want each other's jobs, they want ours as well.

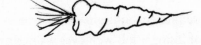

Fig. 1 'The Great Carrot of Retirement'

Some industries are so in thrall to youth that anyone over forty might as well not bother to turn up. Such qualities as we have to offer are less valued than the indiscriminate

---

* The Mash speaks with the authentic voice of the youthful male slacker. The third of its ten quick steps is called 'Meat': 'Take time to appreciate the animal life around you and then eat it in a bun.'

energy and wild arrogance of the young. So who caused the great financial meltdown of 2008, then? People like us staring out of the window waiting for the end of the day, or the young and idiotic? This is what Kevin O'Rourke, Professor of Economics at Trinity College, Dublin, had to say in a well-publicised blog in October 2010:

Most people don't realise that 'the markets' are in reality 22–27-year-old business school graduates, furiously concocting chaotic trading strategies on Excel sheets and reporting to bosses perhaps five years senior to them. In addition, they generally possess the mentality and probably intelligence of junior-cycle secondary school students. Without knowledge of these basic facts, nothing about the markets makes any sense – and with knowledge, everything does.

What the markets ... want right now is for Ireland to give them a feelgood feeling, nothing more. A single sharp, sweeping budget would do that; a four-year budget plan will not. Remember that most of these guys won't actually still be trading in four years. They'll either have retired or will have been promoted to a position where they don't care about Ireland any more.

In lieu of a proper budget, what the country can do – and what will work – is bribe senior ratings agencies owners and officials to give the country a better rating. Even a few millions spent on bumping up Ireland's rating would save millions and possibly save the country.

Bread and circuses for the masses; cocaine and

prostitutes for the markets. This can be looked on as unethical obviously, but since the entire system is unethical, unprincipled and chaotic anyway, why not just exploit that fact to do some good for the nation instead of bankrupting it in an effort to buy new BMWs for unmarried 25-year-olds?

That's a middle-aged person talking, if you hadn't already guessed.

In her 2011 book *The Secret Life of the Grown-Up Brain*, the American science writer Barbara Strauch demolishes several myths about the capabilities of the middle-aged. Her first task is to knock on the head the old saw that our brains lose millions of cells through our life which are never replaced. 'Researchers have now shown that brain cells do not disappear in large numbers with the normal ageing process. Most stick around for the long haul and, given half a chance, can be there – intact and ready – well into our eighties and nineties and perhaps beyond.' We do slow down a bit. When serious chess players take part in a speed game – and are given just a few seconds to make a move – the younger ones always win. We are also slower than we used to be in learning new skills. But the experience we have gained over the years allows us to apply that learning to better effect. We actually get cleverer as we age. 'By middle age, the brain has developed powerful systems that cut through the intricacies of complex problems to find ... concrete answers. It more calmly manages emotions and information. It is more nimble, more flexible, even cheerier.'

Strauch quotes with approval the findings of the Seattle Longitudinal Study, which since 1956 has been tracking the mental skills of the same 6000 or so residents of the grunge capital. In four of the six categories tested – vocabulary, verbal memory, spatial orientation and inductive reasoning – people performed best between the ages of forty and sixty-five, and appreciably outscored their own performances in the tests when they were in their twenties. In her 1999 book *Life in the Middle*, Sherry Willis writes, 'Contrary to stereotypical views of intelligence and the naïve theories of many educated laypersons, young adulthood is not the developmental period of peak cognitive functioning for many of the higher-order cognitive abilities.' The brain cells devoted to 'navigating the human landscape' are 'exceptionally durable'. Thomas Hess, a psychologist at North Carolina State University, puts it like this: 'The fact that middle-aged adults appear to be the most expert is consistent with notions that midlife is a time of optimal functioning ... Basic cognitive abilities are still relatively high, and there's also a fair amount of experience ... [so they] function at high levels in everyday settings.' My favourite result of all is that of David Laibson, of Harvard University, who has established that the middle-aged make sounder financial decisions than anyone else. Indeed, 'his research finds that those who use the best judgement in matters of personal economics are fifty-three years old.'

In the job market, though, none of this means a thing. Young people are cheaper and more biddable than we are, and they work longer hours because they believe it will eventually be worth it.

★

The purging of ambition can be a painful process. Think of it as a form of bereavement. We must mourn our loss of ambition. As is well known, bereavement is made up of five discrete stages: shock and denial, anger, bargaining, depression and acceptance. Stare hard at your friends of a certain age, and I guarantee you will see at least one example of each.

- *Shock and denial*. I am ambitious, of course I am. There is still fire in the belly.* I can keep up with the young ones, of course I can. OK, I've got the odd grey hair.† But I swim thirty lengths every Saturday morning.‡ These young kids don't know they're born. You're only as old as you feel, and I feel great. (*Coughs wheezily*)

- *Anger*. As above, with added swear words, and possibly a new sports car.

- *Bargaining*. I could get into the office before everyone else, and stay later, but I choose not to. With age and experience have come efficiency and efficacy. What I may have lost in energy, I have gained in guile. You're only as old as you feel, and I feel slightly drunk, to tell you the truth.

- *Depression*. Yes, it's a box. Yes, it's very comfortable in here. Now go away and leave me alone.

- *Acceptance*. Did you hear about Dave? Bought himself a sports car. Who does he think he's fooling?

---

* Try Gaviscon, or Setlers Tums.

† The odd strand that the hair dye missed.

‡ And have to go back to bed for the rest of the day.

So what replaces ambition? Contentment? A sort of zen calm, which enables us to sit cross-legged for hours at a time and contemplate the wonders of the universe? I think it might be something even simpler: that the need to strive and achieve is supplanted by a desire to please yourself. Adolf Hitler, I suspect, moved from wanting to conquer the world for pressing ideological reasons, to just really enjoying being in charge and killing millions of people. Great writers and artists think less of their status or their fame as they age, and immerse themselves in the creative process. Top accountants dream less of butchering rival accountants in cold blood, and rediscover the warm glow generated by an afternoon's double-entry book-keeping. Someone I know spends a lot of time on the top deck of double-decker buses, looking down girls' cleavages. It isn't what he had planned for his middle years, but if he could work out some way to get paid for it, he says it would probably be his ideal job.

5

IDLE

'You have been warned against letting the golden hours slip by. Yes, but some of them are golden only because we let them slip by.'

J.M. Barrie

The fiercest desire in middle age is to do nothing at all.

I wonder about this. On the one hand, giving in to idleness feels like the first step on the leafy back-road to retirement, a long slow death of the mind and of the spirit, before the body finally conks out. On the other hand, the prospect of a quick lie-down right now seems rather enticing. Why fight it?

For now that ambition has left us, flying out of the window to latch itself on to some unsuspecting young person, we need something to fill the void. An afternoon nap will fill the next hour or so, but it isn't a long-term solution. Inactivity only works when it is framed by bursts of activity. Otherwise it becomes hard to distinguish from coma.

Why are we so tired anyway? When I was a teenager there was a BBC newsreader called Peter Woods, a huge, mournful bloodhound of a man with massive bags under his eyes that spoke of great trials undertaken and thousands of evenings misspent. His voice and his demeanour could have been expressly designed for delivering news of appalling natural disasters involving calamitous loss of life. I remember thinking, no one can feel as bad as you look. And now I do, most mornings. Later on, after three cups of tea, my brain starts to work, and I feel full of hope and optimism and ideas. This lasts until after lunch, when I want to go to bed. Tiredness overpowers me. It can't be worked through: surrender is the only option. Pillow, bed, snooze. Twenty minutes' sleep and an hour later, I'll feel great. But an hour's sleep and I'll be in a fug for most of the rest of the day. Only too much sleep can make you this tired. So I drink yet more vats of tea and with luck, a few hours later, I may be awake enough to pay the electricity bill. The fact that it is all so out of my control drives me mad. I use up so much energy being angry about being tired, it wipes me out.

If you are sleeping during the day, though, chances are that you are not sleeping enough, or well enough, at night. You won't be alone in this. A great pandemic of sleeplessness now afflicts western society. No one is getting enough. We are all Peter Woods' children, baggy-eyed with exhaustion. And we look back at our youth when, it seemed, we could sleep at will. We could also stay up all night if we wanted to. How did that work? We needed more sleep and we got more sleep, but we could also stay up indefinitely and then sleep it off later. Sleep was plentiful: there was as much of it as everyone needed. No one mentioned that rationing was going to be brought in. Now, even the thought of staying up all night makes us feel sleepy. So we go to bed, and then we can't get to sleep.

A newborn baby sleeps between sixteen and eighteen hours a day. It has a lot of growing to do. A one-year-old is spark out for thirteen or fourteen hours each day, and even teenagers need eight and a half to nine hours. (Their body clocks keep them awake later in the evening and encourage them to sleep later in the morning than most adults. Schools that start an hour later for teenagers report better results and happier pupils.) Most adults need seven or eight hours and make do with less. Who needs sleep, anyway? The idea that sleep was a time-wasting irritant that got in the way of more work was fostered in the 1980s by Margaret Thatcher, who famously only needed four hours a night. But, with respect to some of my more sensitive Conservative-voting friends, Mrs Thatcher was a gibbering lunatic who did well to avoid the padded cell, straitjacket and electro-convulsive therapy her condition surely merited. If she had had eight hours of sleep every night, I suspect that the last thirty years in Britain would have been very different.

It turns out that even a night or two of sleep deprivation can vastly disrupt your need for sleep. Sleep time is not as elastic as we assume. As one sleep-crazed website has put it, 'you can't get used to a lower amount of sleep just because it fits your schedule. If you try to, it will affect your judgement and reaction time, even if you are not consciously aware of it.'* A few decades of that, and you're ready to become Prime Minister.

So if you routinely fall asleep within five minutes of lying down, you probably have severe sleep deprivation or some form of sleep disorder. (Or a bottle of wine in your belly, which amounts to the same thing.) It should take you a while to go to sleep. It's not supposed to be easy! Another sign of sleep deprivation is the so-called microsleep, an episode of sleep so brief you might not realise you have had one. Microsleeps can occur at any time, can last anything from a fraction of a second to thirty seconds, and are best not experienced when you are operating heavy machinery or walking on a tightrope between two skyscrapers.†

So thanks to our habit of burning the candle at both ends, we are all chronically sleep deprived, with no means of making up the shortfall. But shouldn't this get easier as we get older? Is it not true that older people need less sleep than younger people? Most people believe this. Unfortunately it isn't true. If older people sleep less, it's only because their insomnia is worse. The big question among sleep scientists is whether this insomnia is somehow natural, a predictable consequence of ageing, or just circumstantial, an unpleasant by-product of all the niggles and inconveniences of being old. Not that it makes much difference when it's you who can't sleep.

---

* Sleepdex: Resources for Better Sleep.
† Poor decision-making by people working long night shifts was implicated in the nuclear disasters at Three Mile Island and Chernobyl, as well as the *Exxon Valdez* oil spillage. The AA attribute more than 3000 deaths and serious injuries on British roads each year to sleep deprivation: as many as for drink-driving.

As a child I had horrible problems sleeping. I learned that the only way to do it was to take my mind off the fact that I was trying to do it, in fact not to think of anything if I could help it. I was a little frightened of the dark, and having recently watched a lot of *Doctor Who*, I now realise I was right to be. But somehow I developed a sleep technique that worked, and could barely keep awake during my teenage years, when I wasn't eating absurd quantities of toast.

In fact I slept relatively soundly until I was thirty-four, after a brief and damaging love affair with a tall woman with long brown hair. It took me a year to get over her, during which I lost the power of sleep. Night after night I would wake up at four, lie there, feel desolate, toss and turn. The year of awfulness passed, my equilibrium returned, I rediscovered my default mode of slightly irritating good cheer and I met a tall woman with long blonde hair who quickly moved in and started making babies. But I never regained the robust sleep patterns I had previously enjoyed.

Nowadays, in the morning, I ask the tall blonde woman whether she has slept well. She says fine and raises her eyebrow, because she knows that I know that she always sleeps like a log. And that I am just saying that to prompt her to ask me how I slept, because then I can tell her at length, while she sharpens kitchen knives and sighs audibly, imagining what might have been.

Every insomniac has his or her own story, and most of them are as dull as mine. Some can't go to sleep when they get into bed; others wake up in the middle of the night; and one or two, like my friend R, end up manning the Samaritans' phone lines at God knows what time in the morning, because (as he says) you might as well do something. The American Sleep Disorders Association (the alternative ASDA) recognises more than eighty-five sleep disorders, which afflict more than 70 million Americans. One estimate has it that sleep disorders and sleep deprivation add $15.9 billion each year to the US healthcare bill. I love that figure. A round number like $16 billion wouldn't have half the impact, while $15.8 billion would seem trivial, more like small change, by comparison. Do you think their researchers made up the figure on the spot, or stayed up all night working it out?

You can tell that 'sleep science' is becoming big business by the jargon it has started to generate. If you can't get to sleep when you want to, that's Sleep Onset Insomnia. If you can't get up in the morning, that's Delayed Sleep Phase Syndrome. If you wake up in the middle of the night, that's Sleep Maintenance Insomnia. My insomnia history, it turns out, fits a predictable pattern. Sleep Onset Insomnia is commonest among the young, and is usually caused by anxiety or just having a lot on your mind. Delayed Sleep Phase Syndrome 'usually strikes in adolescence'. And Sleep Maintenance Insomnia is common among the elderly (i.e. thirty-four and older).

Insomnia, though, is only one (or maybe three) of our eighty-five sleep disorders. Here are a few more:

- *Snoring.* Don't be silly, I don't snore. Oh yes you do. According to the sleep scientists, snoring is associated with hypertension, cardiovascular disease, diabetes and sleeping on your back like a stuck pig. The only way to cure it is to lose some weight, although being poked in the ribs with a Biro usually sorts it out in the short term.

- *Sleep apnoea.* This is nasty. Associated with serial snorers such as my friend B, whose arrhythmic honks, toots and thunderclaps can be heard two streets away on a clear night, sleep apnoea is what happens when you snore so fiercely that you forget to breathe. Build-up of fat and loss of muscle tone actually cause your windpipe to collapse, so you struggle to breathe for between ten seconds and a minute, which sends your blood pressure and heart rate off the scale, and wakes you up, if you're lucky. You gasp for air, go back to sleep and start snoring again. And this may happen hundreds of times a night. If you're really lucky, your partner will only want to sleep in the next room. There doesn't seem to be any cure. B has tried everything and nothing seems to work, although my own suggestion the other week – try not eating that second pizza – was given predictably short shrift.

- *Narcolepsy.* Like microsleeps, but worse. Even if you are sleeping well at night, you might suddenly fall asleep during the day, for up to thirty minutes, without any apparent reason. You can experience hallucinations, loss of muscle control (oh god please no) or even temporary paralysis when waking. Bad at home, worse at work, unspeakable on public transport. But no matter, because this condition is usually hereditary or caused by neurological damage, and first symptoms usually appear during adolescence. You're probably safe by now. Probably.

- *Restless legs syndrome.* Not serious medically (which means there's bugger all you can do about it). But if you suffer from RLS, you might also experience repetitive movements of the toe, foot, knee or hip during sleep, and there's a daft name for that too: Periodic Limb Movement Disorder. Which at least gives your doctor some initials to write on his pad before giving you the usual prescription for antibiotics.

- *Sleep bruxism.* Or grinding your teeth. No one has a clue why people do this, which I find strangely reassuring.

- *Insomnia caused by fear of sleep disorders.* No scientific name for this yet, but they're working on it.

★

There is more to being idle than being asleep. Doing very little when you are awake is what counts. Having worked so hard for so long, many of us now yearn for high-octane leisure time. And we are not talking about a few snatched minutes in between our many duties and obligations. No, we want hours and hours to fritter away, and absolutely nothing to show for it at the end.

How far we have come, and in how short a time. It is not unknown for stressed middle-aged people to hear themselves uttering the gruesome words: 'There just aren't enough hours in the day.' When we were young there were far too many hours in the day; we had hours and hours, and many more, to fritter away. There were too many days in a week, and an unacceptably excessive number of weeks in a year. My nine-year-old son says, 'Daddy, I've got nothing to do,' and it's a real problem for him. It's too wet to go out, we won't let him watch Sky Sports for more than six hours at a stretch (for which he is threatening to report us to ChildLine) and if I have to play one more game of Monopoly I will go screaming mad. His best friend from down the road is away on holiday. I'm thinking, sort yourself out, boy, it's only a week. He's thinking, a week! That's for ever! I'll never last out!

We have come so far, in such a short time, because life really does speed up as we get older. At the age of eighty, Sir Bruce Forsyth admitted that the previous twenty-five years had passed in a whirr. Whereas, when you are ten, a boring afternoon lasts about three weeks. This is a phenomenon so common, so ineradicably part of our lives, that we hardly give it any thought, but it does make middle age more nerve-wracking than it might be. Just the other day the man who coached the *javeliniste* Tessa Sanderson to Olympic glory died aged seventy-seven. A good age (i.e. very old). The obituary was accompanied by a photo of him in 1984 celebrating her medal at the Los Angeles Olympics, when he was fifty-two, which is no age at all. And 1984, as we all know, was just a few months ago . . . *

---

* What we are experiencing is Decade Erosion, so that every decade we live through feels appreciably shorter than the previous one. If we were mathematically a more advanced race, we would probably talk instead of the differences between the squares. So $2 \times 2 = 4$, $3 \times 3 = 9$, $4 \times 4 = 16$ and so on. The gaps between the squares get larger and larger, but as life accelerates, each gap *feels* about the same. Which is to say that the years between the ages of 4 and 9 feel as long as the years between 9 and 16, and as those between 16 and 25, and 25 and 36, and 36 and 49. I am now between 49 and 64, which means my life is moving about three times as quickly as my son's. If I survive this one it'll be 64 to 81, or the ninth square. It seems only appropriate that if you reach the tenth square you should get a telegram from the Queen.

But as life speeds up, certain aspects of it seem to alter at the molecular level. Boredom, for instance, is easily defined for a child. Daddy, I've got nothing to do. Boredom for adults has a different texture. Daddy, I've got far too much to do, and I don't want to do any of it. In fact, I'm not sure I want to do anything at all. Most evenings now, unless I am out on the town being fellated by Bosnian prostitutes in a King's Cross crack den, I tend to end up sitting in an armchair, reading a book and sipping red wine. Eventually everyone else has gone to bed, I am too tired to read, and the glass of wine is either half empty or half full (delete as preferred). So I sit and stare at my bookshelves. For fifteen or twenty minutes I am almost completely inert, thinking random thoughts if I am thinking anything at all, looking at things I am not seeing and occasionally sipping the wine. They are very nearly the best minutes of the day. I'm sure they help me sleep better afterwards. If you had told me ten years ago that a boozy, bleary reverie at the end of the evening would give me more pleasure than most of the rest of my life, I would have been horrified. But then you will never hear anyone of my age say they are bored when they have nothing to do.

This need for peace and quiet is another feature of male midlife so common that we barely register it. But for most of us it represents a significant shift in the way we wish to live our lives. We may still crave the risks and exhilarations of youth, and think wistfully of our more exhausting old adventures, but the armchair, the book and the glass of wine now have the edge.

It's for this reason that God invented pubs. I have, at the end of my road, what can only be described as an old man's pub. I used to be one of the young people in there hanging out with my friends, and delighted by all the sorry, grumpy old blokes sitting by themselves reading the evening paper. Within ten years, at most, I shall be one of those sorry, grumpy old blokes, who are not grumpy at all and are certainly not sorry. They sit in the pub because it is where they can find peace and quiet. The hurly-burly around them does not disturb them. The jukebox that is far too loud, and the overhead TVs showing lower league football matches on Sky Sports 4, might as well not be there. Armed only with a pint of gassy beer, the *Evening Standard* and the knowledge that their families, if they still have them, are somewhere else, these men inhabit their own meditative bubbles and are at peace. If you are very honoured (i.e. essentially one of them), they may nod at you when you walk by. Once in a while, if they have something to say, they may engage you in a brief, desultory conversation. You should never start speaking to them, though. They have come to the pub to escape from people who want to speak to them. Over the course of their long lives, they have learned that there is altogether too much talking in the world, and far too little sitting quietly and staring into space. They may differ from Tibetan Buddhist monks in a few minor details of lifestyle, but their conclusions are much the same.

Sheds fulfil a similar purpose. As Colin Moulding sang in XTC's 'Fruit Nut', 'A man must have a shed to keep him sane.' I believe these may be some of the wisest words ever written. If I had a garden, I would have a shed. In fact the main reason for getting a garden would be to get a shed. Ostensibly, these modest, leaky and grossly unhygienic edifices exist to help you store the many and various implements you need to help you look after your garden. 'We need somewhere to put the hoes, wheelbarrows and gro-bags,' you say to your family, whereas what you really mean is, 'I need somewhere to hide from you.' Build a largeish shed and you can throw all that gardening rubbish in the corner. Then there's room for a desk, a chair, certainly a kettle and maybe a mini-bar. Most important of all, the shed must have a window. You need something to stare out of for hours at a time, contemplating infinity. You also need an early warning system when someone comes to bother you, thus giving you time to hide your newspaper/beer/secret stash of biscuits and pretend to be working. Because that is the only justification for you asking not to be disturbed there. You are working. Give us a shout when lunch is ready. Need some peace and quiet to be able to concentrate. Not playing internet poker at all. Absolutely not.

Women are right to be suspicious. We are never going to be 100 per cent honest about our need for quality shed-time. There will always be something vaguely underhand and secretive about our behaviour, even if our shed-time activities are entirely innocent. (And let's face it, they never are.) This is a reflection of the Guilt Gap between men and women. Like Virginia Woolf, most women need a room of one's own, but even when they have it, they cannot quite escape the guilt that they really should be doing something else. (Dishes to wash? Lawns to mow? Walls to grout?) Whereas men, I believe, feel no such guilt. We know that the women would like us to feel guilty, but we just can't. So to make everyone's life a bit easier, we pretend that we are doing something sensible and productive in that shed, to conceal our lack of guilt that we aren't.

(Some men do profess to feel such guilt, even to each other, but in my experience they are not to be trusted. They are the kind of Stepford Husbands who say things like 'We do everything together', and pretend not to understand other men's visceral shed-needs. They always turn out to be boffing their wife's best friend, or their best friend's wife, or both.)

Note that a shed doesn't have to be an actual shed. It can be a virtual shed: a room, an office, a corner of a room. Or it can be an internal shed, something you can carry anywhere with you. Take that man at the canal, fishing. He doesn't move at all. Is he making any attempt to catch fish? Clearly not. He just stares and stares, and occasionally breathes. Sips tea from his thermos. Eats a sandwich, as slowly as a man can eat, chewing a hundred times without the tiniest awareness of what he is eating. He is a man who has found peace, who looks as though he is thinking about something, but isn't at all. His internal shed is not only invisible, but sturdier than any real-life, physical shed. Nothing can disturb his meditative state, other than a fish taking the bait, and let's face it, that's not going to happen.

At the kindergarten my children used to go to, there was a fervent belief that kids should not have to sit at desks and learn to read and write at the age of four: it was all too early. Instead the teachers encouraged what they called 'directed play'. In forty years' time, I hope my children come to discover the distinctive joys of directed idleness. We in midlife are idle not with any great purpose in mind. We are weary of great purposes and no longer trust the motives behind them.

Instead, like small children at kindergartens, we rediscover small purposes. Staring into space. Catching a fish, which we then throw straight back again. Gardening. Dismantling things to see how they work and not being able to put them together again. Cooking new dishes not very well. Going for a walk, which just happens to end up in a pub. This is not flabby, undirected idleness, like watching the TV. It's doing something, just.

Somewhere in all this, I believe, is the secret to happiness – or at least, one of them. Psychologists use the word 'flow' to describe what happens when you are so absorbed in what you are doing that you 'lose yourself'. In a state of flow, time seems to pass in an instant. What we are doing doesn't really matter – it's different for everyone – but the degree of absorption does. Children are naturally good at flow. If they lose themselves in a game, the day can whizz past in a trice. Which is why, when children are bored, it's so painful to them. Relatively short car journeys feel as though they last for ever. Whereas we as adults have become inured to our busy, frantic form of boredom, and our opportunities to achieve flow are therefore few. In the 1970s an economist called Tibor Scitovsky wrote a book called *The Joyless Economy*, in which he attempted to explain why so many people were miserable, even when they had enough money. Boredom was his answer. People tended to choose comfort before stimulation. They worked too hard and forgot to find enjoyable things to do away from work. In the forty years since, things haven't changed much, except to get worse.

Flow is the secret. We know that red wine produces a passable substitute, but it's not the real thing. Directed idleness must be our goal. The word 'ecstasy', after all, is derived from a Greek word meaning to stand outside yourself. As Woody Allen used to write at the end of the author biography in his books, 'His only regret is that he is not someone else.' I'm not sure I want to be someone else, but somewhere else wouldn't be a bad start. A shed of one's own: it's not too much to ask, surely?

6

HERMIT

'I live in that solitude which is painful in youth, but delicious in the years of maturity.'

Albert Einstein

The need for peace and quiet, the desire for your own company, the compulsion to build a shed at the bottom of the garden ... what can seem more harmless and reasonable? But there is risk involved too.

I speak not of physical risk. You will have noticed that no mention has yet been made of the words 'Harley' or 'Davidson' in this book. When I first told people that I was thinking of writing a book about male midlife, roughly 63 per cent said, 'What, buying a Harley-Davidson and all that?' (The other 37 per cent thought of saying it, and then stopped when they saw the expression on my face.) Cliché demands that, when embroiled in his midlife crisis, a man will think seriously of buying a motorbike and running off with a much younger woman, possibly on the same day. Abhorrence of cliché, fortunately, stops most of us doing this, even if we wanted to. But I will say this of the middle-aged men I know who have bought motorbikes: all those who had never had a motorbike before drive theirs quite slowly. Buying it and owning it seem to be enough. Driving fast is for the young and expert. Physical risk is therefore minimal.*

In our youth, we were under far greater risk of getting hurt than we realised. Nowadays we are safer than we realise. We don't get into fights. We don't go to places where fights happen unless we want to, and we don't want to. We are less likely to be mugged than the young or the old. We drive more slowly because driving is now a chore. We don't go bungee jumping. We watch people bungee jumping on the television and pretend to our loved ones that we would like to do that too. We might still play sport (of which more later) but it is well known that no sporting injury incurred by a middle-aged man is in any way serious, and that the correct response to the latest Achilles injury or torn hamstring is laughter and mockery. Middle-aged sporting injuries heal much more quickly if publicly ridiculed: it's a matter of record.

So if not physical risk, what? Peace and quiet and sheds answer a deep, almost primitive need, have the power to

---

* That said, my friend Z has been riding bikes for thirty years, and knows of a few first-time midlife bikers who wrapped themselves around trees with fatal consequences. Z is contemptuous of the Harley-Davidson, which he says is 'someone who works in an advertising agency's idea of a motorbike'.

induce 'flow' and can make us happier than almost anything else in the world. But retreating into yourself has other consequences. The rest of the world may start to feel left behind. Your family know you are fishing or in the shed and therefore not to be disturbed. Your friends ring up. 'He's in the shed,' say your family. 'He's not to be disturbed.' Gradually the world grows used to your solitude, expects no more from you. 'He's been in the shed since May,' say your family. 'Occasionally we go out there and deliver sandwiches, and three weeks ago he had a satellite dish installed on the roof, but otherwise we have no evidence that he is alive at all.' At school your children tell their friends that you have gone to live in Ethiopia, while your wife becomes a wow on the local dating circuit. One day workmen appear to board up the door of your shed, so you couldn't leave even if you wanted to. Without your youngest child occasionally passing you packets of crisps through the window when no one is looking, you would starve to death.

Hermit-like behaviour has a long and distinguished history in many otherwise dissimilar cultures. The life of the Christian hermit was rooted in the desert theology of the Old Testament: indeed, the word 'hermit' is derived from the Greek for 'of the desert'. The idea was that, overwhelmed by the love of God, you would take yourself and your loincloth into the desert and there dedicate yourself to prayer, before dying a hideous and prolonged death. If your luck was in, you might find a cave or hovel, in which you would sit or lie down – whatever was more comfortable for your many hours of worship and deep thought. Occasionally people would seek you out for spiritual advice, or to steal your few remaining belongings. Some hermits acquired disciples, who sat at their feet waiting for wise words to emerge, and occasionally brought them meals and clean trousers. Not that you affected to care for such fripperies. In the ascetic life, the hermit disavowed comfort, socially acceptable standards of cleanliness, decent togs and of course sex. The fact that no one wanted to have sex with you anyway was neither here nor there. But it probably made disavowing it a little easier.

The midlife hermit is slightly different, although no one wants to have sex with him either. As we drift into a hermit's life, we do so without any purpose in mind, without meaning to at all, in fact. It just seems to happen. Gradually we withdraw from the world, and the world, miffed, withdraws from us. We are left alone to contemplate our solitude. It's quiet out there. Too damned quiet.

I have noticed this tendency in myself a little, and in some of my friends a lot. Work and family life become all-engrossing. There is less time for running a stable of friends. Such leisure pursuits as you follow tend to be solitary. And as a couple you tend to hang out with your partner's friends. It's easier. It requires less effort. Maybe your partner doesn't much like your old friends, or at least, doesn't like them enough to encourage you to see them independently. Or maybe you and your friends are getting older and grumpier and you just don't get on as well as you used to. I have one friend who, out of sheer bad temper, managed to fall out with almost everyone he had been close to until there was no one left. He retreated further and further into the bosom of family life (and a very fine bosom it was, as it happens). Then the relationship went wrong. Out he went into the world again, searching for company. He tried to make some new friends, but his friend-making equipment had rusted and seized up. Colleagues at work didn't want to start going out for a drink with him after all this time. (I imagine he was just as curmudgeonly at work as at home, which won't have helped.) After a difficult few months, he had to go back to the friends he had neglected for so long and be nice to them. You could see his pain. It didn't come naturally to him. They still irritated the hell out of him, but there was no one else.

We could be ungenerous here and say it's his own stupid fault. But a lot of men seem to go through something like this – certainly enough for us to identify a behavioural pattern. Our friends the sleep scientists would call it something like Self-Isolation Disorder, or Old Git Complacency Syndrome. As we age, we tend to subtract things from our life, without adding anything to take their place. You need energy to add things, energy and desire. You also need to be aware that the process is taking place, that richness and colour are slowly being leached out of life. Most of us haven't a clue. We only notice when it has already happened and it is too late.

Admittedly, some of the things we give up are worth giving up. If you haven't given up smoking yet, maybe now is the moment. On the other hand, you may reason that such damage as was going to be done has been done, that you can't reverse it and if you are going to die, you are going to die. So why stop? If you only have a short time to live, you might as well enhance it with a substantial number of cigarettes.

Among my friends the few remaining snoutists appear far more relaxed about their filthy habit than previously. They no longer feel got at and victimised by polite society. They don't even mind that they are compelled to go outside every twenty minutes or so, whatever the weather. They recognise that there is something noble, even courageous, in their determination to keep smoking, despite the knowledge of certain death. The occasional smokers, the amateurs, gave up years ago. Then the wusses went, the smokers who for some reason wanted to live long lives without even a small cough to show for it. Only the hard core are left. I sometimes see K driving around, flicking his ash out of the window, a picture of midlife contentment. 'Anyway, going outside to smoke gives me some fresh air,' says Z, coughing up a small particle of lung into his handkerchief. 'It's more than I'd get otherwise.'

The problem is that for most of us, our ideas of what constitute 'fun' were defined in our youth, and they have adapted about as well to middle age as we have. For E, it was computer gaming. He loved it, he was good at it, he ended up working in the games business and flourished. Until he was about thirty-eight and found that playing games for hours and hours made him feel a bit strange. He got headaches, and his heart would race. In the morning, after increasingly fractured sleep, he would have what amounted to a hangover, despite physically ingesting nothing that could have caused one. Like any highly tuned match-fit international sportsman, he had discovered that after a certain age, his body could not keep up with what he required of it. He had to cut down, and now thinks he will have to give up altogether. He isn't sure what he will do instead. He thinks taking up smoking might be fun.

Subtracting certain things from our lives is unavoidable,

and may even be desirable. But there's the bathwater, and there's the baby. Some of my hermit friends have returned from their self-imposed exile, at least one after a very nasty breakdown. But others have not. Sometimes I can feel myself going the same way, battening down the social hatches. Do I want to go out on Friday night? I'm not sure I can be bothered. Cocoa? Mm, yes please. Hot water bottle? Now you're talking. Staple me to the sofa for the next thirty years? Oh go on, why not.

7

LEISURE

'I absolutely hate mowing the lawn. When I hear the mowers starting I want to kill myself, it's the sound of death approaching.'

Peter Capaldi, interviewed in the *Observer*,
April 2011

We are not going to play computer games. We are unlikely now to represent our country in our chosen sport. We will watch the television, even though there is nothing on. So what else? How shall we fill our free time? Many middle-aged men end up doing things their younger selves would have laughed at. Here are roughly twenty-six of them.

A is for Ambulation, Purposeful

A brisk walk is good for blood flow, keeps the musculature in trim and makes people think you are actually going somewhere. And you are. You are going to the shop at the end of the road to buy a newspaper, and maybe a bag of Revels. You will walk back home equally briskly, even though there is no hurry at all. Only middle-aged men do this. No one knows why.

B is for Balsa Wood

In the film *The King's Speech*, there is a scene in which speech therapist Geoffrey Rush invites Colin Firth, as George VI, to glue a couple of bits on to an unfinished model aircraft his son has left lying around. Firthy's eyes light up. So do the eyes of all the middle-aged men in the audience. Within seconds they are sobbing for their own lost childhoods, when they used to make things out of balsa wood, and poorly painted Airfix models dangled from their bedroom ceiling, ready to drop on someone's head at any moment. In fact there is hardly any better illustration of 'flow' than model-making, or putting ships in bottles, or whatever mad, pointless activity it was that you did as a child. Hours would vanish as you carefully attached some strut or stanchion to the wrong bit of the wing. The incorrect application of a decal could ruin everything, and even if you were good at it you would be smelling of glue for weeks. (If children smell of glue these days, the social services are called.)

You grew out of model-making, as everyone does. Maybe it's now time to grow back into it. Women may mock, but the beauty of an activity like this is that you won't be able to hear what they are saying. You will be wholly absorbed. There's no point to it, but then that's one of the blissful discoveries of middle age: pointlessness is its own reward. A man must have a shed to keep him sane.

C is for Cooking

Of course anyone of any age can cook and most of us have to. But when certain men of a certain age deal with food, they have a way of letting you know about it. My friend P takes his cheese very seriously. He stares at it from all angles. He decides where he is going to cut it. He tests the knife. He pulls back for a second, to make sure that there is no more elegant slicing solution. In he goes. The incision is made. A surgeon could be no more delicate than this; a watchmaker could be no more precise. The operation is complete. P picks up his slice, stares at it. Is he satisfied with his work? Dissatisfied? It is impossible to tell. He shoves the slice in his mouth and chews thoughtfully. You could hit him on the head with a frying pan and he wouldn't notice. He is communing with his snack. The whole process has taken several minutes of intense concentration and, more annoyingly still, he hasn't offered me any.

P is half-French, which half-explains this. But R has a similar way with a salad. He doesn't just break up a lettuce. He tears it with forensic care along some sort of lettucy ley line that only he can see. He mixes the dressing as though it might explode. It's all a form of peacockery, harmless enough I suppose, unless you are starving hungry and waiting for lunch. The other day I was watching the tall blonde woman grilling sausages for the kids. She did it without really being aware what she was doing at all, while performing several other tasks and also talking to me. You don't talk to R when he is making a salad. Light some candles and put some worshipful music on the CD player, maybe, but the chef must not be disturbed.

Nor is the ability to cook a prerequisite. Watch Barbecue Man, master of all he surveys, wearing a satirical apron and carefully turning over small charred lumps of dark matter that were once burgers. Every man loves a barbecue, as long as he is the one doing the cooking. Everybody else takes care to eat before they arrive.

D is for DIY

Do it yourself if you have to, but don't fool yourself for a moment that you will save money that you would otherwise have spent on real builders. Are there fewer builders and handymen in business than there were before the great unending DIY boom began? I don't believe so. Correcting the bodges of amateurs pays for their holidays, second homes and children's school fees. It's all very well for the non-professional to own one of those beautiful, comprehensive toolkits, with its many plastic compartments full of gleaming new screws and nails, but that doesn't mean you should ever feel obliged to use it.

I am probably not the best qualified person to pass judgement on this, however, having been the subject of a legal injunction that prohibits me from passing within ten metres of an electric drill.

E is for Eating

For every middle-aged man who is cooking, several more are eating. To be fair, not everybody waits until the age of forty to develop a taste for good food, but I have noticed that the subject looms larger in our thoughts and conversations than it used to, in some cases to the exclusion of all else. OK, it's very nice to see you again after all these years, you're looking great, but when are we going to eat? Or, with people you see all the time: shall we go to a film, or shall we just go to a restaurant? (*Licks lips.*) A few midlifers I know have developed a passionate enthusiasm for *haute cuisine*, and wish to sample only the best and most expensive food, especially when someone else is paying. Others just want to eat as much as they can, as often as they can, until they explode. (Mr Creosote, *c'est moi.*) We watch our children expending huge amounts of energy, and needing to refuel regularly. They also have growing to do, and must feed that fire too. Whereas we are just hungry. Our stomachs rumble audibly, which is pretty impressive given how well insulated they are. We tell our children, you mustn't eat between meals because it'll ruin your appetite. Nothing could ruin our appetite. That bag of Revels you bought earlier barely touched the sides.

The worry is that this is somehow pre-ordained. You look in the eyes of the very old, and even if they are thin, ill, angry and gaga, you know that they are only really thinking of their next meal. The living world has receded from their gaze, and all that remain are lunch and dinner. Apparently it's shepherd's pie today. Mm, yum.

F is for Fundamentalism, Religious

Something of a minority interest, this, but when the middle-aged discover God, or god, or gods, they can do so with a fervour that singes people's eyebrows. Like any good hobby, though, religious mania keeps you busy. Praying eats up the hours by itself, and when you add in all the time you might spend knocking on doors spreading the word, or ironing your vestments, or having passionate arguments with people who disagree with you only slightly, your diary is suddenly fuller than it has ever been. God as social secretary: yet another facet of His boundless munificence.

G is for Gardening

Obviously the garden needs to be done, because it's there and it's your job. We could venture beneath the surface here and ask why precisely the garden has to be 'done', as opposed to sat in and enjoyed in all its unmanaged, uncontrolled lushness, as Japanese knotweed encroaches on your house at the rate of an inch an hour and foxes lurk in the undergrowth, chewing on the carcasses of much-loved family pets. But that won't get the lawn mown. And obviously it's good for you to 'do something with your hands'. (Make sure you wash them afterwards.)

For all the best reasons, though, gardening can be a great inducer of flow. Time races past as you successfully pull out a weed whose roots span an entire postal district. The simple pleasure of going to the garden centre, buying lots of plants, planting them in the wrong place and watching them slowly die is apparently hard to beat. I'm not sure I understand it myself, but each to his own.

H is for Hiding from Religious Maniacs Ringing Your Doorbell

They stay there longer if they know you are in.

I is for Installation of New or Updated Software

Can obliterate an entire weekend.

J is for Jalopy

Few people drive their cars for pleasure any more. Midlife man has to do something with his car, though, and if he is a friend's ex-husband, he cleans it. Many are the vast sponges and industrial implements with which he makes the bonnet gleam and the roof sparkle. Three bin bags full of rubbish are removed from the interior, the carpets are hoovered and the steering wheel is polished. (I imagine he slices his cheese very carefully too.) It is a curious fact that men who fail to notice the squalor inside their homes can be so fussy about the inside of their cars. But then I also know women who won't tolerate a speck of dust at home but whose cars are like wheelie bins with an engine. It's only appropriate that one is usually married to the other.

K is for Keys in the Saucer

Does anyone 'swing' any more? Anecdotal evidence for this has been disappointing, I will admit, but gossip and innuendo can usually fill the gaps. No one I spoke to does it, and no one knows anyone who does it, but everyone knows someone who they think does it. The urbanites suspect the suburbanites. The suburbanites think their rural friends are up to all sorts. The village-dwellers think it's all going on in the big city, and so on. But we have all been to that party, far from home, when we have to leave early to get back, and it's clear that the locals are glancing at each other in a way that can only mean, don't worry, they'll be gone soon. And the uglier and more boring they are, the more certain you are that as soon as you are out of the door, the keys will be thrown into the saucer in the middle of the coffee table, and dull Dave will leave with fat Tom's blowsy wife Jane, and poor, sad Alison will be lumbered with right-wing Jeremy yet again. And whether this is happening or (more likely) not, you thank all that's holy that you are yourself, living your life and not theirs: a small consolation, but one to hold on to and cherish during the long dark nights to come.

L is for Looking in Estate Agents' Windows

I spoke to a couple of midlifers whose fathers used to do this. These days only young people look in estate agents' windows, gawping at the interiors of tiny flats on main roads next to the asbestos factory that they will never be able to afford. We, who have moved too many times already in our lives and wish only pain and death to estate agents, accelerate as we walk by. But our fathers would pause in front of estate agents' windows and stare at photographs of show houses with real concentration. And sigh. And imagine the lives they ought to have led, in houses that looked like that one, with wives and children that weren't us. Lives untainted by disappointment and boredom and drudgery. As though such lives were ever lived by anyone. The fools.

M is for Mending Things

Make sure they are already broken before you start.

N is for the National Trust

The only people under forty to be seen in a National Trust property are the children of the middle-aged people who have dragged them there. I vividly recall the intense boredom of these excursions, which were always advertised as 'educational', a word against which there was no argument. And then, at some point in your late thirties or early forties, the midlife switch clicks in your brain and you can see nothing wrong with wandering listlessly around an enormous house its owner can no longer afford to keep, looking at unused armchairs and plates. My friend T favours ruined castles, which he imagines defending against invading hordes by pouring boiling oil over their heads. B likes wandering around enormous gardens, imposing par-four golf holes over them in his mind and wondering where to put the bunkers. My libidinous friend X goes for smaller gardens with lots of hiding places in which he can imagine having sex with someone who isn't his wife. And for everyone there's the promise of the tea shop at the end of the walk, where you can sit down (at last!), eat dry overpriced cakes and sneer at the boring middle-aged people at the other tables. Just don't try and read their lips.

O is for Oenophilia

Impoverished midlifers like me drink wine; rich midlifers lay it down. First you need an enormous cellar. Next you need an equally cavernous space in your mind in which to store the vast amount of information you will need to do this thing properly. Serious oenophiles know which year, which country, which region, which vineyard, which side of which hill, which feet treading which grapes. It's just another game, of course. Buy a dozen cases of Chateau Merchant-Banquère to put down for a dozen years, think about drinking it, then sell it at the height of the market for ten times more. My friend V has a vast cellar, and occasionally opens a bottle of wine so delicious it's all I can do not to burst into tears. But he says he only really enjoys the first glass. And he only *really* enjoys the first sip. How jaded is that? He does love wine, but I suspect buying it and owning it press his buttons more than drinking the stuff. Maybe if I had the option of buying that much and keeping it downstairs in the cool, quietly amassing value, I would feel the same way. Ha! As if.

P is for Pilates

A surprising one, this, because I thought more women than men went to pilates classes, just as more women than men wear make-up, read novels, drink Diet Coke and watch *EastEnders*. But a sizeable minority of (it has to be said) sizeable men have also discovered this highly effective physical fitness programme, devised by Joseph Pilates early in the twentieth century. We have bad backs, do we not? And often the backs are bad because of the weight they are carrying at the front. But instead of eating less, we find ourselves a pilates teacher, who is likely to be female, younger than us and physically at the peak of condition. The timetable is then as follows:

1   Fancy pilates teacher, so go back every week.
2   Fall in love with pilates teacher.
3   Make shambling, desperate pass at pilates teacher.
4   Give up pilates.

The equivalent for midlife women is the hunky guy who works at the gym. The only difference is that the hunky guy is an amoral shagferret, so they usually end up having an affair, which the husband never, ever finds out about.

Q is for Quizzes

When my children were tiny, the local pub quiz saved my sanity. One evening away from domestic chaos, arguing with my friends, drinking beer and eating crisps . . . it may not sound like much, but I looked forward to it all week, and the vicious Wednesday-morning hangover was always worth it. Middle age is more like a dull ache than the piercing pain of new parenthood, but I still find the quiz greatly therapeutic, not to say analgesic. Young and old people love quizzes too, although the young tend to be at a disadvantage because they know sod all, while the old did know it once but have forgotten it. So this is a predominantly middle-aged playground: the ball is ours and we make the rules. It's an opportunity to play, and show off, and dig idiotic snippets of knowledge out of your capacious memory, and come third and win £7.50.*

R is for Recycling and Rubbish

In a two-person, male/female household, it is traditionally the man's job to put the rubbish out. (Is there something intrinsically manly about black bin liners?) The introduction of widespread recycling, however, has transformed a mere domestic duty into a full-scale hobby for midlife men. In my borough, there's dry recycling (newspapers, magazines, plastic bottles, cardboard packaging) and wet recycling (all foodstuffs, including meaty substances). Rumours abound that it's all put in the same hole in the ground somewhere in Kazakhstan, while council officials snigger at our gullibility. But I don't want to know about that: it takes away the fun.

With the dry recycling box, there's the challenge of filling it to overflowing days before it can be collected, while withdrawing any unrinsed jars or inappropriate plastic film your careless, irritable partner may have put in because she simply refuses to read the list of what can and what cannot be recycled. The wet recycling box, which sits outside in all weathers, brings out the bold, devil-may-care adventurer in us, for only the utterly fearless could deal with the vast slugs that live and grow in there as the food festers and mutates into something that may also be alive, although it's not life as we know it, Captain. Sometimes I test my mettle by

---

* For further information see my book *A Matter of Facts*, the definitive work on the subject, probably because it's the only work on the subject.

going out there at night, when the slugs seem more plentiful and very much larger and, if I am not mistaken, make quiet whimpering sounds, although that may be me. Sometimes I take out a kitchen implement and prise one of the slugs off the inside of the box. It comes off with a gentle pop and falls into the rotting food. Then I dump the latest bag of gak on top of it. But does this kill the slug, or does it just supply it with an extra-large late dinner? Does the rotting food assimilate the struggling, squirming body of the dying slug? Or does the greedy slug assimilate the food it finds all around it, enabling it to grow even bigger and leap out at you tomorrow evening, flexing the hundreds of tiny razor-sharp slug teeth that have evolved overnight? I'm not sure I want to find out.

S is for Sexual Reassignment Surgery

There's a lot of it about. One interviewee reports that a colleague of his returned from holiday one summer in wig, make-up and floral dress, announcing that henceforth he wished to be known as Miranda. The company called him a cab and paid him a substantial amount of money never to return. To this day his former workmates have no idea whether he meant it, or whether he was pulling a fast one. They hope the latter, but don't dare find out in case it's the former.

Maybe there were always a lot of men who felt they should properly have been women, but for most of human history, making the change was too expensive, too painful, too socially awkward to contemplate. No longer, it seems. There is a flight from masculinity across the world, in every culture, and middle-aged men are the most visible manifestation of this. That's because a young man who decides to relaunch himself as a woman has a fair-to-middling chance of actually passing as one. Take those hormones, acquire those breasts, and off you go. Whereas the middle-aged man, who has struggled with this for years and years and has only now plucked up the courage to pluck his eyebrows, is unlikely to be very convincing, at least without tens of thousands of pounds of corrective surgery, and possibly not even then. To contemplate this conundrum is to stare into an abyss of misery. Apparently, though, post-op transsexuals are among the few women who really like their own bodies, whether or not anyone else likes them. There may be an important lesson to be learned here, although I have no idea what it is.

T is for Trains

'This is the age of the train,' said a British Rail ad many years ago, incorrectly. The age of the train is, of course, middle age. All those trainspotters you see at the far end of the platform, noting down the number of the train you are on in a little book: none will see forty again. Some midlifers become obsessed with the idea of driving a train, and preferably a steam train. They buy Thomas the Tank Engine books for their children and watch DVDs of Ivor the Engine late into the night. This isn't nostalgia, because steam trains were all but gone when we were little.* This is

---

* Although they lasted longer than you might think. London Underground decommissioned its last steam train in 1971.

part of some deeper, darker folk memory, like T and his boiling oil in ruined castles. T wanted to drive a steam train too. He says it is back-breakingly hard work and as exciting as anything you could imagine.

But there is further to go down this track, much further. If you have an empty attic or a cellar you don't know what to do with, what better use could it be put to than to house a vast model railway? You need money for this, obviously, and time, and a wife who is happy never to see you again, but wouldn't we all do this if we could? I know I would. Consider the case of Rod Stewart. Famed in his youth for squiring blonde lovelies and wearing insanely tight trousers, Stewart now owns and operates a 1500-square-foot model of Grand Central Station and its surroundings. He has 9000 feet of track and several skyscrapers. In 2007 he was on the front cover of *Model Railroader* magazine, and said it meant more to him than making the cover of *Rolling Stone*. On tour in 2011, his dressing-room requirements were a bottle or two of decent red wine and a very large table for his trains. So much more civilised than asking for all the blue Smarties to be taken out.

U is for Up, Up and Away

T did this too for a while. He was single for many years and has no children, and his well-paid job rarely erodes his free time. So he had money and time and for a while used up both in his determination to acquire a private pilot's licence (PPL). He said that the airfield he used was full of deranged-looking midlifers spending their children's inheritance in order to fly around for an hour in what amounts to an oversized biscuit tin with wings. As in the Falklands, you would count them all out and hope to count them all back. Midlifers with PPLs have an odd propensity to fly into hills. What a dangerous hobby, people say – but it's not the hobby that's dangerous, it's the madman behind the wheel.

V is for Voluntary Work

If the pleasure of work is in the doing, then voluntary work should be the most satisfying work of all. At the school my children used to go to, money is desperately tight and any parent with free time is sucked in and put to work. The building is falling down, there's never anyone on reception and one of the class teachers has run away to join the Foreign Legion. (I myself edited the school newsletter for four years, and what a gloomy, navel-gazing journal it became.) But the parents are severely motivated, and the place keeps going, just. What we gain are the pleasure of belonging and a true sense of achievement, and all we lose are our spare time and our wits, because the school's relentless battle for survival drives everyone crackers in time. Normal people going there for the first time see all these crazed, anxious parents running around and, if they have any sense, turn round and walk straight out again. The day I stopped editing that bastard newsletter was the first day of the rest of my life.

The other problem with voluntary work is the other people who do it. My active friend T has recently joined his parish council, which turns out to be a hotbed of rivalry, thwarted ambition and Machiavellianism, much as he had hoped. (He is a great fan of Anthony Trollope's Barchester Chronicles.) His theory is that people behave better when they are being paid, and then let rip when they are doing something only for the love of it. I suspect they are also bored at work, and seek an outlet for all the intellectual energy and naked aggression their jobs no longer ask of them. Someone else I know joined his local neighbourhood watch committee. He said he would rather have spent time with the burglars.

W is for Water Features

Something is always missing from even the best tended garden. For me it's a deckchair and a novel, but for some men it's water. My friend O built a pond. 'A proper one: deep, with lining, pump, filter, mortared rock action round the edge. And I enjoyed it. Mind you, the filter has since packed in, the fish have died, and some of the rocks have come loose, and now I don't want to play any more.' It's the act of creation that matters. Maintenance and repair don't excite the imagination in the same way. For this reason, water features are more likely to be a brief enthusiasm than a lifelong calling. 'My dad had a phase of creating water features,' says F. 'He spent every weekend fiddling with pipes.' Healthier than smoking them, I suppose.

X is for Xcess

H writes: 'My dad has gone through all of the following in the past fifteen years: collecting antique prams, keeping tropical fish, playing on Google Earth, car booting, 'orbing' [look it up – something to do with taking photos on digital cameras that let you see ghosts], getting tattoos, providing aid to a Gambian family and breeding the perfect Yorkshire Terrier . . . '

Y is for Yorkshire Terrier, Breeding the Perfect, and for Yawn

All this leisure is tiring me out . . .

Z is for Zzzzzzzzzz

8

SPORT

'Spent all of last week getting paranoid that I had some kind of muscle-wasting disease as my cycling pace got slower and slower. Turns out I just needed to pump up my rear tyre. Must learn the basics of bike maintenance at some point.'

W's status update, January 2011

You may have noticed that there wasn't much about sport in the preceding chapter. S could easily have been for Sport, just as G could have been for Groin Injuries and H for Hamstring, Pulled. (P could have been for Physiotherapy, L for Liniment and T for Truss.) Midlife men often have a complicated relationship with sport. The most committed sport-phobics are often the ones who feel the strongest need to get fit and stay fit. And the ones who couldn't care less about being fit are the ones watching the most sport on TV. However you feel about it, sport touches all our lives. Some of these lives it enriches, a few it abbreviates. Warning: danger lies ahead.

Golf

Surely the quintessential midlife sport. It may not be fair, but millions of young people across the globe regard golf as the last straw, the final admission that you are old and useless and doomed to wear hideous multi-coloured knitwear and talk tripe to other sad old men. Which is terribly unfair, and also true. B has been obsessed by golf since childhood, and has spent tens of thousands of pounds on it (but not hundreds of thousands yet, he thinks). He admits that his golf club is full of appalling bores, misfits, serial killers and escaped war criminals, but it isn't half as bad as his previous club, where I once went for a quiz night. To join you needed to prove not only that you could play the game to the required standard, but that you referred to women as 'ladies' and had closed your mind to new ideas in 1955. B wanted to win the quiz for normal competitive reasons, but he also wanted not to because it didn't pay to attract too much attention. Coming third, he said, would be about right. Only in a golf club would you have to make such a calculation. We didn't win but, without meaning to, we made such a poor impression I'm sure they all thought we were secretly Jewish, or Punjabi. Those of us who had seen *The Wicker Man* were more than a little afraid.

The shame is that golf is a rather wonderful game, which doesn't require you to be young or fit, or even able to walk more than a few feet without falling over. Its pace and its contemplative air could have been designed purposefully for the middle-aged mindset. Its topography – the fairway to aim at, the rough you always end up in, the bunkers strategically placed to trap you, the cruel randomness of the slope on the green – suggests a number of metaphors for real life, while successfully distracting you from everything to do with real life. Even the balance between skill and luck feels right. There's also the curious paradox that the more beautiful the golf course, and the more pleasant a place it is in which to be, the more beautiful the original woodland or countryside was before it was razed to the ground to allow people like you to play golf on it. B thinks that more landfill sites should be turned into golf courses, if only to increase the risk of personal harm whenever you lose your ball in the deep rough.

Football

We live at an unusual juncture in sporting history, when to say that you don't like football is to admit to something so strange and alien that most people don't get it. Sorry, what was that? No, can you say that again? You were making total sense and then suddenly you were talking gibberish. Is that Estonian, or Basque?

But enough of the wreck that is my social life. The transformation of football from mildly grimy working-class sport in perpetual decline to gobsmackingly lucrative global industry, in what seems like five minutes but was actually thirty years, may be the defining cultural phenomenon of our time. It's defining in more personal ways as well. Men say 'I like football' in the same way that women say 'I would like to have babies at some point in my life'. Football is no longer something you follow in your spare time. It is as tribal as it always was – I support Arsenal, you support Tottenham Hotspur and I spit on your grandparents' graves – but it has become supratribal as well. I belong to football. Football is me. I wear this unpleasant primary-coloured 100 per cent polyester shirt covered with the brand names of venal multinational corporations with so much pride I could burst.

And if you don't buy into it? Well, as I know from experience, best keep your mouth shut. Besides, it's churlish to pooh-pooh anything that gives its adherents so much innocent, if expensive, pleasure. It took me a long time to understand, for instance, that football fans actually enjoy being ripped off by the teams they support, that the greed and corruption of clubs, and the greed and stupidity of players, don't erode their loyalty but reinforce it. Look at the shit we have to deal with, they are saying. But we still love this club. It also gives them someone to blame when it all goes wrong, which in football, as in most sports, it generally does. There can only ever be one winner of a league or a cup; everybody else loses. Again, the midlife man subliminally recognises a pattern in this. We all know one or two people who have won in life, but we know a lot more who haven't, the one in the shaving mirror the best of all.

Football's paradox is that, although the game has changed utterly, it seems to represent something immutable, solid and reliable to its fans. The rest of life becomes ever more feminised: we work in offices and talk about our feelings, and some of us even go on diets. But give or take the odd female linesperson (or assistant referee, or whatever pathetic title they have nowadays), football remains a bastion of hairy-arsed masculinity. For many men it's a refuge, one of the few left. Consider the attempts of the football authorities to impose a mid-season break, allowing players some time off over Christmas and New Year and the coldest winter weather in January. The supporters won't have it. There have been fixtures on Boxing Day and New Year's Day for generations. It's a tradition, a ritual – in short, the only possible way of getting out of the house away from the family. Take that away and there would be revolution.

Midlife football fans don't just watch football. They don't just talk about it, think about it, dream about it and sigh wistfully about it. Some still play it too. I know a handful of fiftysomethings who still creak out for five-a-side on Tuesdays. Needless to say, they are always injured. Debate rages over whether football is more dangerous than other sports, or whether the people who play it are more fragile. One of the players I know had to give up recently, as he had started crumbling to dust. Another would list 'physiotherapy' among his hobbies if he ever made it into *Who's Who*.

But you can see why they do it. Not long ago I was wandering around a town in southern England with time to kill. Down one residential road all was quiet. Birds tweeted, leaves rustled and men wiped down their already clean company Saabs, humming tunelessly. I turned a corner and suddenly, from behind some trees, all you could hear was shouting and yelling, cries of anger punctuated by other people's cries of anger. I skirted the foliage and there it was, a Sunday football match. We think that Sunday football is all about running around, getting some exercise, scoring goals, saving goals and executing the only pinpoint, perfectly timed pass you will manage this year. Nonsense. It's about non-stop shouting. Playing football allows you to release tensions accumulated during a week of unmanly deskwork, and its attendant cups of coffee and soggy sandwiches. It is a licence to scream your head off. Even if you crock your knee and can never walk again, you will have done your spirit a power of good. You could try shouting and screaming in your shed instead, but people might begin to talk.

Marathon running

You never ran for anything before, so why now? An unanswerable question, because the truth is that you're only running to lose weight and look younger, so girls will look at you again. No, don't even pretend otherwise, I'm not listening.

Nonetheless, running can become addictive. The wobbliest old joggers go out and buy decent shoes, run further and faster than before, and somehow manage to overcome the pain of recurring blisters and corns and collapsing ankles, all because they want that rush of endorphins, the runner's high. (It's encouraging to learn that we never outgrow the desire for a cheap thrill.) Before you know it you're running marathons, possibly dressed as a giant soft fruit or the Pope. Many runners publish photographs on Facebook of themselves crossing the line, half-dead with exhaustion. But at least if they publish such photos, their friends know they are still half-alive.

Running knackers the body, particularly the knees. And the only girls who will look at you will be other runners. If they do look at you, make sure you observe the running world's strict courting etiquette. A certain number of mutual overtakings will indicate interest. Then the early, exploratory conversations about injuries, the best routes to run and the efficacy or otherwise of your shoes. If you do end up having an affair with her, it's amazingly easy to arrange: you just tell your partner you are going out for a run. Sex counts as exercise too, and there's a far smaller chance of injury. No need, either, to dress up as the Pope, unless you feel like it, of course.

Cycling

If you think marathon running is obsessive, it has nothing on cycling. I know people who have discovered cycling (usually rediscovered it, to be precise, as most of them cycled as children) and vanished from sight, over the hill, far away. There may be sports that offer a faster getaway, but I can't believe that any gives you the same sense of freedom. Once you're out of sight, you could be gone for ages. No one answers a mobile phone on a bike.

When you next see your cyclist friends, they have lost all their excess weight and become sinewy and weather-beaten. Most of them have a mad light in the eyes, the light of the convert. Dedicated cyclists don't do small talk any more. They just want to go out and do more cycling. Or maybe go to bike shops and salivate over an unusually sleek carbon frame. Out in the garage they keep hidden a small stash of dog-eared bike magazines. They wear Lycra without embarrassment. They are lost to the world.

For a bike is a shed on wheels. Not only can you take it anywhere, it can take you anywhere. There is the problem of the weather, but I'm not sure cyclists notice weather. Even in the cold and wet, I see cyclists scaling the vertiginously steep hill near my home, their muscles, tendons and ligaments stretched to snapping point. It looks like some monstrous form of torture. You can't believe that they are doing this of their own free will. In fact, they have chosen this hill precisely because it is so steep.

When the weather is kind, it is easier to see the point. A forty-mile bike ride, if you are up to it, must be as close as anyone can get to a dictionary definition of flow. Some midlifers take up cycling because they think it'll keep them young, and are surprised to find themselves surrounded by people of exactly the same age. G organises a duathlon each year: a 5km run followed by a 20km bike ride followed by another 5km run. 'The men veterans – over-forties – outnumber their younger counterparts every year,' she says. 'Many of them are doing an event like ours for the first time. Lots of supervets too [over-fifties]. Not the case for the women: we have very few women vets and hardly any women supervets as the attraction of cycling or running through mud seems to pall with age.'

Supervets?

Tennis

Like so many sports, tennis is all in the mind. In your imagination your serve is a thing of grace and beauty. Your ground strokes are a small miracle of speed and agility.

Your backspin is prodigious. Your returns are unstoppable. Without letting you know it is going to do such a thing, your mind imprints memories of old matches seen on the television on to the actual physical process of playing the game. So when you do something a bit nifty, as you surely will sooner or later, if only by accident, not only will you enjoy it enormously (as all bad sportsmen do) but in your mind's eye you will see it as even better than it was, and so enjoy it even more. The fact that the silly old buffer at the other end of the court is playing like a stuffed toy on wheels is neither here or there. And he's winning! Blame it on the run of the balls.

This is why only rich men get tennis coaching, and why tennis coaches are often sad unemployed men who don't understand where it went wrong. A golfer gets coaching because he knows he can improve, because like dentistry golf is about the management of failure. Tennis is about the suspension of disbelief. You cannot get better because you know you are already playing at the very top of your game. It wouldn't be worth all that money just to tweak a couple of minor technical flaws. Rich men are different, as we know. They didn't get this rich without having a clear idea of their own capabilities, and without wanting to win everything, all the time. Women sometimes hire tennis coaches, but that's for another reason entirely.

Rock climbing

Again, it's remarkable how many men in their forties suddenly take this up, having previously shown not the smallest interest in rocks, large or small. Perhaps it's a way of staring your mortality in the face, of challenging the fates to kill you now and save you the bother of slow decline into senility and uselessness. Or it may just be that halfway up a mountain is the only place left you can get any peace and quiet. I read somewhere that in the milliseconds between losing your grip and being dashed to death on the rocks below, you finally achieve a measure of peace. But how would anyone know?

Rambling

That's in the sense of 'walking', rather than 'telling the same story you told half an hour ago to people who have heard it fifty times before anyway'.

The journalist and satirist Auberon Waugh hated ramblers. They were dull, misshapen city-dwellers who wandered half-wittedly across other people's property and generally got in the way. But that's other ramblers. That's not me. I am not wearing an anorak or a rucksack, and nor do I have an Ordnance Survey map in one of those waterproof plastic folders (although I would really like one and keep intending to buy one). You and I are just going for a walk: those other sad fools over there are ramblers. Should we pass each other we will nod and say hello, because that's what people do in the country. Actual country-dwellers say hello to you with an eyebrow raised, as though to say, you don't do this in the city, do you, you fucker. And we smile and say hello back, as though to say, no we don't, you smug bag of fuck, but we have a really good takeaway curry house just up the road and we can get the day's newspapers before lunchtime. The other guy actually knows this because he isn't a real country-dweller either: he moved down here fifteen years ago. Soon, he hopes, people in the pub will start talking to him.

Ramblers are at the bottom of the heap, despised by all, including each other. This is probably just as well, as people need to be discouraged from going for walks in the countryside, to make it more pleasant for those of us who will go there whatever anyone thinks of us. We are not interested in the approval of strangers. We seek only the bliss of solitude, as does everyone. We are a large and disparate community of mutually hostile loners. Oi, get off my land.

Snooker

Each sport, in its different way, demonstrates the body's capacity to turn in on itself. As a professional gymnast you are washed up at twenty-five, as a swimmer at thirty, as a footballer at thirty-five, as a cricketer at forty, as a golfer at forty-five and as a darts player at fifty (or twenty-five stone: whichever you exceed first). In snooker, on rare and beautiful occasions, there is life after fifty, and this cheers us all up. In 2010, aged fifty-two, Steve Davis reached the quarter-finals of the World Championships at the Crucible in Sheffield, beating Mark King 10–9 and John Higgins 13–11 before losing to the eventual champion, Neil Robertson, 13–5. Middle-aged men everywhere were cheering on Davis against this blond-haired whippersnapper who, it was generally agreed, didn't know he was born.

Robertson, though, is a rare young snooker player, in that he actually looks young. Many of his fellow professionals look like nothing on earth. They rarely go out during the hours of light and one or two of them appear to have eaten their lesser opponents. It probably doesn't help that we only see them once a year. So-called snooker fans like me only tune in during the World Championships. For fifteen intense days, we are dragged down into this dank, obsessive subculture, where whole careers can turn on an inadvertent kiss on the blue. These pale men play with such skill and stamina and mental fortitude that by the end of the tournament we feel we know them intimately. Then we forget about them for eleven and a half months. When they re-emerge, blinking, the following April, we are shocked by the ravages time has wrought. Saggier, balder and more defeated, they have done nothing all year but pot long balls and lay crafty snookers behind the black. And the fat ones, defying the laws of physics, are even fatter. Snooker players squander their youth as no other sportspeople do, and we salute them for this, as we did exactly the same thing, except we did it by accident and have nothing to show for it. Still, nice little cannon on the last red; he should clear up from there.

Cricket

For thirty years or so I have been running a cricket team of mixed ability. When we started, we were nineteen or twenty. We aren't now. In the intervening decades, some players have lost interest and drifted away, one or two have died, and a handful have been seduced by the Dark Side (golf). In 1997 the team split into two. All the peripatetic South African bar staff went one way, and the old lags came with me. We still play most weekends between the end of April and mid-September, and our squad – those who can be relied upon to play at least twice a season – has risen to about thirty. We have a handful of young players and some youngish players. But a comfortably upholstered majority of us will not see forty-five again. We enjoy it more than anyone can imagine.

That said, the way we play has changed markedly. Our fast bowlers, as you would expect, are no longer fast: even if they are as fit as they can be (and they aren't), the ball simply comes out of their hand less quickly. For some bowlers, tactics and strategy have replaced cold, hard aggression, while others still just wang it down and hope something happens. The batting, if anything, has improved. Batsmen may not have the strength or power they once had, but they know what works for them and they are certainly calmer at the crease. Even in the most meaningless village cricket match, going out to bat can be an intimidating experience. All eyes are on you. As a young person you are much more worried about making a fool of yourself, and even if you do have the wild and insane confidence of youth, all the older people surrounding you know how easy it is to make you look daft. I am a batsman of no discernible (or even hidden) talent, but I make more runs and stay in longer these days because I am so much less terrified, and I am not the only one.

No, the most visible manifestation of decline is our fielding. Our young players fling themselves around the ground, sprint to the boundary and hurl the ball back, one bounce to the 'keeper. Our older players can run to the boundary, but at about half the speed. (Our oldest player, A, rising sixty-two, looks great for his years until he starts running, at which point you want to say, that's not really running, is it. But it is. It's also what the rest of us will be doing in a few years' time.) Then there's the throwing. On a long boundary, you need two old players to throw the ball back, one positioned halfway. At one ground in Oxford where we played recently, we needed three players. The other team were running fives. It would have made more sense to post it back.

And yet there are consolations. A while ago I watched a couple of young teams, teenagers mainly, playing cricket on a council pitch near my home. Their fielding was different to ours. They did a lot of diving that we wouldn't do, and some of it was spectacular, but only rarely did they field the ball cleanly. In fact it went through their legs more often than not, and they dropped several straightforward catches. I suspect they were slightly more frightened of the ball than we are. But if they did misfield, it was nothing for them to turn round, run eighty yards and fling the ball straight back. We will do anything to avoid this. As a result our ground fielding has become astonishingly tight. We are still frightened of the ball, but we fear looking foolish more.

And we shall keep on going until we can't any more. That's a given, although we don't discuss it. There are a dozen of us in our fifties now. Time is finite. It's a bit like keeping an old car going, replacing its failing components with increasingly rare and expensive spare parts, nursing it along until one day it just won't go any more, and you have to accept the inevitable, and off it goes to be pulled apart for scrap. And you get a new car and wonder to yourself, why did I put up with that ridiculous old rustheap for so long?

9

PEDANT

'The battle against illiteracies and barbarisms ... is not a public battle. It takes place within the soul of every individual who minds about words.'

Martin Amis

Here is something else I left out of the A to Z of Tragic Leisure Activities Taken Up by British Men in the Throes of Midlife. Some men are born pedants. Some achieve pedantry, and some have pedantry thrust upon them. Be not afraid of pedantry. It warms many a chilly, splintered, middle-aged soul.

It can strike at any time. 'Signs of middle age are kicking in,' reports McA. 'I have just shouted "Fewer, not less!" at Radio 4.' McA is in his mid-thirties. He has just been given a glimpse of the rest of his life. At Bank station on the London Underground not so long ago, I heard the following announcement: 'When boarding a train at this station, please use all available doors.' Realistically you can only use one available door, unless they want you to dart in and out of the train through every door until you have collected the set. Even then, if you accept that we are being addressed as a group, why only 'at this station'? At other stations, should we all get in the same door? A response like this is technically known as 'the Pedant's Revolt'.

I accept that not everyone's mind runs in this direction. Millions of us remain free of pedantry for the whole of our lives, just as we manage to avoid tuberculosis and the music of Sting. Otherwise there would be no such thing as the greengrocer's apostrophe. Unencumbered by knowledge, the fruit and vegetable merchant innocently writes 'tomato's' to inform the populace that he has more than one tomato for sale. By doing so he unknowingly suggests that the box of tomatoes thus indicated belongs to a particular tomato: a big cheese of tomatoes, if you like. We realise, though, that the greengrocer has only written 'tomato's' because 'tomatoes' does not 'look' right, and because the apostrophe somehow dignifies the word (in much the same way that some people say 'commence' rather than 'begin' or 'start' because they think it sounds a bit posher). Unfortunately, this construction so riles his pedantic middle-aged customers that they all go to Tesco down the road, and he eventually goes out of business, never realising that it was his stupidity that brought him low, not the quality or otherwise of his produce, or the supermarket's extensive price-cutting.

When Lynne Truss wrote a book about this, *Eats, Shoots and Leaves*, it sold in millions all around the world. I wonder how many people who bought it were under forty. And everyone under forty who did buy it was buying it as a present for someone over forty. I know someone who got four copies that Christmas, and he knows someone who got five.

Why should age make such a difference? Maybe we don't take these things so seriously when we are younger. In the early 1980s, when the heavy metal group Mötley Crüe came into being, with umlauts both on the 'o' of 'Motley' and the previously unheard-of 'u' of 'Crue', it seemed little more than a harmless jape. (They were apparently inspired by the many bottles of Löwenbräu they had drunk the previous evening.) Twenty years later, when I was forty-one, five uninteresting young people won the *Popstars* TV talent show and immediately named themselves Hear'Say. Why the apostrophe? One of the band's members, interviewed on BBC1's *Breakfast*, said it was included because 'it looked good on paper ... it was a design thing.' Lynne Truss called it 'a significant milestone on the road to punctuation anarchy'. But some commentators thought it was a deliberate attempt to appeal to a youthful audience 'by imitating an informal, uneducated style': in other words, an apostrophe-shaped middle finger raised to middle-aged pedants like me who swore never to buy any of their dismal records and cheered when they broke up in acrimony little more than a year later. If anything could be said to be bad punctuation karma, that apostrophe was it.

This was but a minor skirmish in the language wars that have been raging for centuries. For as long as people have been speaking and writing English, other people have been telling them that they are speaking and writing it incorrectly. In the 1660s, the Royal Society put together a committee 'for improving the English language'. John Dryden was on it. He was particularly vexed by sentences that ended with a preposition, to such an extent that when he became Poet Laureate, he reissued all his old works with all the 'stranded' prepositions removed. Thanks to Dryden, what was initially just a matter of taste became a solid and unbreakable rule, loved and honoured by language pedants ever since. In *The Language Wars* (2011), Henry Hitchings quotes 'a well-established American campus joke' that goes something like this:

> On the first day of a new academic year, a freshman approaches a senior and asks, 'Hey, excuse me, do you know where the freshman dorms are at?' To which the senior responds, 'At Princeton, we don't end a sentence with a preposition.' The freshman tries again: 'Excuse me, do you know where the freshman dorms are at, motherfucker?'

In the 1990s I was working as a TV critic for a national newspaper, and made the mistake of quoting what would now be called the 'mission statement' of the USS *Enterprise* in *Star Trek*. 'To boldly go where no man has gone before,' said Captain Kirk. (To boldly go where no *one* has gone before,' said Captain Picard.) The letters poured in. How dare I not only quote the most notorious split infinitive in grammatical history, but fail to explicitly condemn it? Or fail explicitly to condemn it? (Whoops.) I returned fire. Split infinitives are not a grammatical offence, I explained,

with great patience and ill-concealed glee. As Harry
Fieldhouse writes in *Everyman's Good English Guide* (1982):

> Perhaps because a confident grasp of grammar is
> uncommon among native speakers of English . . . con-
> cern for whatever offences the ordinary person thinks
> he can recognise is all the more passionate. Split infini-
> tives are one of these. A split infinitive can inflame a
> businessman who muddles his tenses and upset a politi-
> cian who is blind to a non sequitur. The concern is the
> more extraordinary in that objectors can rarely explain
> why they object. Vague authority may be invoked, but
> the fact is that 20th-century grammarians from Otto
> Jespersen onwards have dismissed the aversion as
> unfounded.

The vague authority might have been an English teacher
many years before, or someone else who told us that split
infinitives were wrong when our minds were young and
malleable.

Midlife pedants complain that teachers don't teach
grammar any more. Harry Fieldhouse said the same thirty
years ago. In 1921 a government report commented that
'grammar is certainly badly taught as a rule'. In 1724, an
anonymous pamphlet called *The Many Advantages of a Good
Language to Any Nation* moaned about the ignorance of students arriving at university, the 'silliness' of women's choice
of words and the inadequacies of the alphabet. We will never
know who wrote this, but I wouldn't mind betting that he
or she had recently celebrated a fortieth birthday. One day,
when they reach a similar age, the former members of

Hear'Say will wake up and think, what on earth were we doing? We should have been shot for that.

There is more to pedantry, though, than applied rage. There can be entertainment too, albeit of a solitary, self-pleasing kind. For some years *Private Eye* had a region on its letters page entitled 'Pedants' Corner', for anyone who wished to correct minor errors of fact, grammar, syntax, punctuation and interpretation. One day someone wrote in and asked, is it a corner for pedants or a corner of pedants? If the former, should it not be 'Pedants Corner' without the apostrophe? Someone else wrote in and suggested that pedants read it and wrote to it individually, not as a group, so really it should be 'Pedant's Corner'. Soon, every letter was about this. No one pointed out mistakes in the magazine any more. The apostrophe, meanwhile, began to move around apparently at random, sometimes popping up in the middle of Ped'ant, sometimes in the corner of Corne'r. The only way to end the argument was to rename the section 'Pedantry Corner'.

Most pubs have a pedantry corner. We stand there with our drinks and bemoan the loss of the word 'disinterested' to mean unbiased, but now used to mean the same as 'uninterested' by the foolish and pretentious. We wonder whether it is now pointless to object to 'decimate' being used as a synonym for 'wipe out', because its original meaning – to punish by killing one in ten men – might now be a little specialised. And to expect people to use 'data' and 'media' only as plural nouns because that's what they were in the original Latin is just picky. My friend U remembers joyous arguments in his local about the differences between pedantic, pernickety and picky.

Pedants don't just consult *Roget's Thesaurus*, they browse through it. If they are lucky, they marry other pedants. 'Steve and I find our pedantry cements our relationship,' writes J on a prominent social networking site. 'Pet hates: young people's shit grasp of English and text speak.' 'I think that most young people have an excellent grasp of text-speak,' writes L in response. And so we are drawn into an argument examining ever smaller and more trivial facets of the original argument. It is the incredible shrinking argument. Honey, I shrunk the argument.

There is more to pedantry, of course, than concern over linguistic niceties. Chambers gives the following definition for 'pedant': 'a schoolmaster (*Shakesp*); an over-educated person who parades his or her knowledge; a person who values academic learning too highly; a person fond of making over-fine distinctions, or one insisting on strict adherence to or interpretation of rules, etc.', which doesn't sound like any fun at all. Wikipedia's Wiktionary recommends that you don't confuse 'pedant' with 'pennant' or 'pendant'. I can't conceive of the pedant who would make this mistake. We are neither flags nor attractive items of jewellery. Readers of the *Daily Star*, however, might confuse pedants with pederasts, paedophiles and paediatricians. God help me should any of them read this chapter. 'Pedant' is also, in Latin, the third person plural present active indicative of *pedō*, *pedare*, and means 'they prop up trees or vines'. (Do not confuse with *pedō*, *pēdere*, meaning 'to break wind, fart'. That would be 'pedent'.)

If you can feel your brain physically shrinking to the size of a brazil nut, you may not be alone.

Nonetheless, I think it would be a mistake to make any

connection between this linguistic pedantry, which at least is about something, and the more instinctive and pervasive pedantry of the jobsworth. Linguistic pedantry is, at heart, reactive. If everyone spoke and wrote 'properly' (whatever that is), we would be happy. Greengrocers would thrive once more, and people would only say 'between you and I' as a joke, remembering the bad old days. There might even be agreement about the use of the word 'hopefully', although I suspect that Arabs and Israelis will break bread over a hearty lunch before that day.

Actual jobsworthery, by contrast, is active, even aggressive in intent. This is the application of rules for their own sake. More often than not, it's an attempt to assert power. It might be quite a pathetic attempt, because the power is so puny, but to the jobsworth concerned, it is usually the only weapon he has available. In *The End of the Party* (2010), his book about the last ten years of New Labour, Andrew Rawnsley tells of an urgent phone call received by the then Cabinet Secretary, Sir Andrew Turnbull, while he was play-ing golf. One of the golf club's staff interrupted him.

'You can't use your mobile here,' he said. 'Believe me, it's very important,' replied Britain's most senior civil servant. 'I don't care,' said the jobsworth. 'What's more – tuck your shirt in.'

This kind of pedantry has nothing to do with age. These pedants were born, not made, and certainly no one thrust pedantry upon them. They achieved all they set out to do as traffic wardens, and looked around for new challenges. They are (thank God) outside the purview of this book.

Or as S put it to me, 'Pedantry means anally following rules, which personally I'm less and less inclined to do as I enter my grand decline.' If we do rant on about language, it's just because, once again, we feel assailed by aspects of the culture that are not on our side. J's pet hate was 'young people's shit grasp of English'. But is it their grasp of English, or is it the young people themselves?

10

YOUTH

'The young may look prettier than we do, but they are also tremendously boring and talk nothing but rubbish.'

Auberon Waugh

Time to grasp the nettle. Our problem isn't really middle age. Our problem is all the young people, and their dreadful, blooming youth. They have what we used to have. We lost it. We put it down somewhere, and now we can't find it anywhere. But they picked it up, and they aren't giving it back. It's not fair, as any toddler will confirm.

'Youth is a blunder; Manhood a struggle; Old Age a regret,' wrote Benjamin Disraeli in his novel *Coningsby*. He was forty at the time. 'Young people ought not to be idle,' said Margaret Thatcher, 'it is very bad for them.' She was fifty-nine. 'How ruthless and hard and right and vile the young are,' wrote the Australian novelist and poet Hal Porter, aged fifty-two. Perhaps you need a few more years under your belt before true perspective arrives. 'Youth would be an ideal state if it came a little later in life,' said Herbert Asquith, seventy-one.

There is another saying, one we have all heard people use, and maybe repeated ourselves from time to time. 'Youth is wasted on the young.' Who said it first? My books of quotations are uncharacteristically hazy on the subject, but whoever it was must have been old enough to feel it. We see the young, with their energy, their beauty, all that time to waste, and we can't help imagining what wonders we might achieve in their place. But we fool ourselves. In our hearts, we know what we would do in their place. We would do now what we did at the time: fritter it away without a second thought.

What we actually want is to be young again but also to know what we have learned since. If I had known that there would never be a second chance with the beautiful woman with the waist-length hair, I would have taken the first chance. Obvious now. But I was foolish and complacent and, yes, a little fearful and too cautious. I was in my twenties. I was a halfwit.

(There is the argument, which I have explored endlessly ever since, that she would soon have realised for herself that I was a halfwit, and the relationship would never have got anywhere. Maybe so, but the chance to fail is better than no chance at all.)

So, was being young so great? Margaret Atwood didn't think so. 'I've never understood why people consider youth a time of freedom and joy. It's probably because they have forgotten their own.' But it's easy to forget. Maybe we are hard-wired to forget, and couldn't hang on to these memories if we tried. Or maybe it's just carelessness. You take your eye off the ball for a moment, and all empathy for youth vanishes for ever. Nostalgia for youth could be a form of mass amnesia. The less clearly we remember our own youth, the more we idealise it, and the less sympathetic we are towards the poor little buggers going through it now. This sounds to me like the beginnings of pomposity, and it's no coincidence that a defining quality of pomposity is a dislike of everything to do with youth. That's not to say that young people aren't annoying. Of course they are. It's just that it may not be entirely their fault.

The problem with being young is that you know nothing about anything. You obviously don't want anyone to realise that – if you are lucky enough to realise it yourself – so you pretend you know it all, often with disastrous consequences. Most young people's arrogance is superficial and easily punctured. Later on it may develop into a deeper, more pervasive arrogance: these are the men who never stop talking at parties. But for now, the swagger is more a stretching of limbs than a statement of intent. In short, most of them don't mean any harm.*

There are genuinely appalling youths in the world, we know that. Many grow into genuinely appalling adults. But rather more young people, I suspect, are vulnerable and terrified and hanging on for dear life. Being appalling may

---

* But how patronising is that? It's like when girls call you 'sweet', meaning 'of no sexual interest whatsoever'. Someone once told a friend of mine that he could see he meant no harm. Friend was incensed. 'I mean harm!' he shouted, 'I mean harm!'

be a coping mechanism. The crucial thing to remember is that youth is temporary, and most of us get over it. Some of the most recalcitrant and unprepossessing young people can become charming and benign in middle age. You and I, for example, and one or two others we know.

It might be helpful, then, to regard youth as a form of disease. Rarely is it fatal: in that respect, old age beats it hands down. It is also more treatable than ever, what with student loans, mortgage repayments, desks and all the other blighted paraphernalia of responsible adult life. Fortunately, symptoms of youth are easy to spot. They include:

- full head of hair;
- disgraceful shortage of wrinkles;
- bright eyes;
- bushy tail.

Extreme youth, which is to say teenagerhood, has its own set of symptoms, some of which recur in middle age. These include:

- surly expression;
- unwillingness to communicate in anything other than grunts;
- constant desire to sleep;
- obsessive but futile interest in girls.

Nonetheless, an entire dimension of teenage behaviour exists to dismay and confuse any adults who happen to be passing. For instance, teens often shout in normal conversation, whether or not they are angry. They wear their hoods up when it's 93° in the shade. They look at you with an aggrieved expression when wearing their hoods up, as though it's your fault. They play hip-hop on mobile phones on public transport.* Some address each other as 'bruv' or 'blood' or even 'geez', often with accompanying devil's horn hand signal; take size eighteen shoes; grow taller than six foot three without written permission; speak exclusively in metric measurements (I am apparently 1.74 metres tall and weigh 67 kg); wear their trousers on the backs of their thighs with their pants showing; and walk as though they have shat themselves (which they have to, in order to keep their trousers up). A new one that gets my goat is that they say 'pissed' for 'pissed off', meaning angry, having heard it in so many American films and TV shows. No, 'pissed' means drunk. They're usually that as well.

Young people have what we envy and are making as much of a mess of it as we did. They can be superficially arrogant, insensitive to the feelings of others, self-indulgent and ruinously expensive to maintain. Some can eat an entire loaf of bread between meals. They are either obsessive about hygiene or unaware that it exists (there is no middle ground).† Even their enthusiasm is oddly irritating. They are discovering things for the first time and assume, not unreasonably, that no one ever discovered them before. Whereas we know we discovered everything years ago, and we are aggrieved, because like everyone, we wish to be

---

* Known as 'sodcasting', apparently.
† One contemporary of mine now believes that he did not possess a sense of smell until his mid-twenties. For many years the dominant aroma in his vicinity was the slightly stewed smell of inadequately dried clothes.

acknowledged. But it is not their job to acknowledge us. It is our job to acknowledge them. Their job is to disregard us completely. The pressure this imposes on a typically battered, dented middle-aged ego can be hard to bear. We bite our lips. We don't tell them they don't know they're born. We want to. Oh, we so want to. We think it. We feel it, with every muscle and tendon and blood cell. Our eyes prick with tears of injustice. Our ears may turn dangerously red.

It's crazy, really. Middle age may be a little low on dignity, but at least we have a clear idea of who we are, where we are and what's going on. Being young is much tougher. It demands a set of skills you usually haven't acquired yet. You have the energy, but you don't know how to direct and use it to best effect. You have the looks, although you can't see them yourself, so they don't count. You have all that glorious time to waste, and not the smallest idea what to do with it. Over the years you will acquire these skills, but by the time you have mastered being young, you are an old fart. Which presents midlifers with an awkward choice. Do we accept and settle into our old-fartitude? Or do we try and relive a youth we never really lived when we had the chance?

11

MUTTON

'You're a grown-up! What do you know about style?'

My son, two weeks before his ninth birthday

A few years ago a man came to my local pub quiz whom we knew as 'the world's oldest punk'. I doubt it was an accurate assessment: he can't have been much older than forty and there must have been one or two older punks somewhere, maybe in eastern Europe, or hiding in a jungle in South America in the manner of those Japanese soldiers who didn't know that World War II had come to an end. Despite his advancing years, the World's Oldest Punk maintained his bleached blond Mohican, as well as a slightly intimidating public persona that had clearly served him well. He also had an attractive girlfriend, which usually shows you are doing something right.

Even so, something seemed wrong about the sight of this

man on the cusp of middle age with his vertical hair and his patent Johnny Rotten leer. We debated this issue at length, as you do in pubs, before it struck us that his adherence to a style associated with extreme youth – and specifically his own extreme youth – actually made him look older. Dressed otherwise, he would look his age. As a punk he looked near double it. He was, in short, mutton dressed as lamb. Or maybe a more surreal variant: mutton dressed as fish.

Image matters. You do not reach middle age without knowing that. We think we have grown up in peculiarly image-conscious times, but tell that to the Cavaliers and Roundheads. Books have long been judged by their covers. Your clothes, your hair and, these days, your tattoos and piercings say more about you than cash ever can. Did I ever have more than a cursory conversation with the World's Oldest Punk? I'm not sure I did. Other than the fact that he was a bit scary, I recognised that his image was for him a form of protection, not only from potential aggressors but from people like me. It cut out the need for small talk, and left him alone with his attractive girlfriend. It also, bizarrely, made him the centre of attention, which he quite enjoyed as well. As my old schoolfriend U said when we were seventeen or so, 'I don't care if I'm liked or hated, I just don't want to be ignored.' This is not something you would ever hear a woman say.

The World's Oldest Punk was taking advantage of a free-dom that didn't exist for our parents. Our fathers, when they hit their forties, surrendered to them completely. There was no other option. Everybody dressed their age, and middle age's wardrobe was not characterised by enormous variation. Pipes, slippers, cardigans and truly awful trousers were what awaited you when youth was gone, and you accepted that. Look at any children's comic from the 1960s and 1970s and all the fathers look like this. In that journal of record the *Beano*, some still do, although most wear trainers and even jeans, which look very odd with their combover baldy hairstyles and natty Hitler moustaches.

Even in the 1970s, though, a midlife crisis might be lying in wait. My father used to go to work every day in a suit, beautifully cut, elegant, with a perfect silk tie, everything laundered to the hilt. At the weekend he dressed in what were called 'casual clothes', an only slightly less formal combo of slacks, sweater and old workshirt, with shoes no less polished than they would be during the week. Then he hit his forties. This man who sat behind a desk all day and employed people to get their hands dirty so that he didn't have to, suddenly turned up one day dressed in denim from top to toe. It was a hideous sight. He was plump and bald and bespectacled and deeply uncomfortable in these dismal clothes, which he wore with the same expensive polished shoes, having not quite done his research, we felt. Trainers didn't exist then, of course. Nor did Shakin' Stevens, and I'm sure I was not the only person who blanched every time this blank-eyed Elvis impersonator appeared on television during the 1980s. Maybe as a result of this, I have never in my life bought a pair of blue jeans, or even tried any on. My father had only ever listened to big noisy classical music at home – Mahler, Wagner, Bruckner, Brahms – but in his car he now had an eight-track cartridge of the Carpenters, presumably purchased to impress the young lovelies. Why have I always detested the Carpenters? A pattern begins to emerge.

My father, I can now see, was in the vanguard of social change, an unwitting pioneer. Over the subsequent thirty-five years, the conventions of middle age have eroded, sartorial rules have been relaxed and no one is expected to wear slacks ever again. (The word has effectively disappeared from the language.) Now we can do what we like. As someone who writes for a living, I am obviously shabbier and more tramp-like than most men of my age.* I shave once a week. I own two suits, both disgraceful, and three dressing gowns.† But I can get away with it, just about, because standards have not so much slipped as plummeted to their doom. Amazingly few people seem to wear suits to work nowadays. Indeed, in my area of north London, if you see someone during the day wearing a sharp suit, he can only be one thing: an estate agent. No one wants to be mistaken for an estate agent. You would be safer from attack if you went out dressed as a Nazi stormtrooper. But the relaxing of the middle-aged dress code has created new problems. Now we can wear anything, we wear anything. Hawaiian shirts, scoutmaster shorts, faded Motörhead T-shirts, baseball caps ... no item of clothing is so debased that a middle-aged man somewhere won't be putting it on with pride, even delight, at this very moment. It matters not that most youth styles were designed with young people in mind – and thin young people at that. Because when we look in the mirror, we

---

* Eleven-year-old daughter: 'But Daddy, if you looked too neat, it just wouldn't be you.'
† A lightweight dressing gown for summer, a heavyweight one for winter and an intermediate one for the intervening months.

don't see ourselves as we have become. We see ourselves as we once were, and sometimes rather better than we once were. Women see themselves as worse than they once were, and often, even more bizarrely, worse than they actually are. And we are all, whether we like it or not, better than we shall one day be.

This gives us the universally distressing phenomenon of the T-Shirt on the Fat Man. When James Dean was alive, no one wore T-shirts other than James Dean. The young people who wore T-shirts in the 1960s grew into older people who didn't wear T-shirts. You stop wearing them because, for all their simplicity, they are garments that demand a great deal. You can be either very skinny or very buff. If, like me, you have weedy arms, you look even weedier in a T-shirt. If you have even a small pot belly, the T-shirt concentrates all attention on it, as though pointing at it with giant arrows. Even the most modest love handles start to look more like love doors.

In the late 1980s, though, came the second Summer of Love. Briefly, and crucially, clubbing fashion dictated that everyone should wear outsized T-shirts. If it didn't hang down to your knees, you were so the-day-before-yesterday. This was good for punies like me who could buy XXXL T-shirts and be of the moment, even though we looked ridiculous. But this was also good for millions of previously disenfranchised fatties, on whom these XXXL and, indeed, XXXXXXXXL T-shirts fitted rather snugly. They may have looked like giant sausages that hadn't been forked before being put under the grill, but that didn't matter. They weren't wearing these T-shirts to look good. Clothes can only do so much. They were wearing these T-shirts because they could. Quite a few of them have never stopped wearing them. Over the years, these T-shirts have become nearly as faded as their owners.*

Shorts, of course, are high-risk apparel at any age. The male knee's innate tendency to knobbliness should rule out all above-the-knee shorts, but rarely does. If they are worn with sandals and socks, law enforcement authorities should be alerted. Really short shorts, as worn by marathon runners in January and footballers in 1972, should not be seen on British streets. They can be as distressing as the sight of middle-aged holidaymakers in Speedos, which may one day be banned by international law.

The leather jacket is another item that should carry a wear-by date. Young men wear leather jackets because they think it makes them look older and cooler. Old men wear them because they think it makes them look younger and cooler. One of these groups is wrong. Leather jackets are acceptable after the age of forty only if you are a hairy biker of the old school, or if it's as old and battered as you are. Luckily, the true awfulness of the brand new leather jacket on the portly middle-aged frame has been brought home to the general populace in recent years by the presenters of *Top Gear*, in what might prove their most significant contribution to the gaiety of the nation.

Baseball caps are fine if you are on television and being

---

* You don't have to be middle-aged to look silly in a T-shirt. In Camden Town, the world capital of youth, I saw an unprepossessing youth loping down the high street, looking like Rodney in *Only Fools and Horses*, only dimmer. On his T-shirt, written in Helvetica 2048pt, were the words 'My Sex Is On Fire'. If I had been carrying a bucket of water, I would have known what to do with it.

paid by some venal corporation to flog its dubious wares, as they are designed principally to carry a logo. It is only their secondary function to make middle-aged men look a bit sad and desperate.

Skinny jeans: absolutely not. And especially not with gleaming new boxfresh trainers.

We have already discussed the catastrophe of the syrup. Just the other day, though, I was at a posh media lunch, and spotted a diminutive long-serving pop DJ whose wig had been 'allowed' to go grey. Or was it a hair transplant? It didn't look like hair. Everybody stared at it. Wouldn't it be better just to be bald?

Somehow, I get the feeling he is never asked that.

This book was twice the length until I cut out most of the stuff about wigs.

One other vital point, though. Have you noticed that in magazines and newspapers people are constantly telling you how the quality of hair transplants has improved immeasurably, to the extent that no one can now tell the difference? The piece is always illustrated by a photo of a sportsman with what looks like a fat rodent sitting on his head. If you looked closely enough you would swear you could see its teeth. The vital evidence in the case *R v Syrups* is a certain singer-songwriter of wide renown. We can be sure that he hires the best. No expense will have been spared. Each hair will have been individually plucked from the heads of hand-picked fans whose only wish is to serve the mighty tunesmith. But it still doesn't look right, does it? Every time you see it, you think, suppose he put that in on a boil wash by mistake. Would it shrink?

There are so many things that can go wrong with middle-aged hair, though. It doesn't need to fall out to make you look stupid. The safest option of all is to keep it short and do nothing with it. Let it be invisible. Alternatively, if you have always had one style, whether it was once fashionable or not, then stick with it. We respected the World's Oldest Punk for consistency if nothing else. Another man I know has had a rocker's greasy quiff for more than thirty years. Even now you wouldn't mess with him, although in truth he is the gentlest man in the world. If he cut off the rocker's greasy quiff, something in all of us would die. I hope he still has it when he is eighty-five and walking on sticks, and I hope I am there to witness it.

Growing it to any sort of length, though, is no longer advisable. Being lazy, slobbish and mean, I tend to hold out for as long as I can before getting a haircut. For a while I get away with it. Slightly longer than average can be rakish and bohemian. But slightly longer than that, and I start looking like John Prescott. The point is that, with each year that passes, the length to which you can safely grow your hair without looking awful gets shorter and shorter. Your margin of error contracts to nothing.

Unless, that is, you just keep on growing it. I know three men who have grown their hair properly long in their forties. Two were seriously bald. The other was visibly thinning. Others mocked them, and I might have done too on occasion, but on the quiet I admired their bravery, the 'fuck you' side of the equation. Wearers of a baldy ponytail do not attempt to conceal or deny their baldness. In fact they draw attention to it, as though to say, it may look awful but I don't care. A wig only shows that you care too much.

I should say here that I myself have ponytail previous. Born in 1960, I was too young to grow my hair long in the late 1960s or early 1970s. My school actually tolerated shoulder-length hair until the term I arrived there, at which point it was banned. Then punk happened. In the late 1970s, after I had left school, you could no more grow your hair long than wear ten-inch bell-bottoms or admit to loving *The Yes Album*. I kept my hair short through the 1980s, but in 1988 I went freelance, and saw my chance. I had always wanted to grow my hair long. I would be thirty soon. As Primo Levi had said about something else marginally more significant, if not now, when?

So I did, and it took a long time, because my hair is very fine and grows dreadfully slowly, and within just two or three years it was about shoulder-length. It never looked that good, and at times it looked dreadful. But I loved it, and I'm glad I did it. My bald friends loathed it more than anyone, for some reason. If it had grown thicker and quicker, I would have kept it for ever, but when I was thirty-three and a half, with a new girlfriend who felt strongly about these things, I gave in and had it cut off. It had served its purpose.

What I discovered when I cut it off was how much younger I looked. How unfair that such a visible symbol of youth as long hair actually ages you. The shirt-doffing pop star and insurance salesman Iggy Pop can only be in his early seventies now, but his long hair makes him look at least ninety. This is the ageing process summed up. The harder you try to look young, the older you actually look.

This particularly applies if you wish to remove some of the grey from your hair. In the 1970s a product named Grecian 2000 was exhaustively advertised on television, with obviously American commercials clumsily dubbed into British English. Grecian 2000 didn't dye your hair, it replenished and restored its real colour (or possibly 'color'). In the ads, a prematurely grizzled and exhausted knitwear model was transformed, with the aid of Grecian 2000, into a younger and more sexually virile version of himself, striding off with his new hair to run wild with all the female knitwear models. We laughed because we would never go grey ourselves and we certainly wouldn't put that foul slop on our hair if we did. Good grief, next thing you know, men would be using moisturiser.

But here we all are, not so prematurely grizzled and exhausted, and worryingly tempted by the Grecian 2000 bottle, or maybe its fiercest competitor, Just For Men. Before we buy it, as full of shame as when we first bought condoms, we should consider the consequences. Can Paul McCartney's hair really be that colour? Is Bryan Ferry's still jet black? Is Ron Wood's? Until a few years ago Tom Jones's hair was as black as crude oil on a dark night in an unlit street when you're wearing sunglasses. Strangely enough, so was his beard, which he must have been touching up daily with felt pen. Then one day he saw sense, went white and looked at least a decade younger. It's strange, because women can dye their hair and get away with it for ever. Men cannot. I think the beard is the problem. If your hair is full and dark and lustrous, and your beard is as white as Santa's, it looks a little odd. And if you start dyeing your beard, we move out of odd and into ridiculous.

We can understand the vanity. We can also understand the need to stay young in a culture that no longer defers to the wisdom of age. Where I think we fall down, as so often, is in our attention to detail. I know a man who dyes his perfectly acceptable grey hair a weird shade of Dale Winton orange every few months. As it grows out he doesn't bother to touch up the roots, and eventually he cuts it all off and goes back to being grey again. God knows why he does it. Maybe he bought the bottle and wants to get value for his money. Maybe it's for a bet. But if you are going to look daft, why not do it permanently? Why look daft in shifts?

The strangest twist on this theme is the trend for young people, particularly famous young women, to dye their hair grey. We are irritated, anyway, by young people dyeing their hair *when they don't have to*. But going grey-out-of-a-bottle is a personal statement so eccentric we feel we have to know what it means. Is it the busting of the final taboo? Or are they trying to tell us something: that student loans and graduate unemployment have turned them white overnight? I would like to think that it's simple delight in being young. They can do anything, even this. It's nothing personal. Don't take it as such. And we will try not to. But to see a 20-year-old girl with dyed grey hair sitting next to a 55-year-old woman with hair the colour of a newly painted pillar box, as I did on the bus the other day, takes a little getting used to.

You are wearing the skinny jeans, the boxfresh trainers and the natty leather jacket, your shirt is hanging out and you have dyed your hair a shade rarely encountered in nature. Where do you go now? To the tattoo parlour, surely.

Marry in haste, they say, repent at leisure. Get a tattoo when you're drunk and spend the rest of your life wondering why. My own feelings about tattoos probably owe something to my age, my upbringing and my morbid fear of needles. But one of the many benefits of middle age is that, if you haven't got yourself a tattoo by now, you are unlikely to get one unless you really, *really* want one. We acknowledge no peer pressure, and we have nothing to prove to anyone. And we know, as sure as we know anything, that if we entrusted the decoration of the only skin we will ever have to a fat, hairy bloke in the tattoo parlour on the high street, he would screw it up. If tattooists could spell, they would be doing something else for a living: forging banknotes, maybe, or subbing this copy. If tattooists could draw, they would be rich. If tattooists had taste or judgement, they wouldn't have all those godawful tattoos over their own bodies. But your tattooist has neither taste nor judgement. He has a perspiration problem, a huge needle and a cheese sandwich he is halfway through. Out, out of the door, as fast as you can go.

How have tattoos become such big business? How and why? If you had wanted a tattoo thirty years ago, the first challenge would have been to find someone who could give you one. Now there are as many tattooists on the high street as Starbucks. Soon there will be degree courses in it. One curious generational shift is that it's now the weediest, specciest boys who seem to acquire the largest, most spectacular tattoos. Maybe, in the absence of genuine physical challenge, this is the only way the weedy and speccy have of showing how hard they are (or aren't). But I suppose that if you hate your body that much, having a rotten drawing of an eagle installed on it is hardly going to make things any worse.*

Beyond that there are only piercings. Again, age protects us from having to understand this, although I imagine it's quite useful to know when there are very large magnets in the neighbourhood. A friend of a friend is a *pierceuse*, and she says that some of her keenest customers are policemen. They are particularly keen on genital piercings, apparently. They jangle when they walk. One or two of them you can hear from streets away. It's not *Dixon of Dock Green*, but then it probably never was.

* The Australian musician and writer Robert Forster, once of the Go-Betweens, has formulated Ten Rules of Rock 'n' Roll, one of which states that the band with the most tattoos has the worst songs. As he told *The Word* magazine, 'Anybody who puts that much effort into their appearance must be diverting the effort from somewhere else.'

12

FACELIFT

'To me, Botox is no more unusual than toothpaste.'

Simon Cowell

'At fifty, everyone has the face he deserves,' wrote George Orwell, who wouldn't live past forty-six. 'It used to be said that by a certain age a man had the face that he deserved,' wrote Martin Amis years later. 'Nowadays, he has the face he can afford.' 'You're never too old to become younger,' said Mae West. But I prefer Rita Rudner's line: 'I don't plan to grow old gracefully. I plan to have facelifts until my ears meet.'

You are pulling a face, I can tell. (Or, if you have had a facelift, you just think you are pulling a face.) But British men, according to daily reports in the newspapers, are embracing plastic surgery with new zeal. Man–boob reductions are the big one, so to speak, but penis extensions, tummy tucks and arseosuctions (I have just thought of that one) are increasingly popular, and cost no more than you might spend on a flash new car, or a divorce. I have yet to meet anyone who will admit to undergoing any of these procedures. But who would admit to a penis extension? All I can say is, don't make the same mistake I have just made, and read all about this on the internet. You won't sleep for weeks.

Ten years ago, in a book like this, a chapter like this would not have existed. But everything moves faster than we can bear, and in ten years' time, who can imagine what will be going on? While interviewing for this book, I was amazed how many of my male friends and acquaintances admitted that they used moisturiser. 'It's really good!' said one. 'It really makes a difference!' It's astonishing what grisly secrets will fall out of men's mouths when you buy them a beer and switch on a microphone. Each had been put on to the moisturising habit by a woman of their acquaintance, although rarely, for some reason, the woman they were living with. (At which point they usually clammed up.) I mentioned all this to a non-moisturising friend.

'You'll never guess who uses moisturiser,' I said. He was agog. 'Only Szygszplodz.' (Names have been changed to protect the guilty.)

'You're kidding me.'

'You could never tell, could you?'

'No, you couldn't.'

We thought for a moment.

'Which shows there's no point to it at all.'

'None whatsoever.'

It might be fun to get together a dozen or so men in

their forties and fifties, and ask a disinterested observer to determine which of them use moisturiser and which fester in their own filth for days on end. My guess is that you wouldn't be able to. Whatever you might slap on your face, you are still going to look bloody awful. Looking as dreadful as we do is our reward for a life well lived. But if it doesn't make you look better, what is the point? The point is that it makes you feel better – and very slightly poorer, but you don't mind that. There are more harmful ways of deluding yourself, I suppose.

One of them is plastic surgery. It doesn't make anyone look better, so what is the point? The point is that it makes them feel better – and considerably poorer, but they don't mind that.

Women are much further down this road. About seven or eight years ago, I realised with alarm that someone I knew marginally, the friend of a friend of a friend, about the same age as me, had had some 'work' done. She is an actress, which makes it almost compulsory, but even so. Her features, always strong, now seemed slightly less defined. She didn't look any younger; she just looked different. Less like herself, you might say. For the first time I could understand those tribesmen from the Amazon basin who believe that when they are photographed, a chunk of their soul is taken from them. A facelift, I fear, does the same thing. And no one ever has the one facelift. In a few years' time the saggy jowls are back, so you go in and have them hoicked up again, and another fragment of your ineffable youness is lost.

More recently, a friend of a friend, whom I know slightly better, has had something done. It might be Botox, or a chemical face peel, or something equally unhinged. Whenever I bump into her I fear I will be afflicted by a condition you might call Facelift Tourette's. Don't mention it. Say as little as possible. Try not to even think of the word.

'How are you doing? You look great. And how's facelift . . . I'm sorry, work?'

Or: 'Nice weather we're having, don't you think? It's such a relief to see the facelift shining after all this time.'

Or: 'How did you get here? I thought of taking the bus but in the end I came by facelift.'

By the end of the conversation, I imagine, I would be unable to say any word other than 'facelift', over and over again.

I worry I am becoming obsessed with this. I see facelifts everywhere. I see a famous married couple on TV. She has clearly had one, he has clearly had one. You look at the face of your loved one in the morning and it's not the person you married, but a smoothed-over, slightly unfocused simulacrum. Did they get a deal? His and hers facelifts? Buy one, lift one free?

In London we see them everywhere. Unusually among licensed forms of self-mutilation, facelifts are an indication of wealth and status. It costs money to have Dr Phibes inject deadly toxins into your forehead and the minced pancreases of haddock and bream into your lips. For the moment, to have cosmetic surgery is to distinguish you from the common herd, but the result is to make you look like everyone else who has had cosmetic surgery. And I don't think my Tourette's is unique: people do see the facelift where once they saw the face.

All this stuff – the misspelled tattoos of international sportsmen, the genital piercings of senior law enforcement officers, the nearly recognisable new faces of people you once knew – seem to say something terrible about life as it is now lived. If we feel so impelled to amend ourselves in these violent ways, it suggests that we never much liked what we were. That's hardly surprising: the underlying message of most advertising and the entire fashion industry is that we are not much cop, and really need to shape up. To be alive in the early twenty-first century is to be made to feel that you are not quite good enough. What's so sad is that by the time middle age creeps along, you would hope that you finally feel comfortable in your own skin. I'm not sure anyone could feel truly comfortable in something so stretched.

As we shall discuss more fully in the next chapter, one of the most tangible symptoms of middle age is the sensation that you are being cast adrift from mainstream culture, that much of film, television, music, art and literature simply isn't for you any more. Tattoos and multiple piercings, which few of us are tempted by, are a more cheering sign that we are no longer young. But facelifts demonstrate that, for some of us, the vulnerability of youth never recedes. I would like to think that, sometime in the future, it will gradually dawn on us all that to undergo unnecessary cosmetic surgery is to broadcast your unhappiness to the world, that it is a cry for help, and a long, keening wail at that. In 2007 the novelist Olivia Goldsmith, who wrote *The First Wives' Club*, fell into a coma and died in New York after undergoing what one paper euphemistically called 'elective facial surgery'. What a grim and pointless way to go. Worse, it is a death that makes your whole life look ridiculous. It's like those men who die in hotel rooms in weird auto-erotic asphyxiation incidents, with satsumas in their mouths and chair legs up their bottoms. Everything they achieved in their lives is deleted by this single absurd act, which speaks to the rest of us only of unfathomable misery. And it does ineradicable harm to the satsuma industry. Many of us prefer clementines nowadays, and who can blame us?

13

CULTURE

'The average British man spends eleven years watching TV and 10,500 hours in the pub over a lifetime.'

Reported in the *Guardian*, March 2011

It is a Sunday night, and I am in the Famous Royal Oak
with my friend C, discussing Jeremy Clarkson. People in
public life cannot imagine how much they are talked about
and found wanting. C says he has an irrational dislike of
anyone called Jeremy, which is an acceptable opinion after
2.7 pints. I say I have an irrational dislike of anyone called
Clarkson. But we can both remember when his
programme, *Top Gear*, was quite good, when it was about
cars, and not about the giant wounded egos of its
narcissistic presenters. We rant a little. We buy another
round, and we rant some more. The barmaid listens. She
is twenty-four.

'But don't you realise?' she says. 'It's not for you.'

What?

'*Top Gear*. It's not aimed at you.'

It used to be.

'Yeah . . . ' she starts, and raises her eyebrows. She doesn't need to say any more. It used to be. It isn't any more. Get over it.

We are silenced. She is not just right, she is stiletto-through-the-ribs right. Six months later I remind C of this conversation and he remembers every word.

Like everything else (except us), popular culture has changed beyond all recognition. For one thing, it's more popular than ever. There's far more of it, more than any one person could ever assimilate. Indeed, there's something out there to satisfy every mood, every budget, every taste, every whim. Some of it demands that you get dressed, put your shoes on and leave the house if you wish to consume it, but an astonishing amount is now accessible without any need for physical movement. If, for health reasons, or for the peace of mind of your loved ones, you had been ordered not to leave your sofa for the next twenty years, you need never be bored for a moment.

A lot of it, though, isn't for us. It never was for us, it never could be, and that's fine. A restaurant menu with one dish I want to eat is a good menu, which makes me happy. A menu on which I would like to eat everything is, in theory, a better menu, but in practice it makes me anxious. I become terrified of choosing the wrong thing. I know that the person I am with will have something nicer. Can we swap? No, sod off. The meal is almost ruined before it has begun.

So we pick and choose, pick and choose. When we were young, and first pushing our trolley through the great cultural supermarket, we tried many things. Several people I knew went clubbing and stayed up all night. Thanks, but no thanks. Foolish and contrary to the last, I had a go at opera. I can't quite believe it now, but I queued for hours outside the Royal Opera House for cheapo tickets with friends who genuinely liked opera. These days I would rather stick my head down the toilet. But it was all in a spirit of adventure and open-mindedness I can barely remember. Now that we know our tastes, we don't waste time on things we won't like. And yet we know that we are who we are because of the mistakes we made when we were young. Was I in that opera queue because of a girl? It's possible.

Our youthful sense of adventure did what it needed to, which was bring us here, where we are now. We have our tastes, and we indulge as many as we can afford. But how much of this stuff is for us? And if less and less of it is, does it matter?

Television

Ah, the telly. Wasn't it great? Four channels, and before that, just three. Once there were just two. And before we were born there was only one! Halcyon days indeed. Once there were no channels at all.

We can find many splendid and entertaining ways of boring the young, but few are more effective than droning on about the 'golden age' of British television. I blame our grandparents. Mine used to ramble on incessantly about how wonderful life was before television, when they 'made their own entertainment'. Conversation thrived and everyone built scale models of stately homes out of matches to while away the empty hours. My grandmother usually told me this in the commercial break halfway through *Crossroads*. She never missed *Crossroads*. Or anything else. I have never met anyone who smoked more cigarettes in a day or watched more television. When she got up to make yet another cup of tea, you had forgotten she could walk.

She reached seventy-five, my grandmother, but not eighty. Everyone who can remember life before television is now dead, or watching a rerun of *Poirot* on ITV3. I am too young to remember life before BBC2. You would have to be over thirty-five to remember life before Channel 4. Whereas I can remember its first day and how excited we all were. I watched my first ever episode of *Countdown*. What innovation. What a bold leap into the unknown.

We all watched too much television, and there was never anything on. So low were our expectations that the act of watching it was enough. Like the Royle Family (a throwback if ever there was one) we saw the television as the focal point of family life. There wasn't anything else to do and the television was on anyway, so you might as well watch it. And when anything half decent appeared, we pounced on it and gobbled it up. The great landmark series of the 1970s were watched by *everybody*. When they were repeated nine months later we watched them all over again. Then we talked about them the next day, and for several days after that. Exciting times.

(I explain all this to my children. They sit open-mouthed. It's like telling them we lived in caves and used flints to make fire.)

The absurd irony of all this was that there was almost nothing specifically for us, as young people, to watch. Television in the 1970s was skewed to the tastes of the middle-aged and the old. Serious documentaries, plays of the month and Wagner on BBC2 for the middle classes; *The Generation Game* and *The Black and White Minstrel Show* for the workers. 'You've got *Blue Peter*,' our parents would say. ('But mother, I'm thirty-two.') If there remains a lingering affection among my contemporaries for *Doctor Who*, Brian Cant and the works of Oliver Postgate, it's because that's all there was. Television infantilised us, but we didn't mind. When is *The Two Ronnies* on? Ten minutes. Quick, eat up.

Leap forward a quarter of a century. We are in our middle years and our tastes have advanced accordingly. We are finally ready for the thought-provoking documentaries and dramas, the live feeds from Bayreuth. We switch on our new, hyper-thin, flat-screen TVs, that somehow take up both more and less room than the old cathode-ray jobbies. And what do we find? Complete bollocks, on all 4657 channels. Reality shows full of cretins. Bloody *Casualty*, still going after half a millennium. Celebrities dancing. Slack-jawed fools singing ineptly on live TV. Chat chat chat. Plug plug plug. *Doctor Who*, with a twelve-year-old in the title role. Endless programmes about celebrities we don't recognise and unusually fat people who only eat lard. And everywhere, on all channels, these charmless tiny Geordie men, as excitable as puppies, as diverting as ingrowing toenails. Apparently Ant always stands on the left, Dec on the right.

Still, what's this on BBC2? A repeat of *The Two Ronnies*? In ten minutes? Quick, eat up.

Music

There's no getting away from it. The best pop music of all – and I speak with total subjectivity, as always on this subject – is the music you hear in your formative years, when music first grabs you by the goolies and won't let you go. I was a late starter: I was seventeen when I bought my first album. Therefore it is the music made between 1977 and 1982 that has the most lasting resonance for me. Music of consequence was made before these years, I am willing to concede. Some exceptional tunes appeared afterwards, too. But of my dozen or so favourite albums, seven or eight were released in this six-year period. I listen to them still. Wait until everyone is out of the house, turn up the volume, and weep for your vanished youth.

My friend C, allergic to people called Jeremy, is eleven years older than me. For him music lost its flavour in about 1973. Funny, that. How many times, I ask, have you listened to Pink Floyd's *Meddle*? His eyes go misty. It seems cruel to press the point further. He is replaying 'Echoes' in his mind, all 23 minutes and 31 seconds of it.

Unfortunately, at seventeen or eighteen we are at our most dogmatic and our least tolerant of other people's opinions. (At least until we reach our fifties.) If our musical taste is formed at around this time, so is our absolute conviction that we are right. As my tastes were (and remain) resolutely unfashionable, I chose to keep my mouth shut. I didn't pretend to believe that The Clash's first album was the best album ever made (or, in the language of the time, the 'most important'), but I didn't actively deny it either. The ferocity of teenage musical tastes is such that whole, coherent lifestyles are created around them, tribal identifications we may later come to regret, or not. A woman friend of mine is now a senior broadcasting executive, respected by colleagues and feared by subordinates. But she and I and her friends know she was once a goth, and anyone with an eye for it can see that, at some level, she still is, and always will be.

Music leaves many of us in our twenties, and the echoes of teenage passion are all we are left with. C listens to some records made after the mid-1970s, but they are Ryvita to him after the five-course *cordon bleu* meal of his musical youth. T, who is the same age as me, discovered classical music in his late teens and never looked back, but put on any of about a dozen glam-rock singles from 1972 to 1974 at a party and his eyes start glittering madly. This is a feature of ancient friendships, that you know where the musical bodies are buried. Which friend of mine would be drawn out to the dance floor by almost any track from Madness's first album, which he used to own on a slightly speeded-up cassette? I'm not telling you.

(This reminds me of those films in which long-dormant Russian sleeper agents are instantaneously transformed into brutal killers when they hear a certain codeword. Or, in this case, 'Echo Beach' by Martha and the Muffins.)

For a minority of us, pop music never loosens its grip.

We go on buying records and CDs, and downloading tracks legally or illegally, and listening to streaming services on the internet and strange radio stations from God knows where, all in the hope of hearing the next killer song that will change our lives. I am one of these people, and I know several others. The music we already have is never enough. Many years ago O'R announced that he had a hundred albums and really saw no need for any more. Every time he bought a new one, he said, he would get rid of an old one. I reminded him of this the other day, in the room he has set aside for the vinyl he never plays. (The CDs are split between two other rooms.) He denied ever saying such a thing.

Older music fans, though, are keeping the music industry going. We are the fools who still hand out money for CDs, because we like having the artefact in our hand. We like sleeve notes and cover artwork. Some of us really like hi-fi sound and the joyous glow of warmth you can only get from very large speakers. I myself have an expensive record player which is only out of action because it now costs £150 to replace the bloody cartridge, and I never feel I can justify the expenditure. The records sit in boxes in the loft, exerting such pressure on the joists we expect them to plunge through the ceiling of the room below any day now.

We keep live music going too. Nobody else can afford to pay the ticket prices, which is why the 'heritage' (i.e. old) acts are permanently out on the road, charging a fortune to all the old sads who bought their records back in the day. Younger acts have younger fans, who have less money. But then older, groovier fans discover the younger acts, who can then put up their ticket prices and buy more expensive cars, drugs, etc. We effectively subvert the young to our own dastardly middle-aged ends. They deserve no less.*

Ringtones

The young regard mobile phones as their own. But who were the first people to get ringtones that sounded like old-fashioned phones ringing? Now everyone does it. We are the trailblazers yet again.

Films

Three quid for a bag of Maltesers and another three quid for a small bottle of water? You are having a considerable laugh.

People who work in cinemas are all young and miserable. Their spirits have been sapped by low wages, bad films starring Bruce Willis and enraged middle-aged filmgoers who feel ripped off and abused by the whole experience. In fact these aggrieved customers and the people serving them have something in common: they all wish they were at home, watching a DVD.

Where, when and how did films go wrong? The simple answer is, a long time ago in a galaxy far, far away. In the

---

* We are even beginning to hear songs written from a middle-aged perspective. Examples from my own record collection include Fleetwood Mac's 'What's the World Coming To' (2003) and Mark Knopfler's 'You Don't Know You're Born' (2002).

1980s Hollywood decided that only the young go and see films. Since then mainstream cinema has been aimed squarely at a teenage audience. Older filmgoers have been ignored. As a result, many of us have stopped going to the cinema altogether, unless it is to take our children to the new *Harry Potter*. And that's not something anyone does for fun. At the end of the new *Harry Potter*, cinema doors are flung open and hundreds of overstimulated children roar out, mainlining sugar and strung out on popcorn. Behind them, a small pack of shuffling, eye-blasted parents, wracked with phlegmy coughs and squinting at the light. They have aged five years in three hours and need a brandy quick. Cinema never used to be like this.

For one thing it's much louder. Is it my imagination or are sound systems in cinemas roughly four hundred times more powerful than they were twenty years ago? Don't get me wrong: I love the clarity of the new digital images, the comfortable new chairs (especially the ones that rock back a bit), the drinks holders, and the wider availability of Aero balls, a family pack of which nearly sees me through the trailers. Surround sound too is a great idea in theory: you can usually hear the sound of the police siren (from behind your right ear) before any of the characters in the film do. But the volume! It's not just Spinal Tap whose amplifiers go up to eleven. Half the time I feel like the man in the old Maxell ad. And the hilarious irony of it all is that, because it's so loud, you can't actually hear anything. Well, you can hear the music and the explosions, the cars crashing and the buildings falling down. Only the dialogue escapes you. You know something is going on – you can see that with your eyes – but what that something is remains tantalisingly out of reach. And you begin to understand why the genuinely old do what they do in cinemas, which is lean over to the next person and say, in a ridiculously loud voice, things like 'What's that he said?' and 'I tell you, it's definitely a wig.'

News

As in film, so in life. You know something is going on, but what that something is remains tantalisingly out of reach. So you read all the newspapers. You listen to the radio. You scour websites. You keep CNN or Sky News or BBC News 24 (or Bloomberg or Sky Sports News) permanently on in the background, a newsgathering white noise. You don't want to miss anything. You try not to ask yourself why.

Again, this is not something young people do. They are all on Facebook, marooned on 498 friends and wondering how to get to 500. News addiction only creeps up on people in middle age. Men are the worst afflicted, but I know a few female news addicts too. Every addiction fills a void of some sort, and it might be that news addiction fills a knowledge void. We don't know enough. We need to know more. Maybe we are frightened of being found out in our ignorance; or we hope that knowing more will make us feel safer. And let's not forget the adrenalin rush of finding things out before everyone else. This is why people become news journalists. They think it will be exciting. They think they will be privy to all the secrets that newspapers cannot print. Unfortunately, most of the middle-aged news journalists I have met are drunk and miserable. They know there are few if any such secrets, which is why they and their rivals make things up. With CNN and Sky News and BBC News 24 permanently on in the background, so they don't miss anything.

If this all sounds a bit rueful, it is because I have been there myself, in a small way. I used to take and read two or three newspapers each day, and I would never miss the six o'clock or ten o'clock news on TV. To be connected in this way was to be serious and responsible, the very least you would expect of a grown-up person and not a bit sad at all. This was before the news channels, high-speed broadband and mobile phones with a million times more computer power than HAL 9000. Technology may not have begun news addiction, but it has enabled and fuelled it. For the first time in news history, our need to know has been matched by our ability to find out. The rest of humanity thinks of it as 'information overload', but to the news addict it's as good as you'll get until you can have access to news channels wired directly into your brain. Then you will never need to speak to a real human being again.

For isn't news addiction just another facet of the hermit tendency? There is no question that man's enthusiasm for facts becomes more pronounced in middle age. I have lost count of the number of men I know who say they no longer read fiction, can't be bothered with it, not interested in stories any more. Instead they read history or biography or true crime or even books like this (for if this was a novel, a made-up story about men in middle age, men in middle age would not read it). Our interest in information grows as our interest in other people recedes. In the end, it is so much easier and more relaxing to look at a screen than at someone's face.

But news is horrible. It has always been bad, it is getting worse, and there is nothing we can do about it. News junkies feel powerful in that they know what is going on, but this power is an illusion. In truth we are mere consumers of news. We have not the smallest power to affect anything.

I myself have cut down to one newspaper a day. I try and minimise the amount of time I spend (i.e. waste) randomly surfing the web, and I never watch news on TV any more if I can help it. Is it too unserious and irresponsible to aspire to a life completely without news, in which we haven't the faintest idea what is going on? Already, I find, things are happening in the world that I simply have no opinion on. It's not that I don't care about the natural disaster here, or the air attacks there. I do, a bit. But I'm not sure I cared any more strongly when I thought I knew exactly what was going on. I can only say that my head feels less cluttered, less full of horror, than it has done for years. Ignorance may not be bliss, exactly, but it has its consolations.

Stuff

Some of us need more than our heads decluttered. One of many programmes I no longer watch on the flat-screen television I never switch on is the one in which the mouthy old trout goes into some poor fool's house and tells him he has to throw out all his stuff, for only then will he know inner peace. This pile to the charity shop. This pile to eBay. (This pile to Sotheby's. Ah, if only.) And everyone watching this programme, you can bet your last 50p, will be sitting in a house or flat no less filled to bursting with assiduously acquired tat they can't bear to get rid of. Male or female, rich or poor, we all own too much, and we keep going to the shops to buy more. It's insane, and we seem powerless to do anything about it.

But look at the magazines that sell us this facile and meaningless 'lifestyle', magazines that are full of ads for things we don't need, and full of articles that are little more than ads for things we don't need. Somewhere, tucked away in the recesses of these publications, there is always a section on 'design'. And this is usually a feature, with numerous photographs, about some bastard's tastefully minimalist home. You turn the pages, sweating with fury. The bastard talks about 'clean lines'. The house is invariably 'light' and 'airy'. There is no mess or dirt: even the children, if any, appear to have been scrubbed down by industrial cleaners. We may not have many belongings, is the message, but every item counts. Books kept to a minimum. No CDs: all our music is on the computer hard disk, backed up by NASA. Original Eames chair. Sofa has self-plumping cushions. You see that cuckoo clock? Cost me 50p in a car boot sale. Turns out it's an original by Le Mouchoir, the Swiss surrealist. Worth up to £400,000 at auction. But we'd never get rid of it. Never.

Would the rest of us like to have our flats and houses examined in this way? I haven't had the call, but I shall be ready when it comes. Here is our shoe rack, newly purchased from a prominent Swedish retailer; I believe it is from their award-winning 'Arsöl' range. Over here, the sofa, lightly torn by the cat, and with one leg replaced by a pile of unreadable showbusiness autobiographies.* And over here, the rest of the books. The ones we both like are on these shelves. The ones she likes but I don't, over here. The ones I like but she doesn't, upstairs in the loft. DVDs of useless action movies? Just behind the out-of-date telephone directories. The metal pigeon with one leg that seems to have melted? A family heirloom. We tried to sell it for 50p at a car boot sale, but no one would have it.

And that's after we have cleared up.

Every couple of weeks I hump a groaning plastic bag of rubbish to one of several charity shops near my flat. Now that all the second-hand bookshops have gone, along with all the other specialist retailers we liked but never used, we can hand over the unwanted Christmas presents we never got round to changing to a mind-boggling variety of aggressively do-gooding charities. I see the clean lines and airy, light space of my local Oxfam shop and – this may be totally unfair – I imagine some flash-suited shit of a chief executive pocketing a six-figure sum and chuckling at people's gullibility. But it's our own fault. We shouldn't have bought all this stuff in the first place.

The polite name for it is 'collecting'. I myself have a collection of *Wisden Cricketers' Almanacks* going back thirty-five years. They are almost valueless and I rarely open any of them. But they look so wonderful and yellow, there on the shelf in an unbroken line, with none missing. If one did go missing, I would probably have to replace it. Why did I write 'probably' in that sentence? I don't fool myself, and I certainly don't fool you.

---

* Including Westlife's and Eric Clapton's.

My son, nine years old, has collected Go-Gos (tiny plastic toys with hideous physiognomies), copies of the *Beano* (still scattered around his room) and now Match Attax football trading cards. I know in my heart that these latter are a colossal waste of money, and his mother tries not to say this out loud, but the fact remains that in 1969/70, I was a fanatical collector of The Wonderful World of Soccer Stars. I bought what seemed like several hundred thousand of these over the season, and at least ten thousand of them were Bobby Stokes of Southampton. They said there were equal numbers of every player in circulation, but we didn't believe them. Everyone I knew had at least a dozen unswappable Bobby Stokeses. Whereas Kenny Hibbitt of Wolves was notoriously rare. I imagined the chief executive of The Wonderful World of Soccer Stars Ltd lighting his cigars with Hibbitts and chuckling at our stupidity. Paranoia starts young. The following year there were no Bobby Stokeses at all, and Kenny Hibbitts were everywhere. And Alan Birchenall had the same photo but a new strip painted over it, as he had moved clubs in the close season. We were not fooled.

The journalist and art historian Mark Hudson, who lives near me and probably takes his stuff to the same charity shops, has identified the four ages of collecting. The first, childhood and early adolescence, is Wanting It All. 'Getting the stuff, treasuring it, possibly even learning from it, are all part of establishing yourself as an individual.' The second age, late adolescence and early adulthood, is Getting Rid Of It All. 'As you head out into the wider world, experiences become more important than objects.' Oh yes, I remember it well. Boxes of junk were binned in a brutal cultural purge, although at least I kept my Soccer Stars albums, and my sixty-odd Peanuts paperbacks. The third age, early middle age, is Buying It All Back Again. Oh dear. He is not wrong. 'The thought that you cheerfully allowed your *Beano* comics/World Cup coins/original Zeppelin vinyl to be given to jumble sales makes you wake in cold sweats.' Apparently if you are a real collector, you will have two original vinyl copies for every significant LP of your youth. One is to play, one is to keep unplayed. Just the thought of this makes my sinuses throb.

Soon comes the fourth age, late middle age and old age, which Mark calls Getting Shot Of It All (Again). I am yet to pass into my zen phase, when the young and callow will seek me out for my worldly wisdom, and I shall address them as 'grasshopper'. But I can already see the sense in this. Do I truly need all these books? 'You feel a renewed yearning for existential freedom,' says Mark, 'to see the rest of the world while there's still time, [to] afford you the opportunity to explore your own creativity rather than acquiring bits of someone else's.' In other words, we shall soon reach an age when we appreciate the true purpose of *Antiques Roadshow*. Those greedy oldsters don't want to keep that beautiful piece of Meissen porcelain. They want to sell it for as much as possible and splurge the cash away on drink, sex and holidays. Anything to prevent the children inheriting it. There might not be much time. Spend it while you can!

14

MONEY

'A large income is the best recipe for happiness I ever heard of. It certainly may secure all the myrtle and turkey part of it.'

Jane Austen, *Mansfield Park* (1814)

We have very clearly been skirting around this subject for a while. I would like to think that this has been extreme delicacy on my part, and not blind terror. For money, as they now say, is the elephant in the room. It was the elephant in the room before rooms had elephants. In my flat it's the elephant in every room. It was never a particularly large flat, but with all these pachyderms roaming about, it feels like a matchbox. I just looked in the matchbox, and there was a tiny little elephant in there too.

I knew one or two people at university who Had Money. No one made a fuss about it, and it may just have been coincidence that those with money often had nicer rooms than those of us who didn't. When we left, most of the monied went off in search of more, and some of the unmonied decided it was time to play catch-up. I myself floundered like a dying fish. It didn't seem to matter. There would be time later on to make some money, once I had worked out how to do it. It couldn't be that difficult, could it?

Whoooosh! Twenty-five years go by, and it has long since become clear that some people can make money and others simply cannot. Having it in the first place was clearly an advantage, but many others have acquired it with a single-mindedness I continue to marvel at. They figured out early that it was the only sensible thing to do. I am not going to argue with that, although I do wish that someone had tipped me the wink. But some of us were never going to pile up the cash, however hard we tried. There's no point complaining about it, although we do. We complain that society only rewards those who make money, but as those rewards *are* money, we are wasting our breath. Money is the only measurement left. We may not be judged on how much cash we have piled up when we reach St Peter's pearly gates – if we reach them, if they exist – but before that point, we seem to be judged on little else.

Teachers, for instance. If you teach for a living, an amazing number of supposedly intelligent people will assume it's because you can't do anything more lucrative. Or that you can afford to do it because you have other sources of cash to hand. The idea that you might actively prefer to do something so inadequately remunerated is laughable. Thus, inexorably, the status of teachers has declined, from pillars of the community to self-deluding pillocks who haven't spotted that all notions of 'public service' are defunct. Well-off parents don't see them as equals any more. Teachers are just another service industry: house cleaners with a degree. You no longer entrust the education of your children to teachers, you outsource it. There's an arrogance here I suspect I have become too sensitive to, seeing it sometimes when it isn't there. But with money the only measurement, it's no surprise that many of the monied have come to think rather well of themselves. We are not quite as degraded in this respect as our friends the Americans, many of whom believe that enormous wealth and moral superiority are essentially indistinguishable. But we might be soon.

I should calm down. The die is cast, after all. Money is not just one of the great imponderables, it's also one of the great uncontrollables. Anyone who says they have a handle on their money is probably lying. Give a middle-aged man a drink and he will tell you how worried he is about money. While doing the groundwork for this book, I was amazed to discover that this even applies to people who are appreciably richer than me. One, who has literally millions salted away, worries that it won't be enough, and everything is going to collapse, and they'll be after him. He lies in bed at night fretting about cash. So do I. So does everyone. Whether or not you have any doesn't seem to be relevant.

On the face of it, then, we are all in the same boat, worrying about money all the time. Unfortunately some people are in first class and the rest of us are in steerage, singing Irish songs and waiting for the iceberg to hit. At a fiftieth birthday party not so long ago, I was hanging out with a couple of writer friends, both of them on the impoverished side of skint. At half past ten, N stood up and said, 'Everyone's too rich here. I'm going home.' Q went with her, but I thought I would hang around a little longer. I went to the bathroom, splashed some water on my face, steeled myself (as you have to sometimes), strode out, picked up my glass, and headed for a little knot of fiftysomethings, one of whom I knew slightly. I could hear her talking as I approached.

'And then we bought the house near Toulouse . . . '

It wasn't what I needed to hear. I turned on my heel, put the glass down on the nearest occasional table and was out of the house in twelve seconds flat.

We all worry about money, but some people have more to worry about. The great divide is between those who are waving and those who are drowning. An enormous wedge of experience is thrust between these two groups. Of course, some people may be drowning who appear to be waving, for bourgeois pride demands that we admit no weakness and put our best foot forward at all times. Maybe after they bought the house near Toulouse, their business went belly up, their children were kidnapped by aliens and the new house was overrun by garlic-munching rats with a taste for human flesh. I doubt it somehow. Even if any of this did happen, it would be turned into a jolly little anecdote about the recalcitrance of French bureaucracy and the impossibility of finding Weetabix in the local shops. But it's no coincidence that I spent most of that party loitering in the margins with N and Q, who are both hanging on for dear life in ways I can identify with. If anyone told us about the house they had bought near Toulouse, our first and only thought would be: can we go and stay there for free, please?

When you start making friends, as a child and as a teenager, you form bonds with people on the basis of mutual interests, shared experiences, similar backgrounds and all the rest. There are also deeper patterns that only emerge over time. A few years ago I was working on a project (doomed) with a fellow writer, and we ended up spending a lot of time together, although we didn't know each other that well. To distract ourselves from the job at hand, we talked about anything, everything. His parents, both now dead, had been together, happily married, for decades. His wife's had been too. My parents divorced when I was fourteen and I hadn't spoken to my father since I was fifteen. His best friend's parents were still together. His wife's best friend's parents were still together. My best friend's parents had divorced when he was in his early twenties. All my close friends but one had either lost a parent young, or had had a fractious and difficult relationship with one of them. The endless reiteration of these patterns was fascinating to us both, and later, I would say, it helped us rationalise the long-term failure of our writing partnership. We still get on well, but we never became very close friends. Whether that's because we realised we couldn't (because of this fundamental difference between us) or because we decided we couldn't is impossible to determine. In fact, it gives me a headache just thinking about it.

The point is that, if the hermit tendency does not kick in, you should carry on making new friends throughout life. But these later friends are different. While you may have many things in common, not all of which you will immediately be aware of, you won't necessarily share the same background, and shared experiences are less likely. No, the most significant factor now will be money. Our newer friends tend to have similar incomes (or standards of living, call it what you will) to our own. The rich make friends with the rich. The famous form unshakeable bonds with the famous. If you have recently moved into a cardboard box, chances are that your intimate circle will soon be drawn almost exclusively from those who also use sturdy packaging material as their primary residence.

I am not saying this is a good thing or a bad thing. It's just the way it is. I have spent much of the past fifteen years standing in pubs eating dry-roasted peanuts. A remarkable proportion of the friends I have made in that time do something similar. Some prefer pork scratchings, other swear by the Thai chilli crisps, but what we have in common is what you might call 'acquired status'. Wherever each of us started, we all ended up here. Our common ground is the ground on which we walk.

Old friendships are different. They need to be cherished and nurtured, and never more so than in middle age. We are naturally more casual about our friendships in our teens and twenties, and we value them more as the mists of youth begin to clear. Our old friends know us; we know them. Each of us tolerates the other's glaring character flaws, or at least takes account of them. I have drifted apart from old friends, but never so far away that rapprochement became impossible. I have fallen out with a few too: the closer the friend, the more violent the argument. But eventually you make up. One of you sues for peace. Life is too short. A weary old cliché, this, worn down by centuries of overuse, but one day you realise with a shudder that it is also one of the wisest sentences ever written, encapsulating a truth too profound and disturbing for many human brains to grasp. Life is far, far too short, certainly for daft feuds with annoying, stubborn, deluded old bastards you have known for decades and hope to know for many more.

What can get in the way is money. Envy can corrode old friendships as little else can. (There's always Having Sex With Your Friend's Wife, but isn't that a form of envy as well?) As some of my friends became appreciably richer than me, I realised that, if I was to stay sane, I would have to dampen down my God-given talent for resentment and bitterness. The writer Jon Canter has a nice way of putting it. His relative happiness, he says, is affected by people he grew up with, by university contemporaries, by friends. And, in particular, 'by friends who were poor when I was poor and now ... are far, far, far richer. It's that third "far" that does it. I'm OK when they are far, far richer. But far, far, far richer makes me want to weep.'*

The challenge is to avoid being eaten up by envy. Well, we can let it have the odd nibble now and again. There doesn't seem much harm in envying casual acquaintances who delight too publicly in their financial advantages. We have to express ourselves somehow. As for enemies, there's no close season on them. But our true friends must feel we are on their side, just as we feel we are on theirs. 'Whenever a friend succeeds, a little something in me dies,' said Gore Vidal, possibly his most famous utterance, because it is so unpleasant and self-defeating. Whenever a friend succeeds, we rejoice with them. Otherwise, what kind of friends are we?

Oh, that's so easy to write, and so much harder to do.

* *Guardian*, 28 March 2010.

As it happens, I feel I am doing quite well with the envy. I haven't flushed it entirely out of my system, but I would like to think that I am on the way. Continued mental health and happiness demand nothing less. But what midlife gives with one hand, it steals away with the other. Envy recedes, like a hairline, but the worry doesn't. In fact, it seems to become entrenched. It has laid in provisions and is preparing for the long haul. The only thing worse than constantly worrying about money is realising how boring it is to be constantly worrying about money. Stress and boredom: an unbeatable combination. I am worn down by them. I am tired when I wake. I am even more tired the rest of the time. But I am not giving in to it. I refuse.

When I was working on the project I mentioned earlier, with the fellow writer whose parents had never parted, we would spend many, intermittently fruitful hours in his study. He would sit behind the computer, staring at the screen in the hope that the solution to our many problems would magically appear there. I would stomp around the room, stare at the walls, dream of chocolate and sleep. One day I was looking out of the window and I saw someone else I knew, a divorced man, coming out of one of the houses opposite. His ex-wife and son lived there. He was taking the son out for the afternoon. This person I knew was, in normal life, ebullient and confident, a bit of a braggart in fact, but a good and gentle soul underneath. His son, who was about six, ran on ahead. The father lit a cigarette and slouched along behind. I was taken aback. I had never seen anyone look more resigned and defeated. It was the slouch of despair. It was, in truth, the way an awful lot of middle-aged men get from one place to another, especially when they don't think anyone is looking. But I thought then and think still, I am never going to do that. I am never going to succumb to the slouch of despair, nor its close relative, the shuffle of despond.

This is why we make new friends among people who live similar lives to us, because we can have a good moan with them, and they will understand. The slouch of despair is the lonely man's walk. And they will understand because they know, as we know, that little is going to change now. Either we are rich, or we are not. Some of us might yet become much richer, and others might yet become much poorer, but most of us will stay roughly where we are. This is the true end of youth. Not when you stop feeling young, or when the young start looking at you in that pitying way they have, but when all those options to make your life better simply are not there any more.

Money can buy you these options, and so, in a way, can help you stay young. The rich don't just look younger than us because they have had expensive surgery. I sat on the other side of a table from Sting a few years ago, in a radio studio. He gleams with vitality and good health, and the primary reason, I would suggest, is that he has an extremely nice life. You too would gleam and glow if you never, ever had to do anything you didn't want to do.

And the rest of us? We are waiting for something. We may not know what, but we are waiting anyway. My mother expects, any day now, to win £1 million on her Premium Bonds. She knows exactly how she would spend the vast pile of riches that will never come her way. She allocated it all in her head years ago. Daydreaming about it makes her nearly as happy as the actual money would. I rather envy her.

She may not have any money, but quite a few ageing parents are really quite comfortable. They bought their houses when property cost buttons. They have their pensions and their holidays and, with any luck, their marbles as well. Their children, ageing themselves, love them dearly and are waiting for them to turn their toes up. If they could do so cleanly and neatly, without going ga-ga or incurring the crippling fees of nursing homes or sheltered accommodation, that would be ideal. Jane Austen understood all this, two centuries ago. Disregard the surface frippery of her novels, the pretty costumes and well-appointed country houses we see in glossy film and TV adaptations. Austen still speaks to us because almost every character in her books is waiting for someone older to die so they can inherit their money. No one has jobs, so there aren't any other ways of getting the stuff, unless it is by marrying it, which can work if, like Fitzwilliam Darcy, your intended owns a house the size of Leicestershire. But it won't work for us. That ship has sailed. Inheritance is our last hope. It seems unfair that the only way we can get our hands on all that cash is by burying a beloved older relative or two, but like Jane Austen we live in cruel times. A house, a house, my kingdom for a house, whether or not it is near Toulouse.

15

WHATEVER

'One half of the world cannot understand the pleasures of the other.'

Jane Austen, *Emma* (1815)

Too true. If Austen was the first person to say something
like this, she wasn't the last. The great humorist Miles
Kington once wrote that you can divide the population of
the world into two halves: those who habitually divide the
population of the world into two halves, and those who
don't.

Fortunately, however you care to define these two halves,
we usually know which half we are in. On the first sunny
day of spring, do you immediately put on a T-shirt and
shorts, even though it's not quite warm enough, or do you
still wear slightly too many layers and shake your head
wearily at all these idiots in shorts? It has to be one or the

other: you can't do both. If you smell Kentucky Fried Chicken in a public place, do you think, mmm, delicious, or do you have about five seconds to get out of there before you start heaving? Or when you cut your toenails, do you snip them straight into the wastepaper basket or do you pile them up on the side of the sofa and look at them for a few moments, satisfied by a job well done? Whichever you do, your partner will usually do the other, which means that the one who forms a pleasing pile has to do so when everyone else is out of the house, to forestall their cries of mockery and disgust. How sad it would be if both of you piled up your toenail cuttings but did so only in private, unable to inform the other of this small but significant source of gratification. Such tiny disparities can drive a wedge into the most outwardly harmonious of relationships.

Becoming middle-aged, as we have discussed, only confirms you in most of your habits and opinions. It hardens your attitudes, as well as your toenails. (One of my little toenails is so thick I keep expecting to be hunted for ivory.) Things we just did a few years ago become the way we do things. I put on my pants before I take off my dressing gown. It means nothing, but if they inscribed my grave with the words 'He put on his pants before he took off his dressing gown', I think I would take that. (It would also mean that they hadn't found out about some of the other, far more appalling things I do.)

But middle age is also a time of change, voluntary and otherwise, and it can be around now that some of us leap from one precisely defined grouping to another, maybe even its exact opposite. Maybe you did once like Kentucky

Fried Chicken, or even doner kebabs. Maybe you ate them everywhere, and wilfully disregarded the pained expressions and retching noises of people a few years older than you. Then one day, for no obvious reason, the smell made you want to barf too. Some little biochemical switch clicked, and you changed sides. If you saw your younger self eating that shit, you would gladly see him choke on it.

Which brings us, like a guided missile, to the question of litter. As a young person you may not have had any strong feelings about litter. You may have put your Coke can or your sweetpaper in the bin because you were well brought up – or you may not have because you weren't – but either way, it wasn't something you gave much thought to. Who cares? Litter exists. Someone will clear it up. Whatever. Get over it.

Then one day, without warning, the biochemical switch goes click. From that day on, you will never let a piece of plastic packaging flutter to the ground. On the rare occasion you drop one, you will intercept it before it lands. No one would believe you could move so fast. Because litter now matters. Not for what it is, because, in the end, we know it is a trivial crime, it will be cleared up, and no children or animals will be harmed in the process. No, litter matters for what it represents. It says 'I don't give a monkey's'. Litter is blinding arrogance combined with absolute thoughtless-ness. It can make you so angry you fear for your health.

Five or six years ago, with partner and small children, I was walking along the towpath of Regent's Canal near Camden Lock in north London. It was a balmy Sunday in midsummer, late in the afternoon, and several groups of young people were sitting on the grass next to the canal, talking and drinking and enjoying the summer haze. One young man, his back to me, drained the last of a can and dropped it in the canal. It floated away. It wasn't an aggressive act, you could see that. He was finished with the can so he disposed of it. The canal was convenient, so in it went. I doubt he ever thought of the can again. Only I remember it, five or six years later, in full Technicolor and Dolby surround sound. My mind's eye can still see the arc it made as it hit the water.

Needless to say, I didn't do anything. You will have deduced that from the fact that I am not serving a twenty-year sentence in Wormwood Scrubs. There are a number of excellent reasons why middle-aged people do not carry guns, and here is one of them. I did toy briefly with pushing him in, but that would have been more trouble than it was worth too. Braver and more pompous men than I would have gone up to the snivelling little turd and pointed out where he had gone wrong. Even then, you would never get the response you wanted. Get over it. Whatever.

How to deal with this menace? Execution would be the cleanest and simplest solution, although it does occur to me that reducing a living, breathing young person with silly piercings to an oozing bloodied corpse is itself a form of littering, and arguably a more environmentally damaging one than dropping a can of Diet Sprite into a sludgy old canal. Camden Lock being a place where young people congregate, sometimes for purposes other than littering, it might be feasible to station snipers on the top of nearby buildings. But it wouldn't be a long-term solution. Once the first littering little turd had been downed, the area might start to develop a bit of a reputation. The turds wouldn't sit there as before and not litter. They would go somewhere safer and litter as before.

It was some days before I formulated a workable plan. You employ a litter inspectorate, who wear peaked hats and confront anyone who drops litter. The inspector takes a photo and records the felon's personal details. The felon laughs this off as pitifully ineffective and pointless. Wait a fortnight, then send round the death squads. Really, no one would notice or care they had gone.

At which point in the conversation your psychotherapist, if you had one, might raise a troubled eyebrow and press the red button on his desk. You had always wondered what that red button was for.

Your therapist would be right. Such towering fury probably does say more about us, the litter vigilantes (and putative commanders of the litter militia), than it does about the litterers.

But like the littering, our litter rage has deeper meaning. What offends us is not so much the wrapper fluttering to the ground as the lack of thought behind the action. How can people be so self-centred, so unable to see the consequences of their carelessness? Very easily. It's the work of a moment. Stay there and I'll show you how.

Middle age is the state we arrive at having lived quite a number of years. On the face of it, though, that is all we have in common. There are as many types of middle-aged people as there are middle-aged people. So I am not going to say that we all obsess about litter. It would be untrue. But it does strike me as interesting that, given this near-infinite range of experience and temperament, so many of us of a certain age should have arrived, after a long journey, at what is essentially the same conclusion. Pick it up, you little bastard.

Same conclusion, but not necessarily for the same reasons. There are those of us, for instance, who feel more drawn to order and formality than we once were. People I know who could not bear to wear ties and jackets a few years ago now wear them by default. It's easier, they say. No, say I, you just like it more. Formality allows you to put some distance between you and the rest of the world, to withdraw into yourself a little (and the hermit tendency is a corollary of this). Civility and politeness, you realise, have their virtues. You can see why your parents wanted you to be better behaved than you were: it was easier for them that way. Order equals peace of mind, which you now understand is your final goal. Litter does not engender peace of mind.

Alternatively, none of this might apply at all.

Rage and resentment might be the overpowering emotions. Hatred needs no justification. The angriest man I ever knew died young, enraged to his final breath that he wouldn't get the last word. The angriest man I now know keeps it all bottled up. Whenever I hear a car backfiring, I wonder whether it's him, going off like a firework. If he does go, he will take a large chunk of north London with him.

For many people, middle age brings humility. The world doesn't revolve around you. It never did. In fact, you are wholly insignificant. What a relief. Humility can give you the peace of mind you seek, even happiness if you are lucky, but it also imposes a sense of responsibility. We are responsible to the world around us, and to the people around us. Soon we find we have higher standards of behaviour than we used to have. These standards do not include dropping litter.*

This issue of respect seems to me fundamental. My friend McR was on the 43 bus with his ten-year-old daughter, and behind him a teenage girl was on her phone, swearing like Gordon Ramsay. McR turned round and asked her, as amiably as only he can, to tone it down a bit. The girl gave him a mouthful. 'It's a fuckin' public place, innit? I can do what the fuck I like!' But the point is, in a public place, you *can't* do what the fuck you like. You would like to think that that was obvious, but to a moron, obviously it isn't. Similarly, the sodcasters, playing their terrible music on phones in buses, cannot expect to be treated with respect when, by their actions, they so unequivocally show disrespect for everyone else. Their 'freedom', as they see it, actually imprisons others.†

Selfishness is the curse of the age. People behave badly because they can. Someone I know has the neighbour from

---

* Interviewed about his loves and hates in the *Sunday Telegraph* in October 2010, the comedian and actor Alexander Armstrong cited 'bad manners' among his hates: 'They rile me more than anything else. I extend it to include litter dropping, general insolence and not saying thank you. Life would be so much easier if everyone was prepared to put other people first.' He had celebrated his fortieth birthday six months earlier.

† You don't need to swear excessively or play music to be annoying on a bus with a mobile phone. Last February, also on the 43, I heard a young bloke with a beard tell his mate about his holiday. 'You'd love San Francisco, man. Los Angeles didn't do it for me, but San Francisco is wicked, man. All these guys on motorbikes, fuckin' 'ell, basically man.' (That's verbatim.) The rest of us in the bus glanced at each other, united for a moment by our shared loathing.

all our worst nightmares, who blasts out music at deafening volume at all hours of the day and night. Is it a wilful act – a violent act, even – intended to destroy people's peace of mind? Is it just extraordinarily thoughtless? Or indifferent in a cauterised, Aspergic kind of way? After much discussion, we theorised that it might be a form of subconscious suicide. Maybe he is sitting there, torturing himself with Slipknot, waiting for someone to go round and club his head in with a baseball bat. It's a mansion block: a hundred and fifty or so people live there, and every evening maybe a hundred of them will seriously contemplate murder. You wouldn't necessarily do it yourself, but you would support to the hilt anyone who did. Sooner or later, I suspect, someone will crack and club a neighbour's head in exactly these circumstances. It would be a test case. Surely no jury would convict. And if one person got away with it, others might try it too.

Our world is overcrowded, and for the moment at least, we adhere to the bizarre notion that every human life is in some way valuable. Meanwhile, our elders, who are even angrier than we are, tell us how much better life was when they were young. There was more respect. People were less brash and rude and didn't swear all the fucking time. And they might be right, to some extent. But their premise rests on at least one faulty assumption. It assumes that the world changes but we don't, really. The litter issue, I believe, proves otherwise. As fast as the world is changing, we are changing too, but we are moving in the opposite direction. We are genetically programmed to age physically, we know that, but we are genetically programmed to age culturally as well.

It's not such a bad thing. At least it means we will be comfortable at whatever age we fetch up. Slippers beckon. Horlicks calls from the kitchen. Trousers with elasticated waistbands whisper from the wardrobe. It is as it was always meant to be. We have to take it on the chin – or, increasingly, chins. As the young people would say: whatever.

16

CRUMBLED

'Men are OK from thirty to forty-five; if they're care-
ful they can stay about the same. After that it's an
increasing struggle because of jowl and neck lines,
even if the waist can be restrained. And the bruising
of repeated sexual rejection starts to show in the eyes.'

Alan Clark, in his diary, November 1983

Physical decay in middle age can be swift. Since Chapter 3
we have both aged visibly. And you have just been reading
the book. I have been writing it, and I look years older.
Can't be much time left now.

Teeth

Since the last time I broached this subject, I have been to
the hygienist to get my teeth cleaned. (Even at their most

gleaming, they are now a dull banana yellow.) I asked her if my gums had receded much recently. She said no. She lied. I reckon that between five and ten per cent of every meal gets stuck between my teeth, where, unless it is removed immediately, it quietly ferments until, about two hours later, my breath smells like an unwiped bottom. I bulk-buy dental floss. Sometimes I brush my teeth three times a day. My gums are probably in better health than they ever have been. If there was only a little bit more of them, life would be perfect.

Hygienists, though. We are the first generation in human history to have been ministered from childhood by dental hygienists. Obviously we don't see the same hygienist all our lives. We see a progression of hygienists. The first is apocalyptically strict. If you don't floss and brush regularly, all your teeth will fall out and you will look like Albert Steptoe. The next generation is more emollient. You really need to look after these teeth. They won't last for ever. Her signature is the resigned sigh. You clean your teeth rigorously in the week before seeing her because you don't want to disappoint her. I have now progressed to the third age of hygienists. My current one doesn't nag, or sigh. It's too late for that. She reassures, she avoids confrontation, she crosses her fingers behind her back. They look warped from constant crossing.

My question is this: are there three distinct varieties of hygienist, or are they all the same hygienist, responding differently to people of different ages? I can't believe there is any worse job in the world.

Eyesight

Whatever did happen to Shakin' Stevens? I'm not sure I care that much, but the other day I saw a photo of him singing at someone's benefit concert and was pleasantly surprised to see that he looked much the same, except that he was wearing glasses. Of course he was wearing glasses. Everyone wears glasses in the end.

That is not to say that everyone wears them all the time. A remarkable number of my interviewees report holding a book further and further away from their eyes until their arms are simply not long enough. They know they should put on their glasses/look around for them because they're here somewhere/get eye-tested in the first place, but it's more convenient to contemplate getting some sort of extension affixed to their arm, until you're sitting on the sofa and the book is nearly out of the window. By this stage you don't need glasses, you need binoculars – and possibly a slap around the head.

What we cannot change, we have to accept. After the age of forty, our eye muscles are less able to exert the pressure needed to ensure sharp focus. The lenses change in consistency and elasticity. Eventually they transmit colour less effectively. Blues and blacks become harder to distinguish. Then the cells on the retina become sparser. Someone of sixty needs three times as much light to read comfortably as someone of sixteen. Our eyes also become slower to react to sudden light or sudden darkness: we become more easily dazzled. Playing cricket in high summer, I now have to wear sunglasses the whole time; otherwise, just give me the guide dog and be done with it.

According to Dr Tom Stuttaford, the sage of *The Oldie* magazine on medical matters: 'Everyone in their forties needs to have their eyes tested regularly, preferably annually, by a good optician or optometrist.' But what chance have we of getting there? We could easily find ourselves in a mobile phone emporium by mistake, or one of those shops selling overpriced candles. All those things you were going to do with your life, and you end up as Mr Magoo.

There are other perils involved in this. OK, it's not strictly necessary to read the lyrics on CD inserts, but it comes to something when, as my friend O'R admitted, you no longer bother to read the tiny instructions on medicines and just assume that two tablets will do. It's usually two, isn't it? Every four hours? Should be fine.

All of us, then, are afflicted by age-related long-sightedness, including those who were already short-sighted. For years the short-sighted have been half-looking forward to long-sightedness, in the belief that they might become slightly less short-sighted as a result. But it doesn't happen. They are just as short-sighted as before, but now they are long-sighted as well. These are misnomers, anyway. 'Short-sighted' should be rebranded as 'long-blind', 'long-sighted' as 'short-blind'. After the bifocals – two strengths of magnification in the same lens, one for not being able to see bus numbers, the other for not being able to read instructions on medicines – we will need trifocals, covering distance, middle and near vision. I think I'll stay at home and watch TV, if I can find the bloody thing.

Hearing loss

My teeth are OK, my eyesight is hanging on by a thread, and did I mention that I still have a full head of hair? But my hearing is knackered. As far as I can ascertain, the actual ears seem to work quite well: I can hear music with the same pinpoint precision I always could, and (unlike my brother, who used to be a DJ) don't need to turn it up to deafening volumes just to be sure it is on at all. But since late 2005 I have loud and persistent tinnitus in both ears. It is like high-pitched white noise, it is slightly louder than normal conversation, and it never stops. Given that this is a form of randomly imposed torture, I am not doing too badly with it.

Its origins are clear enough. In the late 1980s and early 1990s I reviewed gigs for a national newspaper. In three or four years I probably covered fifty or sixty: not a huge number, but enough to impose permanent damage. After the loudest of them – I remember David Bowie's dismal art-metal band Tin Machine playing at what was then the Town and Country Club in Kentish Town with particular lack of fondness – my ears would ring for a couple of days and then recover. In 1992, though, I had to cover the first date of Tina Turner's European tour in Antwerp. (Was it her third farewell tour or her fifth? I can't remember.) The volume was unspeakable. Afterwards my ears rang for ten days. I took this as a warning, and retired from gig reviewing instantly. Nonetheless, I was left with low-level tinnitus of a type many people suffer: a mild annoyance, but nothing that would bother you unless you were in a very quiet room with the windows closed at three o'clock in the morning with far too much to worry about.

In 2005, however, one of my oldest and closest friends died in unusually grim circumstances, after he and I had fallen out rather badly. It was a dreadful time, and over one night the tinnitus increased tenfold in intensity. I could see that it was some kind of physiological reaction to impossible stress, but then the tinnitus itself is highly stressful. On bad days you think you are going mad. I went to the doctor. Usually when I call the doctor's surgery, it's for something urgent, something you need to see someone that day for. So you never actually get to see your own doctor: you only ever see the locum. In five years signed on at this practice, I had never met 'my' doctor. But on this occasion I felt the need to see 'my' doctor. I needed comforting. I needed a cure. I also wanted to make sure he existed. What had he been up to all this time?

So I went along. He took notes. Had I been exposed to intolerably loud noises at any point? Road drills? Concorde? I told him about Tina Turner, and you could see his eyes glaze over. This was injury by misadventure. All my own fault. Should have worn earplugs. Fine, but what can we do about it? Nothing at all, he said. It isn't curable. With which words, I was ushered out. Next!

This doctor was a year or so older than me. The next time I asked to see him, they said he wasn't well and would be away for a while. The time after that, they said he was dead. So this was the only time I ever saw 'my' doctor. I can't tell you how unsettling this thought is. Doctors aren't supposed to die, let alone at forty-eight. I wonder who 'my' doctor is now. I don't dare find out, just in case my seeing him (or her) reduces his (or her) life expectancy to a few months as well.

The tinnitus, though, goes on. It will outlive many more members of the medical profession and probably me as well. I will be lying in my coffin and the mourners around the grave will be looking at each other and asking, what's that noise? I shall present myself at St Peter's pearly gates and ask him, why have I still got the tinnitus? And he will say, why are you assuming this is heaven?

I can manage it now. You learn techniques, and I can sometimes forget about it for hours at a time. It seems to decrease in intensity when I am less stressed, and after two largish glasses of red wine. When everything gets too much, it is deafening. Chicken, or egg? I don't know, but the stress and the tinnitus have become so intertwined it hardly matters any more. Each is a manifestation of the other, in some way. The tinnitus is at its worst when there is a lot of background noise. In a group of people in a pub or at a party, I can only hear clearly the person next to me. Maybe it is time to engineer the return to fashionability of the ear trumpet. Given a sharp new design and a good polish, it could be the hearing accessory *de nos jours*. Alternatively, I shall just have to get used to saying 'Come again?' a lot.

I have noticed one minor and unwelcome consequence of all this. You are walking through the streets of the city, and everyone is in their little survival bubble, forcing their way through the crowds they don't feel part of, because crowds are always other people. You make a nasty little comment under your breath. It may have the word 'fuck-wit' in it. It doesn't matter. No one can hear you. But hang on. Why is that man turning around and giving you such a dirty look? Why did that woman pass you and say

'Fuckwit yourself'? Because their hearing is keener than yours, and yours is worse than you think it is. From now on, great care has to be taken with your running commentary on the inadequacies of your fellow man and woman. Try thinking it rather than speaking it. I sometimes have to ask others whether I just said that outrageous thing out loud, or merely thought it. I have always said it out loud.

Bombast

In *Brief Lives*, John Aubrey spoke of 'Edward de Vere, Earl of Oxford (1550–1604)', who, 'making his low obeisance to Queen Elizabeth, happened to let a Fart, at which he was so abashed and ashamed that he went to Travell, 7 yeares. On his returne the Queen welcomed him home, and sayd, My Lord, I had forgot the Fart.'

It's a mistake anyone could make. To be mortified by your guffs, though, is a young man's game. Oldsters don't worry a fraction as much. They fart here, they fart there, they fart everywhere. It worries us much more, because what old blokes are doing today, we will be doing the day after tomorrow. We know that our eyesight, hearing and 100 metres times will decline, but no one wishes to face up to gradual loss of sphincter control. Yet we may be all right. My tinnitus has revealed to me an important truth about the trumping habits of the elderly. Because of loss of hearing, they believe they are farting in silence, as they always used to. At the same time, inevitable but mild loosening of the guff-dropping musculature means that a greater effort needs to be expended to produce the Silent But Deadlies of old. They can't hear them, they probably can't smell them, so they think they have got away with it. This process seems to accelerate as they get older, with appalling effects on their reputation and the air quality in their vicinity. No longer is it enough to look innocent and try to deflect the blame on to the nearest baby. You see it on the bus. Oldster plants one, then leaps off at the next stop, grinning evilly. Baby in pushchair gets a whiff, bursts into tears, everyone looks daggers at baby. Disgraceful, really.

Leakage

Did you notice that it was only male, middle-aged TV critics who worried that Jack Bauer never once went to the toilet in eight series of *24*?

Try taking a holiday in Jersey. Lovely beaches, good seafood and unbelievable numbers of public conveniences, all clean and fully functional. The oldies love it. They are never more than a brief shuffle from bladder relief. If you ever go on holiday to Chile, by contrast, make sure you take loo paper. Chilean public loos don't have any.

The real annoyance, especially in public loos, is the need for drastically increased dribble time. You do your pee, and think you are done with it, but the bloody thing dribbles away, drip by drip, molecule by molecule, until you finally get bored, shake off the last few drops and zip up. Whereupon the bastard thing dribbles a bit more, thus creating a telltale wet patch on your sexy boxer shorts. This is why middle-aged men end up sitting on the loo like girls, reading three or four magazines at a sitting and barking at anyone who dares to disturb them.

That single ear hair

It was there a long time in the end. Tall and proud and tenacious, it grew like a lone cactus in a desert. I would feel it there with my thumbnail, and after a day or so to pluck up courage, I would rip it out with a single sharp movement that made my eyes water. I would always have tissue handy to mop up the blood, but astonishingly there never was any. Then, when I wasn't paying attention, it would grow back. It never gave up.

And it is alone no longer. A small carpet of soft, baby hairs covers the inside of my ear. No longer a lone cactus, but a shrubbery. Desert becomes jungle. One can imagine the many and varied fauna that might find a home there. Microscopic equivalents of insects and lizards and colourful parakeets, all doing their utmost not to be scoffed up by microscopic Venus flytraps. It's a cradle of life. Higher and higher the shrubs grow, into tall slender trees. Send in the loggers!

Wrinkles

So, no facelift, because only Silvio Berlusconi wants to look like Silvio Berlusconi. Wrinkles are our scars of battle. Like Mick Jagger, we can call them laughter lines if we wish. (George Melly: 'Surely nothing's that funny.') If, like

George Michael, you spent your youth looking serious and tortured, you develop a deep vertical furrow between your eyebrows, the Serious Furrow. Horror at the way the world is going gives you those two deep crevasses going down from the sides of your nose, and so on.

Nonetheless, what you wouldn't do in real life can still be done in cyberspace. On Facebook, for instance, you can (as I do) put up a ridiculously old picture of yourself, or (like my friend S) you can put up a new picture of yourself and Photoshop the wrinkles away. No one will ever know. It's easy.

BEFORE   AFTER

Strange, incomprehensible but trivial ways in which the body can let you down

My brother has started sweating down only one side of his body. Right side, bone dry. Left side, sweats like a pig. He saw a doctor, who said it's terribly rare, but nothing to worry about; just the way the brain works. My brother says he is used to it now, and his deodorant expenditure is down by an amazing 50 per cent.

My friend McL has gout, on and off. Crystals of uric acid build up on certain joints, in his case the knees. The pain is excruciating. But gout has a poor reputation. Historically it was known as 'the rich man's disease', or 'the disease of kings', as people believed you only got it through overconsumption of rich food, red wine and particularly port. People still believe this. As it happens, out-and-out self-indulgence accounts for no more than 12 per cent of cases; genetic predisposition is a far likelier cause. Gout is a by-product of the middle-aged body's fantasy that it can still repair itself, which leads it to work overtime in vain producing all these redundant urates. McL is stick thin and vegetarian, although he would be the first to admit that he likes a drop. But everyone behaves as though the gout is his fault. His ears glow red with the injustice of it.

At around the same time my tinnitus hit, I also developed some psoriasis on my scalp. It doesn't itch, much, but if I lose concentration and scratch it in public, you could be excused for wondering whether it had started snowing. It is like comedy dandruff. You could probably make a nice little pile of it. I wonder what would happen if I added water. I might not need to buy wallpaper paste ever again.

More worryingly for me, the patch of psoriasis shifts around. It started off on the right side, just above my ear, but has gradually migrated, and now forms a ridge running from just above my forehead straight back to my crown. If I went bald overnight, I would look like a Klingon.

Fortunately, there's always someone worse off than you. C has to shave the side of his nose. They don't tell you about that in kindergarten.

Is it worse for women?

I threw the discussion open to my friends on a certain social networking site. Here were some of the contributions:

Γ: Pelvic floor after four babies gruesome enough?

Θ: The first grey eyebrow hair. Just wrong. So wrong.

McT: The realisation, for women, that unless you have a really great bone structure, it's better to be a bit overweight than underweight.

F: Absolutely. After forty it's face or figure. Madonna chose figure: well, she's basically a dancer. Being a bit fat would send her over the edge, I imagine. I chose face.

L: Eyebrows that need plucking almost every day to avert a Gallagher-style monobrow.

F: I hate all those headlines in women's mags with Liz Hurley on the cover saying 'How to Look Great after Forty'. They never print the honest answer: 'Lots of money'.

Δ: Can you write your message in big type? I can't read it.

G: Finding out the hard way that not doing your pelvic floor exercises in your twenties and thirties means you cannot sneeze during middle age without crossing your legs first. Oh, and steer clear of trampolines on a full bladder.

Γ: Running for a bus has its moments too.

J: Sadly my pelvic floor was like a drumskin in my thirties, but a child put paid to that, and now I can't even find it to exercise it. My physical shape is sadly ropey and I have just been told by my GP that my ovaries are shrinking – ugh!

McT: To my original comment, I would add the rider, 'If you want the tits, you've got to pay the arse tax.' Plus, I just tweeted Kew Gardens to ask when was the best time to see the rhododendrons. That is the ageing process made flesh.

17

PARENTS

'There are various ways of dealing with approaching old age: the Anglo-Saxon way is to be ironic.'

Justin Cartwright, *To Heaven By Water* (2009)

They have been many things to you: nurturers, nursemaids, supporters, role models, blank cheques, cooks, launderers, mini-cab drivers, landlords and landladies, fans, critics, teachers, wilful squanderers of your inheritance, embarrassments, assets, liabilities. Now, finally, they perform their most valuable role yet: as early warning systems for your own old age. To do this they need to be still alive. If they are not, that's another kind of warning, a rather shrill, insistent one you probably shouldn't ignore.

When we are in our forties and fifties, our parents start dying. One or two will have left the stage earlier: I have at least three friends who were orphans before the age of forty. But many of us, as we negotiate the lower slopes of midlife, have two parents who are still going, who are hale, possibly hearty, and concerned we are eating the right things. Twenty years later, these parents are appreciably less likely to be around and on our case.

Not that it makes any difference how old you are. C was approaching sixty when he lost his parents, aged eighty-seven and eighty-nine, within a year of each other. He was knocked sideways. The next eighteen months, he says, were a blur. My grandmother was seventy-five when her mother went, aged ninety-seven. She never recovered. A few weeks later she had the first of a series of strokes, and spent the next five years miserably waiting to die. Children who lose a parent may seem 'braver' than these collapsing oldsters, but they could spend the rest of their lives trying to come to terms with the loss. When I look at my two children, with the usual overpowering surge of love, I understand that my primary responsibility to them is to stay alive. And I have no control over that at all. If I cock it up, I won't even get the chance to apologise.

Given that middle age is so challenging, demeaning and at times plain miserable, how come more of us do not end it all? Why do so many more young people commit suicide? Because they don't have children, that's why. Once you have them, your responsibility to them to stay alive outweighs your natural desire to do away with yourself as quickly and painlessly as possible. The underlying paradox is that it's the weight of responsibility, the tiredness, the lack of money, the loss of hope, all brought about by having children, that make you want to top yourself in the first place. Young people finish themselves off for different reasons: feelings of inadequacy, the meaninglessness of existence, personal failure and lack of achievement, the contempt or indifference of others. We are long past all of these. What took us past were the children. They made us see that feelings of inadequacy are almost universal; that the meaninglessness of existence is a huge relief; that lack of achievement is trivial; that the contempt of others is irrelevant. Some problems are laid to rest, and others arise in their place. This is the normal rhythm of life: one step forward, two steps back. Just make sure you don't fall down the whole flight of stairs.

Having children is not compulsory, of course, or even always possible. My friends B and Mrs B worry about who will look after them when they are old, something no parent of small children ever thinks about. (On the contrary. They wouldn't be surprised if their children moved to Australia to get away from them.) B says he would like to have been a father, but he knows he can say that in the safe knowledge that he was never going to be. Mrs B didn't want to be a mother. B loves Mrs B, so that was it. They live a comfortable life in a largeish house they would never have been able to afford if they had had the children they haven't filled it with.

Before I became a father, at the relatively advanced age of thirty-nine, I rather sneeringly thought that having children was just a device to stop you worrying about what you were going to do with your life. And it is. I was right. Where I was wrong was in believing this was a bad thing. Why worry? What you are going to do with the rest of your life is clear up after your children. Parenthood is a form of indentured servitude, without end. Fortunately, there are rewards. The love of those children, both conditional (on your giving them money) and unconditional (once you have given them the money). Your love for your children, a resource that never runs out, and makes you feel more alive than anything else in the world. And this wondrous distraction from self, something the young me saw as an imposition, and the gnarled old me sees as liberation. A fellow parent said to me the other day, have you got a pension? No, said I. No, neither have I, said he, and we laughed until the tears flowed.

Next up are the teenage years. I am not too worried. This may be a mistake, and writing it here is tempting fate, I realise that. But there is nothing I can do about any of it, and worrying about it now won't make it any easier to handle when it arrives. Besides, I think I know what they will be going through. Middle age is rather like a second adolescence, only it takes you in the opposite direction, from virile, potent adulthood towards drooling incompetence. My children will be struggling their way upwards through the hormonal fug, and I'll be meeting them on the way back down.

At the age of fifty, though, you could be the father of a 35-year-old, of young adults, of teenagers, of toddlers. You might even be contemplating parenthood for the first time. Our sperm may not swim as fast as they once did – I imagine them pausing for a rest and a chat every now and then – but they are tenacious little blighters. And if they are slightly out of condition these days, carrying one or two extra pounds, we know from experience that that will only make them more buoyant. Younger, fitter spermatozoa are more likely to throw in the towel: it's all too much effort. The middle-aged sperm will swim on and on. For God's sake, men, there's an egg to be fertilised. In 2004, more than

75,000 babies were born to fathers older than forty in the UK, and of these, 6489 were born to fathers over fifty. We all enjoy those occasional stories in the press of some gummy old wreck who can barely walk and believes Mr Churchill should come out of retirement, photographed dandling the bouncing baby he has just sired on his arthritic knee. Pablo Picasso became a father at sixty-eight, Des O'Connor at seventy-two, Anthony Quinn at eighty-one, Saul Bellow at eighty-four. Charlie Chaplin fathered babies at the ages of 30, 36, 54, 55, 56, 59, 62, 64, 68, 70 and 73. He made fewer films in his later years, and this may be why. James Doohan, Scotty in *Star Trek*, was eighty when his seventh child was born. The engines obviously could take it after all.

Older fathers have their strengths and their weaknesses. The latter include not being able to pick the baby up after its first birthday. I would not be able to lift either of my children (twelve and nine) off the ground without incurring life-threatening back injuries. Older fathers can also, by all accounts, be pompous, distant, uncommunicative and overly formal. But then so can younger fathers. All I know is that I felt far more equipped for fatherhood at thirty-nine than I would have done at twenty-five. It's not so much about wisdom gained – although there may be the odd smattering – as foolishness jettisoned, and fear put to the sword. The point is that whatever age we first become fathers, we are not ready for it. Women have been thinking about motherhood, on some level, for most of their lives. (My daughter has been talking about having babies almost since she was a baby herself.) Whereas I believe that most men only start thinking about fatherhood when it is too late. 'Congratulations, it's a boy.'

From that moment on, we are playing catch-up. Most of us are still trying to work out the rules of the race while our womenfolk are sprinting over the horizon. This can be difficult for the male ego. No one wants to come second in a race of two. Many men drop out of the race altogether. Again, though, older fathers are more likely to show staying power than their younger counterparts. Our egos are less vulnerable. Coming second isn't the disaster it once was.

Nonetheless, we remain a minority. Most of my contemporaries have older children than mine, and to judge by their bemused expressions, they can't quite believe it either. It seems like five minutes since these babies were born, but already they have grown into vast hairy teens and young adults, with their mysteriously different personalities and their own tranche of daft opinions. If they are not actively engaged in sexual relations with other young people, they are masturbating themselves to death as a stopgap. Soon they will be wandering off to start living their own lives. We understand this. Part of our job as parents is to loosen our hold on our children, to let them go off and make their own mistakes, having learned so much about making mistakes from watching us. And yet, even though we know they are going to go, it can come as a shock when they do. Why should that be? I am beginning to think we can prepare for nothing in life. Even things that are inevitable seem to take us by surprise.

Thus we encounter Empty Nest Syndrome, a condition so widespread it merits its own three-letter acronym, ENS.* The house that previously seemed far too small will soon seem far too large. Empty nesters report that their homes

* TLA is the three-letter acronym for 'three-letter acronym'.

feel 'echoey' after their children have left, as though all the carpets have been taken up. Some of these echoes are obviously emotional. All those familiar noises you can hear in your mind's ear: children refusing to do their homework, calling '*Daddddyyyyy!*' from the bath because they forgot to take a towel with them, smashing valuable vases with footballs you banned them from kicking indoors, drivelling on the phone for hours to their friends while you try not to say what your parents said to you thirty years ago ('You'll be seeing them again tomorrow so why not talk to them then?'), forgetting everything they need for school for the fourth day in a row, playing their music too loud, objecting when you play your music too loud, having a friend round whom you immediately identify as an emissary of the Devil. All these have gone for ever, or until your child runs out of money and moves back in.

These are the legendary 'boomerang' kids, or FUCs (Freeloading Unemployed Children). Suddenly the house is too small again. Offspring you distinctly remembered waving off have returned to eat all your food and propel you, kicking and screaming, into one of the lesser 1970s sitcoms. The bonds between parents and children are made to be broken. They are not supposed to grow back. But youth is stressful and overpriced, and home is cheap and safe. You can't blame them for making the most of the little they have, which turns out to be the little you have left. You should be flattered. You must have done a terribly good job as a parent for them to want to come back.

I quite enjoyed broaching this subject with parents of teenagers, if only to gauge their reaction. For every one that dreads the departure of their babies, another lives in mortal fear of their return. I met a couple of old acquaintances recently after a number of years, and before we had been talking five minutes we had started totting up how much our kids had cost us. It wasn't a competition, yet it was. Each of the other two claimed to have spent hundreds of thousands of pounds on their progeny, 'and still they won't go,' said one, almost with pride. Once we boasted of our children's reading age or academic achievements; now we boast of their complete uselessness.

Are we comfortable, though, turning into these Sitcom Dads (SCDs)? Terry out of *Terry and June* (*TAJ*) was never an obvious role model for my generation. Being parents, though, brings something out of us we didn't know was there. That something is our own parents. However hard you resist turning into your father, a part of you always has been him. You are your mother too, which might be even tougher to accept. I can see my father in the mirror, and my partner sees my mother in some of my expressions and reactions. H, aged twenty-eight, says she knew she was turning into her mother when she found herself putting leftover food in Tupperware to save space in the fridge, *even though there was nothing else in there at the time*. We hear it in the slightly old-fashioned phrases we sometimes use, and in things we say to our children. You're not sitting indoors on a lovely sunny day like this. You can't have that now, it'll ruin your appetite. You're not going out looking like that. It's your hormones. Don't answer the door to anyone. You'll be seeing them again tomorrow, so why not talk to them then?*

---

* McL: 'When you've got your own house you can do as you like, but since you're under *my* roof . . . Ha ha ha, waited my whole life to say that.'

What's particularly comic is that we believe we have some choice in the matter. We work so hard over so many years not to turn into our parents; we think we have beaten them, and broken the mould. Then we turn into our parents. Choice is an illusion. Free will is an illusion. Resistance is futile.

There are so many examples in all our lives. The friend who was forced throughout childhood to play a musical instrument, practising endlessly and unwillingly, and giving it up the first chance he had, now coercing his own child to play a (different) musical instrument, and practise long and hard. The other friend, whose political opinions were diametrically opposed to his father's twenty years ago, and are identical to them today. The small boy who was a picky eater and yelled at by his omnivore father when he wouldn't eat a Brussels sprout. Now, when his own son will eat nothing but toast, the almost ungovernable rage and frustration. (This last one is me.)

The line my father always used, as an alternative to explaining (let alone justifying) his actions, was: 'You'll understand when you're my age.' That is not a line I plan to use with my own kids. Maybe it's the thin red line, the last line of my defences. You may not mind turning into your father in some ways, and may not even notice others, so trivial are they. But there is a core of your self that must remain yours, that will resist until death. Resistance isn't futile: it's absolutely essential. By extraordinary coincidence, I know a lot of people who have spent a lot of their lives battling one or other of their parents. This list includes both of my own parents. Is it possible to break the pattern? Do our children inevitably come to see us as implacable opponents? I so hope not. When the boy refuses to eat his food, I don't shout at him. Well, I try not to. I wrap myself up in knots to avoid doing so. By the end of some meals I am a human pretzel.

Salmon have a pleasing variety of names for the different stages in their life cycle. A young fish starts as a *parr*; when it goes down to the sea it's a *smolt*; if it returns to home waters after a year's sea-feeding it's a *grilse*; after it spawns, it's a *kelt*; and so on. Maybe we should have different names for us, as we turn into our parents. Children who go back home in their twenties are our grilse. Kelt salmon are characterised by their shabby and exhausted appearance, as are kelt humans. But salmon only live for eight years at most, so we need names for the subsequent stages in our life cycles. I am at the *pretzel* stage, trying to defy my programming. If I fail, maybe the *sitcom* stage will be next. Our children grow, our parents age, and other, as yet unnamed stages lie in wait for us.

One we can observe at close hand is the affinity that develops between our ageing parents and our younger children. Our parents are further down the road into second childhood than we are. While we can identify with adolescents, they see something of themselves in the smaller ones, so they spoil them rotten. 'They never indulged me like that,' you think, trying not to pout or stamp your feet. Which shows that they are still the parents and you are still the child. But probably only just. The balance is changing, and so slowly that few of us notice it happening. Your parents are slightly more doddery than they used to be. They may also be more crotchety. It takes greater humility than most of us are capable of to cede your independence, especially to your children, whom you can remember in nappies. (My great-grandmother, in her nineties, never referred to her sons, in their sixties and seventies, as anything other than 'the boys'.) Your parents turn to you only with the greatest reluctance, and often with singular ill grace.*

And they will understand this long before you do. C says it was a 'blinding revelation' the day he realised that his parents were no longer looking after him, he was looking after them. The revelation came some time after the fact. We become the responsible ones. We worry about them as they worried about us. (Don't answer the door to anyone. You're not going out looking like that.) They are our dependents, and we are alone in a way that we have never been before.

In our cricket team, players tend to vanish from the radar for a year or two after they become fathers. The rest of us are sympathetic. We know that you cannot run around a cricket field on a warm afternoon if you have not slept for three months. Who will look after the baby? Its mother desperately needs some time off. So players drift away for a while, and drift back only when some form of domestic equilibrium has been reached.

Now, I find, something similar is happening as players' parents grow older and frailer. All spare time seems to be taken up by motorway driving, because so few of us live near our mummies and daddies any more. Every weekend of the year, Britain's roads are unfeasibly clogged. Where are all these people going? A lot are going shopping for things

---

* Of course, you may already be a grandparent yourself. The average age to become a first-time grandparent in the UK is forty-nine.

they don't want or need, and I'm sure a few have forgotten it's the weekend and are driving to work by mistake, but I wouldn't be surprised if a majority weren't going to see elderly parents who need the lawn mowing. We thought it was such a good idea to move so far away; now we curse our youthful impulsiveness.

Frail is one thing; ill is quite another. Denial monkeys that we are, we blithely assume that our parents will live for ever. When they become ill, we are more shocked than they are. But look around: everybody else we know seems to be dealing with the failing health of an elderly parent. If you are between forty-five and fifty-five, I would suggest that you know at least one person who has a seriously ill parent, you know one whose parent is palpably dying, you know one whose parent has recently died, and you may know several who aren't close to getting over it. I also know one who has been cut out of the will, thanks to a villainous, witch-like stepmother, but that's another story.

Some people say you don't really become a grown-up until your parents have died. I have always hated that idea, which seems small consolation for the fact that your parents have died. And what is a grown-up, anyway? Is it such a good thing to be that it is worth paying such a hefty price? Find me anyone who says yes and I'll show you either a liar or a pompous, emotionally cauterised middle-aged man whose inner child is lonely and crying and as lost as anyone can be.

18
GONE

'Life cover for the Over-55s: leave behind more than just memories.'

Leaflet in Nationwide Building Society, May 2011

So much in our lifetimes has, quite simply, gone. Parents are almost the last of it. Things have been disappearing for far longer than that. It's quite surprising that there's anything left.

Loss, though, is a basic ingredient of life, one of the sub-atomic particles they haven't found yet. Nothing lasts for ever, other than possibly honey and a few game show hosts.* But how much loss do we allow ourselves to notice when

---

* According to legend, archaeologists once unearthed some 2000-year-old honey in one of the Egyptian tombs. Someone tried it, and it tasted fine. Did they butter the toast beforehand?

we are young? How much do we let through our defences? In our youth we embraced only the new, and forgot the old ever existed. Now, in midlife, we remember the old, and want it back.

These feelings can strike at any moment. I was in the kitchen, reaching up for the biscuit tin, which we place on a high shelf to stop us helping ourselves to the contents more than twice an hour. And I suddenly had a vivid memory of the biscuit tin we had when I was a child. It was round, and red and white. What happened to it? I rang my mother. Oh, I threw that away years ago, she said. You did what! I said, a little unreasonably. I'd have had that. Yes, she said, but have you thought about that biscuit tin even once in the last twenty years? Irrelevant, I blustered. I liked that tin. Kept the biscuits crisp. Like every other biscuit tin in the known universe, said my mother.

A small loss, then. A very small loss, although I am now foggily aware at the back of my mind every time I reach for a biscuit that I am one biscuit tin down on the deal. (I think I am in the denial phase of the bereavement process.) Smaller losses have their uses, though. They help us not to be overwhelmed by the larger losses, which seem to occur more and more frequently. Our lives are full of absence. So much has gone that we cannot remember how much, let alone what most of it was.

Imagine walking down a city street, one you know well, and seeing that an entire block has just been demolished. Where once there was building, there is now only air and space, with a mild whiff of rubble. Men in hard hats walk around looking pleased with themselves, for knocking down buildings carries a high level of job satisfaction. The young person within you looks at the site and wonders, what will they build there next? Hospital, office block or enormous water slide? Your middle-aged self looks at the site and wonders, what did that building look like before they knocked it down? You cannot remember. There was definitely a building there – you have walked past it count-less times – but every detail of its existence has left you. The gap in the skyline corresponds precisely to a building-shaped gap in your mind.

Gaps in the mind, of course, get us worrying. Is this the first sign of Alzheimer's? Some of us can't even say the word. That would be the ultimate loss, the gradual and unstoppable draining away of self. Have we worried about this before? Maybe we have, and forgotten all about it. Could it be that believing that this is only the first time we have wondered whether this is the first sign of Alzheimer's, when it isn't the first time, is in fact the first sign of Alzheimer's? If we can remember that thought, the next time we forget something and wonder whether this is the first sign of Alzheimer's, we will probably be in the clear.

Forgetting is normal. It keeps us sane. Forgetting saves us the boredom of remembering, and the horror of remem-bering. It can also allow us the pleasure of remembering, of rediscovering things we have forgotten. This is why we have old friends, who remember things we don't, but who have forgotten things we can remind them of. There is only so much room in a head, even one as well stocked with brains as yours or mine.

(This is why memory tests are the stuff of youth. So you can remember π to eighty-three decimal places? Hot diggety dog. I'd rather go for a walk. It's not that young people are better at learning things off by heart, although they may be, I don't know. It's that they can see a point to it.)

Forgetfulness, though, is temporary; other kinds of losses are more permanent. As I started writing this chapter, it was announced that the last company in the world making typewriters had just gone out of business. Of course it has. No one needs a new typewriter any more. (Or 'acoustic computer', as I believe they are now called.) But if you are, say, fifty, you can remember the workplace when (predominantly male) executives had (predominantly female) secretaries who used (predominantly noisy) typewriters, and everyone started letters (letters!) with sentences like 'Thank you for your letter of the 14th inst.' Computers have swept all this away, in just a few years.

There have been so many changes to everyday life. Children look at phone boxes and wonder what they were for. I remember buying a pile of French phonecards for a trip to Paris in about 1994 and thinking I was terribly sophisticated and up to the moment. Francs and pesetas and German marks and the Irish punt are only memories now. 'Tell us about the old days, Daddy,' my children say. What, quill pens, open sewers and high infant mortality? 'No, Daddy, the Angel Delight flavours you could have ...' Well, there was Mint Chocolate, say I, and Banana, which resembled real banana only in that it was yellow, and if you were really lucky you'd sometimes find Raspberry flavour ...

Nostalgia, of course, is an astringent. You wouldn't want to drop any on your clothes. Far too many of us have suffered at the hands of the 'Ah, remember Spangles?' school of stand-up comedy, which has shifted whole generations out of comedy clubs and into the bar next door. I remember Spangles, but only in order to forget them again. (They were horrible.) Whereas I genuinely mourn the passing of Opal Mints, which were a minty version of Opal Fruits, later rebranded as Pacers. I bought a lot of packets of those, but not quite enough to keep them in business. I remember the Picnic bar before it became Peanut Picnic, when it was a tastier and more sumptuous alternative to Toffee Crisp. I remember when four Trebor Fruit Salad chews cost an old penny. I could go on about this for hours. Sometimes I do.

Each man's feelings of nostalgia and loss, however, are his own. Comedians, like TV ads, seek to repackage our memories and sell them back to us again, because it's easy and they think we are mugs. But they never get it quite right. They cannot. They have no access to the inside of our heads. Their memories of Spangles are their own; they cannot impose them on us. Nor can I impose mine on you, or anyone else. My children think I am mad as I snarf up a bowl of Butterscotch-flavoured Angel Delight in a few frenzied seconds. They can't imagine why anyone would want to eat anything so disgusting.

But so much has gone, and still more is going. We have lost typewriters and Opal Mints, politicians appreciably older than us, TV newsreaders you intrinsically trusted, modesty and honour in sport, bus conductors, slide rules, Alphabetti Spaghetti and Steve McQueen. We have lost our innocence and our belief in so many things. We have lost several single socks and a number of teaspoons that have fallen down the back of somewhere. I have lost the earbuds to my iPod, which is driving me mad.

We are losing second-hand bookshops, almost all notions of public service, our hair and our hearing. We are losing bakers and butchers and greengrocers, the integrity of our towns and villages, our jobs. We are losing the endless battle with inertia. I hate to say it, but some of us might even be losing interest. Let's not even think about losing hope.

And I am losing patience with all this negativity. Not everything we have lost was worth keeping. Having shed most of my ambition, I find I have also lost the shame I had when I was young. I have lost fears, I have lost jealousies, I have lost that awful feeling that the centre of things is somewhere else and I have somehow been excluded. I have lost the self-consciousness and self-doubt that make you second-guess all your own reactions, and never just loosen up and enjoy yourself. But the shame is the worst. Over the past ten years or so, it has simply gone. I just don't care what anyone else thinks any more. If you don't like this book . . . well, if you don't like it you won't have read this far, for one thing . . . but if you really don't like it, there's nothing I can do about it, and to be honest I don't care. Ah, the liberating, deep-breathing joy of being able to say that.

Fears are more complicated. On holiday some years ago, I remember saying how happy I was to have shed certain fears I realised I had been harbouring since childhood, and my friend S^2 said maybe, but new fears always arise to take their place. How right he was. When I was a child I thought flying in an aeroplane was wonderfully exciting. Even as a youngish adult it caused me no grief. Now, before a flight, I am a nervous wreck, gulping down the red wine as though it were mineral water and trying not to yelp during take-off. What is that all about? These are not rational responses to practical problems. We know, intellectually, that the plane is not going to fall out of the sky. We know that this is a far safer mode of transport than almost any other. And yet we know that if the plane does fall out of the sky, (a) we have no chance of survival, and (b) our death will be terrifying. Whereas if I am run over crossing the road outside my house – a distinct possibility given all the anxious middle-aged parents breaking the speed limit in 4×4s to take their awful precocious children to school – it will just be a huge CLUMP! and I'll be dead before I hit the ground. Probably won't feel a thing. If we had to die, I think most of us would choose a method that gave us the absolute minimum of screaming time.

Still, I am more than happy to have lost many of the fears I once had: fears of humiliation, of failure, of impoverished sexual performance, of being laid bare. The ambition never did me much good, and the professional jealousy was a complete time-waster. (Some people are going to do better than you in life. You'll recover.) And when the jealousy goes, it's suddenly much easier to see it in others. That's fun. Jealousy cannot be contained. People cannot stop themselves expressing it. It might be a single sentence, or just a look, but once you have clocked it, you have a key to their soul. Competitors with a weakness are the best sort of competitors to have. Middle age, I believe, gives you the eyes to see these things. As never before, you can identify who is on your side and who really isn't. There are surprisingly few rewards for surviving this far, but one of them is clarity. To replace perfect eyesight, we get perfect hindsight, and much improved foresight. This is not such a bad deal.

Whether we choose to use these gifts is, naturally, up to us. We all have middle-aged friends who are angrier and more frightened than ever, who will turn into tiny, terrified old people hiding under the dining table with lots of tins and a shotgun. I am not a stranger to irrational rages myself, as you may have spotted, but I know I need to find a balance between the productive expression of my righteous fury and the crazed bottling-up of frustrations, grievances and straightforward terrors, until I start yelling at random passers-by and breakfasting on bleach. But since I started writing this book, it has become clearer and clearer to me that middle age represents a chance to throw off all this rubbish. At last we can free ourselves from who we have been, which in most cases was rather annoying young people. There are annoying middle-aged people as well, but maybe not as many. Although I would say that. Younger people might have a different view.

The litmus test is the school or university reunion. Nostalgia may be an astringent, but is it acid or alkaline? Most of us attend these occasions in a state of trepidation, and possibly against our better judgement. And yet we are driven by irresistible curiosity, a *need* to know what happened to these people we once knew. If you go to a reunion too early, say in your twenties or thirties, you might be put off them for ever. Your contemporaries are either more successful than you or less successful than you, and a lot of them are so far up themselves you can't hear a word they are saying. The early reunion is an exercise in display and delineation of status. The shitbags of ten or fifteen years ago are even bigger shitbags. Battle lines will be drawn. People you only used to find irritating might become enemies for life.

Far more sensible to stay at home. Throw a sickie. Wait ten years or so.

Nowadays reunions are less complicated pleasures. It may be that the shitbags of twenty-five or thirty years ago were not invited, or are too busy running the imposing fortified islands they have since bought. But everyone who turns up seems so much *nicer* than they used to be. (Don't worry, they will be saying the same thing about you.) Most of us are more relaxed, less determined to make an impression, more open to making contact. In the past five years I have reactivated friendships that had lain dormant for decades, and formed new friendships with people who were only ever passing acquaintances. We have all been through it, you see, and come out the other side. And it's gone, a lot of that stuff, it's gone for ever, and we miss it not at all.

19
LOVE

'Twenty years of marriage: I'm on my own for two weeks, and I'm still putting the seat down.'

Friend's status update, April 2011

Another room, another elephant. That would be a bad one, wouldn't it? You wake up one morning, and you're married to an elephant. (Maybe your wife already is.)

I was going to call this chapter 'Regret'. 'A short, evocative and achingly beautiful word,' says the poet and philosopher David Whyte, 'an elegy to lost possibilities even in its brief annunciation.' *Moi, je ne regrette rien*, at least until I have had a couple of cups of tea in the morning. Whyte believes that the rarity of honest regret is due to 'our contemporary emphasis on the youthful perspective', that it takes maturity to experience the depths of emotion if you are not to be debilitated by it. You need to have lived a little, in other words. 'To regret fully is to appreciate how high the stakes are in even the average human life.' Oh yes. Whyte believes that regret can 'embolden' us in middle age, can help us look to a better future by showing us, under sharp neon lights, some of the godawful fuck-ups we have perpetrated in the past.

But what actually do we regret? What really lingers in the mind and the heart and, in my case, the pit of the stomach? Years ago I went out with a woman who might be described as a professional *regrettiste*, or maybe *regretteuse*. The anti-Piaf, anyway. She regretted everything she had done: the 'A' levels she had taken, the university course she had chosen, the deadbeat boyfriend she had somehow acquired. The grass was always greener on the other side. In addition, the flowers were more radiantly beautiful, the slugs had been vanquished and feral cats did not piss up against the trees. Life was a battle for her, and therefore for me too. I couldn't solve my own problems, let alone hers, so after a few years I left her to it. At that point regret seemed an awful thing, more like a disease than the transcendent state of being David Whyte describes. She and I are still friends, and I am delighted to say that her regret habit – you might even call it an addiction – has left her in middle age. Under mild torture, she might even admit to being happy. But I doubt she has ever felt 'emboldened' by regret. Quite the reverse.

My own regrets are all about love. They are about the lovely women I didn't go out with, the lovely women I did go out with but was too stupid to appreciate, the missed opportunities, the errors of judgement, the cavalier idiocy of youth. I look back and I think, you prize dickhead. How could you? Why didn't you? Why did you? Mine hasn't been a particularly full romantic life. The desert was always encroaching on it, and tumbleweed sometimes blew through it for years at a time. I wasn't alone in this, although it often felt like it. Asked towards the end of his life whether he had any regrets, Sir John Betjeman famously said, 'Yes I have. Not enough sex.' The reason we remember this reply is that it applies to all of us too.*

In November 2010, psychologists from Harvard University published a major study into mental well-being. 'Happiness is found by living in the now,' reported the *Guardian*, 'particularly if the now involves having sex.' Researchers had collected information on the daily activities, thoughts and feelings of 2250 volunteers. 'They found out that people were happiest when having sex, exercising or in conversation, and least happy when working, resting or using a home computer.' They also discovered that, on average, people spent 46.7 per cent of their time thinking about something other than what they were actually doing. And when their minds were wandering, they were less happy. Reminiscing, thinking ahead and even daydreaming made them gloomier. 'A human mind is a wandering mind,' they wrote, 'and a wandering mind is an unhappy mind.' So that's that then.

What this does suggest, though, is that the theory of 'flow' is a sound one. If we can lose ourselves in whatever we are doing, if time speeds by and we are beyond distraction, then

---

* It is therefore possible to regret all the dreadful things you have done, while at the same time regretting you didn't do more of them when you had the chance. This seems a reasonable summary of the human condition.

that's as useful a definition of happiness as we can find. If we spend 46.7 per cent of our life thinking of something else, that's not good. Even people doing voluntary work allow their minds to wander for 30 per cent of the time. Whereas people engaged in carnal activity report just a 10 per cent distraction rate. And how much of that is men trying to think of incredibly unsexy things for obvious reasons?

And what of the equally groundbreaking and generously funded research conducted in 2007 by the University of Warwick and Dartmouth College? These researchers analysed data from mental health studies in seventy-two countries, and concluded that levels of happiness follow a 'U' shape throughout life, rising in the twenties and the seventies but dipping significantly during middle age. When the human race sups from the cup of happiness, we midlifers are right at the bottom, with the sediment.

There is only one possible conclusion to be drawn from all this sterling effort, and that's that middle-aged people aren't getting any sex whatsoever. Not a sniff. Not that many of us would admit to this publicly, because between the ages of fourteen and ninety, people don't. You need to buy them a lot of drinks, and I have done this on your behalf and in pursuit of a higher truth. Roughly five glasses of wine in, their resistance crumbles like a biscuit and they admit all. Obviously people in long-term relationships aren't getting any, unless it's with someone else. They love their partner dearly, they know everything about them, they know exactly what they like. And after a decade or so, 'exactly what they like' is turning over and going to sleep. So is everyone having an affair? A few daft young people might be, but midlifers know that if they are caught, they will lose everything: family, money, self-respect and years of their lives in the divorce courts. The divorce figures, which were crashing through the roof a decade ago, are now in decline. Excellent, say finger-wagging newspapers and the foolish politicians who read them. But there are two good and coherent reasons for this: one is that not so many people are getting married in the first place (generally, people get married nowadays because they want to and not because they are compelled to); and two, because once married, no one can afford to get divorced any more. Ten, fifteen, twenty years later, you may barely be able to stand the sight of each other, but neither of you wants to rot in a bedsit, eating baked beans on toast and crying yourself to sleep each night. So you stay together, and neither of you has an affair, unless you are rich and can afford all the hassle, or unless you are poor and have nothing more to lose.

The same half-witted politicians – my God, the quality is so low – talk about 'providing a financial incentive' to get married and stay married. But no one is going to get married for money (given how much even the most modest wedding costs) and there is already a financial incentive to stay married: the avoidance of poverty. I thought that by now a lot of my contemporaries would be in the divorce courts and addressing what my twice-married friend McV calls 'the Neil Young question' (is this your Neil Young album or is it mine?). But the only two couples I know who have divorced are loaded, and the two unmarried couples to split (each with two children) are penniless. Everybody else keeps going, practising their Stepford-spouse rictus smiles and waiting for inspiration, or maybe a judicious traffic accident.

As I said, I have spoken to a few people about this, and it's remarkable how many of them are reluctant to dunk their head in the bathwater when their partner is in the room, in case said partner succumbs to unbearable temptation and pushes their head down until they drown. Paranoia is rife. Mention words like 'toaster' and 'extension lead' to these men and they visibly blanch. One husband had an argument with his wife about whether they should put a gas oven or an electric oven in the new house that neither of them much liked anyway. He wanted electric, she favoured gas. She said it was cheaper, but he knew she wanted gas because electric ovens don't explode. Some people stuck in long-term dysfunctional relationships are starting to lose their minds.

But you can always tell when your relationship isn't going as well as it might. She is driving along a road with humps and you are in the passenger seat. At each hump she makes sure her side of the car goes over the flat bit of road and you go over the humpy bit and leap three inches in the air. If she accelerates before the hump you are in real trouble. Watch out that your breakfast cereal doesn't smell of almonds, and that the milk doesn't fizz as it hits the bowl.

In fact, surprisingly few British marriages end in cold-blooded murder. Millions of women are tempted, but pull back from the brink. Some are playing the long game. They feed their captive husbands heart-bursting quantities of greasy, fatty food, washed down with buckets of lager. (Another trick is to set the husband up with what he believes to be a secret stash of pork pies, which are then constantly replenished.) Only when they have fed their man up as you would a goose for foie gras do they drop the toaster in the bath, and everyone assumes he has died of natural causes because he is fat. But wives need patience to prosecute this course of action, as well as the acuity, foresight and ruthlessness of a criminal mastermind. I'm not sure I know more than a couple of dozen who qualify.

Anyway, most women can't be bothered. They know you aren't as bad as all that. If they did get shot of you, there aren't crowds of potential replacements queueing round the corner on the off-chance. As all single women over thirty-five will tell you, the standard is not high. If you discount opportunistic married men (of whom there is apparently an infinite supply), the only males left out there are weirdoes, dullards, milksops, morons, loons, oiks, toughs and shits. This is why so many attractive, intelligent women seem to end up with daggy men. There just isn't the choice.*

That doesn't stop women wishing and hoping, and maybe even praying. In January 2008, 40,000 women told UKdating.com exactly what they were looking for in a man. Their preferences, all rolled together in a big ball, created a twenty-point guide to Mr Right. He must be at least five feet ten inches tall. He must be good-looking, weigh twelve and a half stone and earn more than £30,000 a year. He must have blue eyes and short, dark brown hair, be of medium build, have a degree, never have been married, have no children, have had no more than three serious relationships, have no facial hair whatsoever, drive a silver Mercedes (yeah, right), like going to the cinema and eating out, have had no

---

* Frenchmen have an expression for it: 'as unhappy as a dog in Turkey or a woman in England'. They have a solution for it, too: Frenchmen.

more than six previous sexual partners, own a house worth at least £300,000, not smoke, dislike football, and like pets. (Only 1 per cent of women questioned said that their Mr Right could hate pets.) Not only does this man not exist, but if he did, the rest of us would torture and kill him. Then we'd trash his house, crash his Mercedes, eat his pets and stick a false beard on his corpse.

Mr Right would have his choice of any woman in the world. Miss Right repeatedly makes do with Mr Wrong. It may not be fair, but it is potentially good news for us. One of the stranger features of the heterosexual male midlife is the sense that there are more attractive women than ever, far far more than there were when we were young. Yet again, I was under the impression I was the only person who thought this, and therefore the only person who suffered to the point of physical pain while walking down a city street between April and September. Where have they all come from? Where were they when I was young, skinny and ridiculous? After everything else that has befallen us, you could easily interpret this as the final insult.

First, though, I established that everyone else feels the same way. Then I worked out why. When you are, say, twenty, you generally fancy girls of roughly your own age and slightly younger. This continues throughout life. So at twenty, you will be gawping at pretty women between the ages of fifteen and twenty-five. When you are fifty, you will be gawping at pretty women between the ages of fifteen and fifty-five. That's four times as many. Really, it's a disaster. The more women there appear to be, the less we can do anything about it. (Either we are unavailable, or we look like hell, or both.) And it gets no better. See that man in his seventies or eighties shuffling along the pavement, with the tears flowing down his cheeks? In his imagination he is striding at a healthy pace, fast enough to overtake that beautiful young woman ahead of him with the exquisite buttocks. Even the word 'buttocks' gets him going. The flesh is weak, but the spirit is half a century younger and gagging for it.

The trick, I think, is not to take any of it too seriously. Be at one with your inner Leslie Phillips. 'Hell-o!' you say to yourself as you pass one of the 'attractive' stops on your regular bus route. (Why is that? Why do prettier women get on and off at certain bus stops?) My friend Y once admitted to me, in a weak moment, that he would change carriages on the London Underground if he saw a good-looking woman in the next one along.

'Do you still do that?'

'Of course.'

Sex has always been as much in the mind as in the body: the balance has shifted a little, that's all.

In 2010 the *Sunday Telegraph*'s magazine *Stella* commissioned an exhaustive survey on British sexual behaviour. Given that everybody lies about it all the time, we should probably come well armed with salt when we consider these statistics, but they are interesting nonetheless. People rated trust as most important in a relationship, followed by companionship, humour and financial stability. Sex came a distant fifth. Seventy per cent of men looked at pornography, compared with 21 per cent of women. More Liberal Democrats (30 per cent) than Conservatives (22 per cent) or Labour supporters (24 per cent) owned a sex toy. (But 44 per cent of women who had watched *Sex and the City* owned a sex toy.) More men had had sex at work (20 per cent) than paid for it (13 per cent). Eighteen per cent of respondents had been unfaithful while married; 12 per cent had not had sex for two years or more while in a relationship. (And that's just the people who were telling the truth.) Twenty-eight per cent of men thought about sex at least every hour, compared with 4 per cent of women. More women wanted to have sex with George Clooney (23 per cent) than Brad Pitt (11 per cent) or Daniel Craig (10 per cent). Men's favourite position was Woman On Top (32 per cent); women's favourite was the Missionary (26 per cent). (Isn't it supposed to be the other way round?) Men had had an average of 8.3 sexual partners, women an average of 6.5. More Conservative and Labour voters (14 per cent each) than Liberal Democrats (10 per cent) had used Viagra. Overall, 22 per cent of men over fifty-five had used Viagra.

(Do we want to think about erectile dysfunction? No, I don't think we do.)

One particularly mesmerising 'statistic' – and I think it merits the quotation marks – is the response by various groupings to the question 'How often do you have sex in an average month?' Of single people, the largest group (25 per cent) said one to five times, and 11 per cent said none at all. Of married people, the largest group (35 per cent) also said one to five times, and 5 per cent said none at all. Of divorced people, the largest group (45 per cent) said six to ten times, and only 1 per cent said none at all. Yeah, right. It's crazy out there. Get your divorce papers and a whole new world of untrammelled shaggery opens up to you. In your bedsit.

It all gets a bit much after a while, don't you think? Shut

your eyes and all you can see are sex-crazed hordes of divorced Liberal Democrats running through the streets brandishing dildos. I begin to see the appeal of life within an enclosed religious order, where no one even speaks, and certainly no one watches *Sex and the City*.

And yet we all believe in love. Trust, companionship, humour and financial stability are the four cornerstones of love, it seems, with sex as an optional extra. (A decorative flourish on the edifice, as opposed to a supporting wall.) We believe in love, because what else is there? We have the evidence of our senses, which is that some relationships simply flourish. Some people meet, get together and stay together for good. 'We have to work at it,' they always say. Yes, of course you do. But you are still exceptionally lucky to have found the one for you and kept them.

We all expect too much. As a society we are captivated by the cruel myth of Happy Ever After. Anything less is seen as a failure. (Relationships never 'end', they always 'fail'.) But as Kate Figes says in *Couples: The Truth*, Happy Ever After is a relatively recent phenomenon. In the eighteenth century, a quarter of all marriages were remarriages. Lifelong marriages were usually shorter because lives were shorter. And as more people lived in extended families, couples weren't thrown together for so many hours of every day, so many days of every year. The quality of the relationship, and maybe even the relationship itself, was simply not as important.

Figes is unflaggingly optimistic about modern marriage, which she describes as 'a castle with a very wide moat'. Although a third of all marriages now end in divorce, half of these divorces take place in the first seven years. After twenty years together, only 15 per cent of couples split. But is this because the rest truly love each other, or because it's too difficult to do anything else? How many people are subsisting in a state of Unhappy Ever After?

It's always easier to stay where you are. Inertia has much to be said for it. Better the devil you know. While women always seem keener than men to get married in the first place, the evidence suggests that men are happier than women within marriage. (If they have any sense, they know they couldn't have done any better.) Outside can seem scary, for all kinds of reasons. Many of the single people you know seem to have been single for a long time. And who is to say that if you did find someone else, it wouldn't be just as unsatisfactory as this relationship? Maybe the relationship isn't the problem. Maybe it's something about you.

If you are the dumped one – and men increasingly are – you will need time to recover. The last time I received the heave-ho, I was a basket case for the best part of a year. Women, when dumped, tend to retreat into solitude and possibly cake. Men move into rebound mode. We are never more toxic. The memories of my own year of hell still make me cringe. Did I claim earlier that I had lost all shame? Not for this. The year was 1994, and I hereby apologise to anyone unlucky enough to have met me then.

Your confidence deserts you. No one wants to be by themselves for good, and yet most of us seem to end up that way, whether deprived of a partner through natural causes, accident or misadventure. As a single friend of mine said to me, 'It takes enough courage to take all your clothes off in front of a stranger when you're twenty. Imagine how much braver you have to be to do it at forty-five.' Previous owners of a body beautiful are at the gravest disadvantage here. You have a mental image of what lies beneath your clothes that, tragically, does not square with the sagging, bloated, piebald reality. To disrobe and reveal only a body risible feels like one humiliation too many.

So marriages prevail, and Happy Ever After becomes This Will Do. You stay together for the sake of the children (I have heard of one couple who stayed together for the sake of the dog). And what is to come? Probably very little, because everyone feels uncomfortable about the idea of old people falling in love and having sex. Including the old people. Which is why they tend to pursue young people, chasing them down the road so slowly that the young people don't even have to accelerate to get away.

20
SCYTHE

'I like collecting words that don't have an equivalent in English. There's one in Icelandic that means "man reduced to the level of a pig through drink" and another that translates as "man left to die a solitary death on a small island".'

Joanne Harris, interviewed in the *Observer Magazine*, March 2010

Marathons, motorbikes and mistresses: these, according to my friend G^2, are the three Ms of midlife. He has left one out, of course. Or maybe the first three are merely facets of the fourth. The one we don't want to think about; the one we think about all the time.

First, though, the constituent parts. If we have touched on marathons in these pages, and cast a slightly jaundiced eye on motorbikes, we have paid suspiciously little attention to mistresses. What a wonderfully old-fashioned word that is. Great men used to have mistresses (often in the plural) in the days when you could smoke enormous cigars indoors and Roger Moore bestrode the narrow world like a colossus. Power defined this relationship, as it did all others. 'If a man marries his mistress, it creates a job opportunity,' said Sir James Goldsmith, the businessman and occasional politician who died in 1997. Men like this might go to their graves unmourned, but at least their graves are very much bigger than yours.

Nowadays we would probably prefer a word like 'lover' or 'girlfriend', or (one I heard used in all seriousness the other day, and thought I might throw up) 'special friend'. We might be less respectful of someone else's 'bit on the side' or even 'shagpiece'. Not that we discuss this sort of thing much. To a man, the interviewees for this book said absolutely nothing about extra-curricular relationships, would not be drawn. Looking at my friends, I can guess which of them might play away, but it would only be a guess. Women find this hard to believe. They think that when men get together in pubs, it is for a prolonged bout of sexual boasting. That may be true of the under-25s (who are all lying anyway) and the likes of Sir James Goldsmith and their penis-shaped cigars, but it's not of any men I know. Even the most incontinent rumpo merchants and tottyhounds seem to cover their tracks. We are men, so we compartmentalise. Even our closest friendships are conducted on a need-to-know basis.

Often, then, the first we know that one of our friends has been up to no good is when it all blows up in public. Wives are left, families torn asunder and the new girlfriend is displayed in public for the first time. 'You must have known,' say all the women. 'Well, obviously I had a clue,' you say, to hide the fact that you hadn't. 'Well, I guessed ages ago,' say the women. 'You could tell by his eyes.' That's not true either, but at least you are both lying for the same reason: to save face. And also to avoid the question in everyone's mind: who will be next?

Because break-ups are contagious. One couple calls it a day and all the other couples sit and watch. And people get to thinking, do I want to stay with this person for the rest of my life? Or would I rather eat my own liver? Sitting in judgement upon others, we might presume that they take such decisions lightly, even irresponsibly. Only when we find ourselves taking the same decisions do we realise how serious and weighty they are.

We are, of course, in a realm beyond cliché here. That middle-aged men will sooner or later think of running off with someone new and probably younger is acknowledged by everyone. Naturally, the middle-aged women feel put out by this. They have given the best years of their lives to this dolt. But if so many men do this, and so many, many more are tempted to, is it not a phenomenon worthy of serious appraisal? Disapproval gets us nowhere, blinds us to the truths lying somewhere in the long shadows cast by people's 'bad' behaviour. I would admit, I have been as disapproving as anyone. I have shaken my head and tut-tutted when men I knew left good women in the lurch. My father did it to my mother. There seemed no excuse for it.

But these behaviours, the marathons, the mistresses and the motorbikes, are nothing more than intimations of the fourth M, mortality. They are the tall and imposing figure of Death looming over our shoulders, carrying an enormous scythe in his bony fingers. Middle age is when we truly know we are going to die. It may be in thirty-five years' time, it may be next year from some horrible, as yet undetected cancer, it may be tomorrow under a bendy bus. All the life experience we have diligently collected, all the safeguards we have put in place, will count for nothing. In the prescient words of Private Fraser, we're doomed.

Of course it's one thing to be aware of your oncoming demise, and quite another to worry yourself to death about it. Our doom is inescapable, but an overpowering sense of impending catastrophe may not be the brightest way to approach it. Midlife crises are essentially panic attacks. Oh my God I'm going to die. What have I achieved? Nothing. What will I leave behind me? Very little. Who cares? No one. What am I going to do? Make a complete fool of myself. Because, having realised you are going to die, you also realise that it no longer matters whether or not you make a complete fool of yourself. It isn't going to change anything in the long term. So why not, if the opportunity arises?

So from being a panic attack, a man's midlife crisis swiftly mutates into a problem that needs to be solved. Since we are going to die, we must now try to live. And since the primary biological purpose of life is to create more life, it makes sense to seek out young and fertile women and impregnate them willy nilly. Hooray, we are hard-wired after all! There is nothing we can do about it! Bye bye!

(And yet, not so long ago, at one of the many reunions I now attend, I met two old acquaintances, both rising fifty, both gay, one in a relationship with a 32-year-old, the other in a relationship with a 24-year-old. They were both a little sheepish about it, but I thought, why not? There's no biological imperative there: an opportunity has arisen and been taken. And what does the disapproval of others matter? Isn't that something we have managed to outgrow, worrying about what other people think of us?)

But this is all displacement activity. Even arguing about it is displacement activity. Death is still behind us, lurking in the most distant corner of our peripheral vision. Has he always been there? Maybe we just didn't notice him before. Whereas if he has just arrived, I would say we have rather more to worry about.

Not that a little good, honest morbidity will do you any harm. I am not suggesting you sleep in a coffin, but it is useful to be conscious of the fragility of life. When the mother of my children and I started going out with each other in the mid-1990s, we quickly had a conversation about death. I felt I should warn her. It seemed the kindest thing to do. In her thirty or so years, she had lost no one of any consequence. Funerals were unknown to her. But she needed to know of my own, rather more besmirched track record. When I was eleven a boy I knew had a hole in his heart; one morning he just didn't wake up. Another developed galloping bone cancer; one term he came back with a leg gone, and not long afterwards the rest of him was gone too. Later on, some friends of a friend went on holiday to Switzerland and drove off a mountain. A history teacher had a fatal heart attack, aged twenty-eight. A boy whose mother had died leapt out of a third-floor window. Another went at twenty of leukaemia. Someone I knew at university was caught in the Harrods bomb in 1983, having heard there was something going on and gone out specifically to find out what. The teacher I was closest to at school had a heart attack at the age of thirty-nine. One of my closest friends at university died of Aids in 1992. Another went of a brain tumour in 2003. Yet another, who I had known since the age of nine, died of lung cancer in 2005. An old cricketing friend, aged forty-nine, had a fatal heart attack at the crease, while hitting a four to go from 75 to 79 not out. ('Retired deceased.') Most recently, my friend Matthew, a former priest and the gentlest, kindest man I have known, died in his sleep, also at the age of forty-nine. And these are just the friends. My mother's friends are almost all gone, my brother has just lost his best friend (suicide) and a large chunk of the 1980s was spent burying various relatives. There are serial killers abroad who have seen less death than this. I am surprised the police haven't tapped me for my DNA.

At Matthew's funeral, his ten-year-old son made a speech so moving and dignified you could barely hear a word of it under all the weeping. Afterwards a dozen of us went to the pub. It was what Matthew would have wanted. A career smoker, he had given up drink a handful of years before for health reasons, and concentrated thereafter on food. I once bumped into him in a café near the school where he taught, tucking in to one of the vastest meals I have ever seen. While his death had been a terrible shock to us all, it hadn't been a complete surprise. Over eight or maybe more hours we got pissed and argued and had a fantastic time, renewing old friendships that had fallen into abeyance, and wondering where all the time had gone. And not asking the question that was on everyone's mind: who will be next?

Once we went to weddings. By the time I was thirty-seven I had been to thirty-eight of them. I know, because I made a list. (I also like keeping things in alphabetical order.) Last year the list turned up in an old notebook I was leafing through to avoid doing any real work. How many more weddings had I been to in the subsequent dozen years? For a happy, rainy afternoon I trawled through old diaries to update the list and came up with a final figure of forty-seven. I would still like to crack fifty, but it might take a while. I rather like weddings. Sure, they cost a fortune and can be very dull if you end up on the wrong table, but at a wedding everyone suspends irony for a day. Something profoundly private, even mysterious – an intimate relationship between two people – is briefly glimpsed in public. Things happen at weddings. For a single man, as I once was, they were a valuable resource.*

We don't go to many weddings any more. We go to funerals instead. Here's another formalised social ritual, at which everyone suspends irony for a day, which marks not the opening of a gateway into a new life, but the slamming of a vast, heavy oak door that will never open again. As at weddings, emotions are high and people drink too much. The food is less lavish at funerals, but you don't have to stay all day, or talk to anyone you don't want to, and no one requires you to dance. For a single man, I am reliably informed, they are a valuable resource.

---

* I met at least one long-term girlfriend at a wedding. And at another, while taking a brief rest from the proceedings with my head on the table, I overheard two friends of mine, each in a relationship with someone else, discuss the sex they had just enjoyed in an adjoining hotel room. They believed I had passed out. When they read this (twenty years later) they will realise I hadn't.

Each death is a singular disaster. Each one takes a chunk from your life and erases it as though it had never happened. Well, it happened in your memory, but we know how selective and unreliable that can be. While the acute pain of bereavement evens out into a chronic ache, you can never quite compensate for the loss. The conversations I used to have with Matthew or Esther or Harry, I can't have now; there are just gaps where those friendships used to be. The gaps will only become more plentiful, assuming that we ourselves can stay alive. Long life is a pyrrhic victory: you reach the winning post only to find that you're the only person left in the race.

Everybody else's death, though, pales beside the prospect of our own. Do we believe there's anything else afterwards? Might oblivion not be the best option? I have a horrible fear that the afterlife, if indeed it exists, is a little like the Sunday afternoons of my childhood. Everything is shut, there's nothing on the telly, my father is playing Bruckner at top volume up in his bedroom in a furious temper, and the less time I have left in which to do my homework, the more I don't do it. Heaven is hell, in other words. But if heaven is heaven, let it be our own individual notion of heaven, as opposed to someone else's. Mine would be a little like Lord's cricket ground, bathed in sunshine on the first morning of a four-day game, with good company and a pocket full of money for beer and pies. If I can keep that image in my mind as I slide towards death, maybe it will come true.*

* A doctor friend says that Lord's is a very good place to die. Hundreds of buffers sit out there, soaking up the sun after a long lunch, and almost every day one of them neglects to wake up. At the end of play, the buffer-wagon rolls up and body-bags him. It's all part of the service.

In the meantime I read obituaries with growing fascination. Who cares what else is happening in the world when another of the Carry On cast has died, or a much-loved 1970s footballer, or someone who once played with Black Sabbath? People who were famous when we were young are now croaking at an alarming rate. Obviously their deaths mean far less to us than that of a friend or close relative, but every one who goes takes a sliver of our past with them. To us it feels like a form of slow cultural erosion, because the newer, younger celebrities who replace these people in public life don't have the same resonance. How can they? They are newer, and younger.

The deaths come in waves. At one point in the 1990s, stars of Hollywood's golden age seemed to be pegging out on a daily basis. A few gnarled old veterans hung on to life by their exquisitely manicured fingernails, but hardly any are left now. Those still alive as I write this will probably be dead by the time you read it. You begin to understand what it must have been like for Hal Roach, who produced Laurel and Hardy's short films, but didn't die until 1992, at the age of 100. He had outlived Laurel by twenty-seven years, Hardy by thirty-five, and his only wife by fifty-one.

Sometimes the wave passes before you have had time to acknowledge it. A decade or so ago, it became apparent that nearly all the men who had fought in World War I were gone. A hundred were left, fifty, a dozen, a handful. Then one or two. The old, who are survivors of their own great cull, were unfazed by this, but the middle-aged, whose dreams are now full of scythes, found it all unbearably poignant. You might survive the battlefield, with a little luck. But you won't survive the old people's home.

There are three types of obituary, as far as the reader is concerned. There's the very old person who has died, who lived a long life, whose time was clearly up. The photograph in the paper may be of someone extraordinarily ancient with enormous ears, or it may be of the deceased as a young, vibrant person sporting the fashions of the 1950s, or even earlier. These obituaries can be fascinating to read, even a little comforting, but they excite no profound emotional response in the middle-aged reader, which, given all the other stresses he has to endure, is probably just as well.

Type two is the slightly younger person who has died. This can be anyone of your age up to about twenty years older than you, and the underlying theme is a life cruelly cut short. These obituaries are the hardest to read. Your moles itch, the pain in your abdomen won't go away and you might need to pee seven minutes after you last peed. Worse than the knowledge that Death is stalking you is the certainty that you haven't done enough in your own life to merit the obituary this smug overachiever has been given. How many column inches? Bet he was a nasty piece of work in real life.

Type three is the best of all: the obituary of someone appreciably younger than you. These you read with a smile on your face and joy in your heart. All the fame and the money in the world couldn't save him. Ha!*

---

* Not everyone takes this view, though. A commuter friend of my friend Ψ opens the *Times* obituaries page every morning on the train and works out the mean age of the people who have pegged it that day. If it's higher than his age, that's a good omen; if it's lower, he prepares himself for the worst. The fatalities he dreads most are those of extreme sports practitioners who have perished in mad base-jumping incidents and rappers who die in drive-by shootings. On such days it takes at least a major-general to bring the average up to safety.

No obituary can tell the whole story, or anything more than a small part of the story. It may even tell the wrong story. The traditional code of obituaries – 'he was unmarried' for 'he was a rampant homosexual', or 'he didn't suffer fools gladly' for 'he was an arrogant monster' – has not vanished completely. But every obituary tells some sort of story, and many of them tell the same one, of complicated lives that were no easier than our own, and often much more difficult. Even the most glittering and magnificent of careers include failure, disappointment, even great sadness. After checking the facts about Hal Roach earlier, I looked up Laurel and Hardy on Wikipedia. I never liked them much myself, but my daughter worships at their feet. Seventy-five years after their heyday, their short films are still loved and esteemed. But how long did that heyday last? Fourteen years. Their first short film was made in 1926, and their last full-length film for Hal Roach came out in 1940. Before 1926 they were striving. After 1940 they were sliding. In that year Stan Laurel celebrated his fiftieth birthday and Oliver Hardy his forty-eighth.

Obituaries, then, are comfort reading for the middle-aged, as I hope this book has been too. Writing it, certainly, has been a bracing experience. I had no idea, until I started talking and listening to people, how many of us were feeling the same way, experiencing the same things, not really talking about any of it to anyone. Feelings of failure, disappointment and sadness are obviously better shared, but they can also be offset against a strong sense of liberation, of having finally thrown off the shackles of youth. Being young is a pretty miserable existence, we now realise. Each of us struggles through it alone, supported only by his own unshakeable ignorance. In middle age, though, we might find that we have more in common with each other than we imagined. The sheer fact of our survival brings us together. Life has humbled us all. Death stalks us all, the bastard. How does he spread himself so thin? Only by working much longer hours than any of us can now be bothered to. If it weren't for his prominent bone structure and the complete absence of visible flesh, you might suspect that Death was actually a young executive on the make, trying to impress his superiors with his exceptional diligence. Maybe so. They are usually the most dangerous ones.

Asked by *The Word* magazine what lessons he had learned from a long and fulfilling life, Sir Terry Wogan replied, 'Kindness, kindness, kindness.' Twenty years ago I would have thought this answer bland and smug; now it seems the very essence of wisdom. I would expand it a little, though. We are younger than Sir Terry. We are thinking not only of our past and our present, but of our future too. So, with due humility, I proffer the following three lessons of middle age:

- We only have the one life.
- Our main duty to others is to be kind.
- Our main duty to ourselves is not to be bored.

My friend T says he would drop the third, which he thinks is effectively the same as the first, and add this:

- It's relationships that matter.

I tell him he is talking rubbish. He says I am a platitudinous idiot who should get a job writing the verses in greetings cards. I kick him in the shins, and he gives me a dead arm. The barmaid declares it a draw. A pint or two later, we agree that you just can't get good masking tape any more. It always tears vertically, and what's the use of that? And so we talk, on and on, into the long dark night that will envelop us both one day, but not yet, let's hope, not just yet.

ACKNOWLEDGEMENTS

Thanks, for their ideas, observations and deep howls of terror, to Cliff Allen, Stephen Arkell, Fran Bell, Justin Berkmann, Hazel Bingham, Luke Bingham, Patrick Bingham, Gaynor Bond, Nick Cohen, Tim Cooper, Georgia Coops, Thomas Coops, Richard Corden, Sam Craft, Amanda Craig, Oliver Crick, Claire Daly, Bill Dare, Alan and Selena Doggett-Jones, Frances Evans, Nigel Farrell, Sally Ann Fitt, Rod Gilchrist, Dave Glenn, Tania Glyde, Petrina Good, Mel Griffiths, John Haydon, Sarah Hesketh, Ian and Victoria Hislop, Tom Holland, Elgar and Mary Howarth, Patrick and Ruth Howarth, Theresa Howarth, Mark Hudson, Sarah Jackson, Caroline and David Jaques, Bob Jones, Michele Kimber, Pauline and Richard Last, Andrew 'AJ' Leonard, Oliver Lewis-Barclay, Nick Lezard, Sarah Long, David McCandless, Alison McKenna, Leo McKinstry, Howard McMinn, Adam McQueen, Veronica Marris, Teresa Maughan, Mike Michael, Tim Minogue, Jenny Naipaul, Nick Newman, Peter Noble, Simon O'Hagan, Julian Parker, Francis Peckham, Ivan Polancec, Chris Pollikett, Fred Ponsonby, Susy Pote, Richard Poynter, Neal Ransome, Lucy Reese, Elisabeth Reissner, Judy Reith, Andy Robson, Kerstin Rodgers, Frank Romany, Simon Rose, Patrick Routley, Sir Kenneth and Susie Runciman,

Terence Russoff, Joanna Ryan, Kate Saunders, Louisa Saunders, Christopher Silvester, Rose Smith, Daniela Soave, Phil South, Richard Spence, Leisa Steele, Cath Sutton, Anthony Sycamore, Mitchell Symons, David Taylor, Russell Taylor, Sam Taylor, David Thomas, Hilary Todd, Stephen Walker, Robin Welch, Roger Wesson, Francis Wheen, Alan White, Helen White, Yasmin Whittaker-Khan, Ceili Williams, Rukhsana Yasmin and anyone else I have forgotten.* Also to my friend and agent, Patrick Walsh; to my friend and publisher Richard Beswick, and everyone else at Little, Brown; and to the blond(e)s at home, Paula, Martha and James. This book is dedicated to my mother, Jean Berkmann-Barwis, whose unfailing good cheer and passion for chocolate biscuits inspire us all.

---

* Incidentally, the letters in the text do not correspond to any of these people's names. This is intentional.

To buy any of our books and to find out
more about Abacus and Little, Brown, our authors
and titles, as well as events and book clubs,
visit our website

www.littlebrown.co.uk

and follow us on Twitter

@AbacusBooks
@LittleBrownUK

To order any Abacus titles p & p free in the UK,
please contact our mail order supplier on:

+ 44 (0)1832 737525

Customers not based in the UK should contact
the same number for appropriate postage
and packing costs.